That They Be One

That They Be One:

The Social Teaching of the Papal Encyclicals 1740–1989

Michael J. Schuck

Georgetown University Press
Washington, D.C.

Copyright © 1991 Georgetown University Press
All rights reserved
Printed in the United States

Library of Congress Cataloging-in-Publication Data

Schuck, Michael J.
    That they be one : the social teaching of the papal encyclicals,
1740-1989 / Michael J. Schuck
        p.   cm.
    Includes bibliographical references.
    ISBN 0-87840-488-0. -- ISBN 0-87840-489-9 (pbk.)
    1. Sociology, Christian (Catholic)--History of doctrines--18th
century. 2. Sociology, Christian (Catholic)--History of
doctrines--19th century. 3. Sociology, Christian (Catholic)-
-History of doctrines--20th century. 4. Sociology, Christian
(Catholic)--Papal documents. 5. Catholic Church--Doctrines-
-History--18th century. 6. Catholic Church--Doctrines-
-History--19th century. 7. Catholic Church--Doctrines-
-History--20th century. I. Title.
BX1753.S377   1991
261.8'08822--dc20   90-44235
                                                              CIP

CONTENTS

3. THE POST-LEONINE PERIOD: 1959–89   117

Preface

On the eve of his arrest and crucifixion, Jesus contemplated his disciples' future, praying to the Father "that they may be one, even as we are one."[1] In this rare example of a gospel prayer, Jesus affirmed the centrality of fellowship for his followers' ongoing existence. Since then, stimulated by Jesus' Spirit, Christians have sought the same: community with God and each other.

But what kind of community did Jesus will? How can it be created? By what means can it be sustained? In part, these questions concern the order and operation of Christian worshipping communities. Yet they also bear on the wider political, familial, economic, and cultural spheres of human interaction within which Christians conduct their daily lives. What, if any, communal responsibility exists for Christians in these realms?

Over two millenia, Christians have answered this question in many ways. One response is the encyclical letters of the Roman Catholic papacy. Since Benedict XIV's decision in 1740 "to preserve the Catholic faith and either preserve or restore the discipline of morals" through new emphasis on the medium of encyclical letters, 284 letters by seventeen popes have resulted in a remarkable body of observations and recommendations concerning human fellowship in society.[2] Whether one regards them with favor, disdain, or indifference, the papal encyclicals are a major piece in the history of Christian social ethics.

This book explores the social teaching of the papal encyclicals. While many fine books have traversed this ground, this work does so in three new ways. Unlike the typical method of analyzing papal teaching by focusing on a few conventionally designated "social" letters, this study takes stock of all the encyclicals. This approach expands the panorama of papal social concerns and properly situates the conventionally designated "social" encyclicals in their wider literary context.

Second, contrary to the common reduction of encyclical social teaching to issues in economic relations, this book includes papal discussions of human interaction in the religious, political, family, and cultural spheres of social life. Delimiting social ethics to economic relations is a holdover from the nineteenth century, when focus was on the plight of European workers following the Industrial Revolution. Much is lost by sustaining this narrow understanding of social teaching. The popes simply have more to say.

Third, as opposed to the usual practice of beginning the study of encyclical social teaching with the letters of Leo XIII, this book moves the discussion back to its true origin: the seventy-seven encyclicals predating Leo XIII. The textually inclusive and topically broad-gauged method used in this study allows these earlier texts to resurface. Their retrieval exposes the degree to which conventional neglect of pre-Leonine letters has skewed the interpretation of encyclical social teaching as a whole.

These new methods serve two purposes. One is to acquaint the reader, in a coordinated way, with the fascinating array of social observations contained in the papal encyclicals. Thus, chapter 1 treats the 138-year period of encyclical writing before Leo XIII, called here the "pre-Leonine period." Chapter 2 covers the eighty years of papal letters between Leo XIII and Pius XII. This is called the "Leonine period." The encyclicals of the "post-Leonine period," from John XXIII to the present, are investigated in chapter 3. Each chapter begins with a brief overview, moves to an extended discussion of the problems and solutions offered by the popes, and ends with a summary interpretation.

The second purpose of this book is to address a particular question. Since the Second Vatican Council, critical analysis of papal letters has challenged the conventional notion that encyclicals offer a coherent social message. These analyses have noted substantive changes in encyclical sources, methods, and conclusions over time. Thus, in a 1981 speech marking the ninetieth anniversary of Leo XIII's *Rerum novarum*, John Coleman asked if it was any longer possible to view encyclical teaching as a coherent body of social thought. "The logical unity of the teaching," he said, "still needs to be shown."[3]

This book addresses Coleman's question. It argues that the papal letters cohere, but in a manner previously unrecognized in commentary literature. Unlike theories locating encyclical coherence in natural law moral theory or the concept of human dignity, this study holds that the letters cohere around a shared—though variegated—communitarian understanding of the self and society. The popes' theological communitarianism further yields a cluster of convergent recommendations and judgments concerning human relations in the religious, political, family, economic, and cultural spheres of social life.

This is not to say that papal teachings have remained unchanged over 249 years. Significant changes and reversals have occurred. One responsibility of this study is to point them out. The evidence for these claims accrues in chapters 1-3, with full discussion of coherence theories in chapter 4.

Four technical remarks must be made at the outset. Due both to the paucity of data and limitations of space, the precise historical context of every encyclical treated in this study cannot be provided. Readers are encouraged to follow the notes, where as much available historical information is given as thought pertinent.

This study explores patterns in papal thought. These patterns were uncovered by exhaustively gathering and assembling papal ideas, then critically examining their resemblances and reversals over time. Limitations of space make it impossible to provide a complete list of every encyclical reference supporting these patterns. In lieu of such a list, major representative references are given in the notes.

The main source for the encyclicals cited is Claudia Carlen's *The Papal Encyclicals*, 5 vols. (Wilmington, N.C.: McGrath, 1981). This is the collection most readily available to North American readers. The numbers appearing after encyclicals cited in the present study are the section numbers given in the Carlen translations. Exceptions to this rule include John XXIII's *Mater et Magistra* and *Pacem in terris*, as well as Paul VI's *Populorum progressio* and *Humanae vitae*. In these cases, the numbers cited are those in the translations provided in Joseph Gremillion's *The Gospel of Peace and Justice: Catholic Social Teaching since Pope John* (Maryknoll, N.Y.: Orbis Books, 1976). Four encyclicals have appeared since the publication of the Carlen collection: John Paul II's *Slavorum apostoli*, *Dominum et vivificantem*, *Redemptoris Mater* and *Sollicitudo rei socialis*. Here, the translations and paragraph numbers provided are those given in the journal *Origins*, specifically vol. 15, no. 8, vol. 16, nos. 4 and 43, and vol. 17, no. 38. Instances where I use my own translations are indicated in the notes.

All scriptural references are from the Revised Standard Version unless otherwise noted. The upper case word "Church" is used in this study as a pronominal short form for "Roman Catholic Church," with no judgment against other Christian churches implied.

NOTES

1.   Raymond Brown notes that John 17:11 is a gloss, "more at home in the third unit of the prayer (see 21-23)." Raymond E. Brown, *The Gospel According to John* (Garden City, N.Y.: Doubleday, 1966-70), 759.

2.   Benedict's full quote, inaugurating modern encyclical literature, reads: "Neque illud a Nobis praetereundum est Romanis Pontificibus morem perpetuo fuisse, ut episcopos universos vel alicujus tantam provinciae ad catholicam fidem custodiendam, morumque disciplinam aut servandam aut restaurandam, Litteris encyclicis excitarent." Cited in Paul Nau, *Une Source Doctrinale: Les Encycliques* (Paris: Les éditions du Cedre, 1952), 42, note 1. See also Sean O'Riordan, "The Teaching of the Papal Encyclicals as a Source and Norm of Moral Theology: A Historical and Analytic Survey," *Studia Moralia* 14 (1976): 140.

3.   John A. Coleman, "Development of Church Social Teaching," in Charles E. Curran and Richard A. McCormick, eds., *Readings in Moral Theology No. 5: Official Catholic Social Teaching* (New York: Paulist Press, 1986), 176.

Acknowledgments

Journalist Francine du Plessix Gray once observed that "It's a myth that the writing of factual prose is more objective and less intensely personal than fiction." I agree. Underlying the scholarly issues which first triggered this study is a trove of episodes and conversations with remarkable people in my life which have prodded this work in tacit ways. Because these mentors go unnamed in the text, I acknowledge them here.

My thanks, in memoriam, to Rev. Francis J. Ketter, Rev. Joseph A. McCallin, S.J., and Rev. Charles J. Carmody. Thanks also to Sr. Modesta Clemens, O.S.B., Rev. John Pickla, Dr. Lawrence Barmann, Dr. James Hitchcock, and Dr. James Gustafson. To facilitate final preparation of the manuscript, Loyola University of Chicago provided a summer research award for which I am greatly appreciative.

My deepest thanks also to my family: to my parents, without whose constant support this study could not have been crafted; and to my wife, Lojzka, and children, Mateja and Aloysius, the daily sustainers of my faith, my intellect, and my life. Such have been my personal tutors in the community for which Jesus prayed.

1

THE PRE-LEONINE PERIOD: 1740–1877

Students of papal social thought rarely examine the encyclical literature written from 1740 to 1877. Only embarrassing, retrograde compositions are thought to exist here, characterized by Gregory XIV's *Mirari vos* and *Singulari Nos* on the errors of Lamennais, or Pius IX's *Quanta cura* with its infamous appendix, the *Syllabus of Errors*. According to Richard Camp, the pre-Leonine period popes "had little to contribute to a Catholic doctrine of social reform."[1]

Yet, dismissing the pre-Leonine period encyclicals is a mistake. Rather than a useless corpus, these letters inaugurate a critique of Enlightenment claims concerning society and individuality central to subsequent papal thought. Positively, the popes' communitarian understanding of the self and society establishes a precedent which survives 249 years of encyclical composition.

This chapter examines the pre-Leonine period letters. It begins with an overview of the texts, noting their general historical context. Then, two aspects of the encyclicals are studied: the problems they identify and the solutions they offer. The chapter concludes with a summary interpretation of pre-Leonine period social teaching.

Overview

Following Benedict XIV's inception of modern encyclical writing, nine popes produce seventy-seven letters antedating Leo XIII. Most addressees are bishops. There are thirty-four *litterae encyclicae* (letters to all bishops) and thirty-six *epistolae encyclicae* (letters to bishops of specific countries). Exceptions include five letters written to "all the faithful," one letter to missionaries, and one to heads of religious congregations.

The popes' major interests are morality and worship. Only one pre-Leonine period encyclical exclusively treats a doctrinal issue: Pius IX's *Ubi primum* on the Immaculate Conception. Of the sixty-three letters concerning Christian morality, twenty-four focus on clerical discipline and thirty-nine address the moral life of the laity.

Pre-Leonine period encyclicals can be grouped in three chronological clusters: the "prerevolutionary" letters occurring before the French Revolution; the "interrevolutionary" letters appearing during the Revolution and the rise of Napoleon; the "postrevolutionary" texts spanning the European Restoration to the accession of Leo XIII.

The twenty-four prerevolutionary encyclicals are produced by Benedict XIV (1740-58), Clement XIII (1758-69), Clement XIV (1769-74), and Pius VI (1775-99). During this period, Tridentine Church reforms begun in the sixteenth century continue, while new external forces challenge ecclesiastical discipline. Bourbon monarchs expel the Society of Jesus from their territories and the Hapsburgs claim legislative control over the Church in the Austro-Hungarian Empire. Absolute monarchs (Maria Theresa and Joseph II in Austria, Frederick the Great in Prussia, Catherine the Great in Russia, Louis XV in France) govern lands still emerging from feudalism, populated by subjects vaguely aware of national identity. Vitalized by precious metal imports from Mexico and Peru, the European economy accelerates. For a time, the commercial revolution reinforces mercantilism, the state-controlled halfway house between medieval economic traditionalism and the modern market system. The philosophical Enlightenment begun in the previous century by men such as Thomas Hobbes, René Descartes, and John Locke spreads through the polemical tracts of the French *philosophes* and Italian *illuministi*. Jean-Jacques Rousseau and David Hume produce this movement's first internal critique. Culturally, Fragonard and Chardin bring baroque art to its final stage, Bach and Handel dominate European music, and Voltaire's writings enliven the Continent's literary salons.

Only two encyclicals, one by Pius VI and the other by Pius VII (1800-23), represent the interrevolutionary corpus. This forty-eight-year lapse is caused by the eruption and aftermath of the French Revolution. During this period, numerous French clergy and laity are imprisoned, killed, or deported; papal communications are restricted or banned; and Church property is appropriated. At the same time, the English steam engine and factory system unleash economic forces requisite for nascent industrial capitalism. Adam Smith surveys the phenomenon in 1776, launching classical economic analysis. In Prussia, Immanuel Kant challenges Continental philosophy, while English politicians and philosophers discuss Edmund Burke's conservative response to the French Revolution and Jeremy Bentham's radical utilitarianism. Mozart's neoclassicism and Beethoven's romanticism mark the period's musical development. Goethe, Schiller, Byron, Shelley, Goya, and Géricault reflect literary and artistic forces inspired by this revolutionary era.

The postrevolutionary encyclicals are the work of Leo XII (1823-29), Pius VIII (1829-30), Gregory XVI (1831-46), and Pius IX (1846-78). These popes revive the genre with fifty-one letters in fifty-five years. At the same time, a new generation of English, German, French, and Italian theologians spark a Roman Catholic intellectual revival. Social forces unleashed by the French Revolution still incite political upheaval, now against the restored governments of Prince von Metternich's Holy Alliance. Significant political changes occur with the 1830 bourgeois revolution in France; the independence movements in Belgium, Poland, and Ireland; the socialist revolutions of 1848 and 1871; and the unifications of Germany and Italy. The second stage of the Industrial Revolution exacerbates these trends. New steel production, rail transportation, and agricultural machinery alter work and home life. An impoverished, volatile industrial proletariat rises. David Ricardo adjusts Smith's economic analysis, but Karl Marx's scientific socialism demands a radical intellectual and practical revision. Philosophers debate Hegel and Schelling's idealism, Auguste Comte's new positive science of society, John Stuart Mill's refined utilitarianism, and Charles Darwin's biological studies. Chopin, Strauss, and Schumann continue the romantic movement in music, while Millet, Daumier, Dickens, Balzac, Flaubert, and Dostoevsky create a new "realism" in art and literature.

Responding to these tumultuous events, encyclicals first emerge as a major genre of papal communication during the pre-Leonine period. Already by 1832 Gregory XVI must publicly apologize in *Mirari vos* for delaying the "customary" inaugural encyclical eighteen months.

Problems

"It is very often the best way of understanding ideas and beliefs," writes John Herman Randall, "to realize what they are reactions against."[2] With this in mind, the practical and theoretical problems discussed in the pre-Leonine period letters require investigation.

Problematic Practices

The popes identify many troublesome practices in European social life. For the sake of analysis, these practices can be grouped in five broad areas of human interaction: religion, politics, family, economics, and culture.

Religious Practices. The pre-Leonine period popes consistently identify four problem areas in the religious practices of the Church: episcopal leadership, clerical discipline, lay religiosity, and theological study. Several specific papal criticisms touch each area.

Concerning episcopal leadership, the popes admonish bishops for imperiousness and vanity, deficient church upkeep, poor catechesis, and laxity in administration of sacraments.[3] Absence of bishops from their appointed sees and neglect of diocesan visitation are also reproved. Additional problems are created by schismatic bishops, some joining the postrevolutionary French Constitutional Church and others creating the Old Catholic Church in protest over the First Vatican Council definition of papal infallibility.[4]

The discipline of lower clergy also meets encyclical scrutiny. Two major problems are clerical ignorance and avarice, the latter involving employment in secular business, changing money, renting land, selling products at markets, and charging fees for religious services.[5] In addition, the popes protest the involvement of priests in Polish uprisings against Russian political and religious oppression in 1768 and 1830.[6]

In the popes' view, the religious life of the laity is threatened by neglect of marriage regulations, Sunday observance, fasting, and religious instruction.[7] The laity are also warned against participating in Protestant "Bible societies," intermingling with Jews, and adopting "Mohammedan names" to avoid taxes levied against non-Moslems in Albania.[8]

For their part, theologians are warned against inappropriate research methods and contentious public behavior. In the former case, the popes reject interpretations of Scripture, doctrine, and canon law which "arise from private reflection, outside the mind and spirit of the Church." In the latter case, the popes admonish public dissent from Church teaching.[9]

Political Practices. Political problems receive significant attention in the pre-Leonine period letters. These troubles can be organized into three areas: state encroachment on Church affairs, government oppression of citizens, and civil violence.

Three forms of state encroachment on the Church successively concern the popes. The first form occurs before the French Revolution when imperious yet otherwise loyal Roman Catholic rulers move against the Jesuits and develop national, state-controlled Church structures. Between 1759 and 1768, Bourbon monarchs of Portugal, France, Spain, Naples, Sicily, and Parma expel the Society of Jesus from their domains on charges of state intrigue and corruption. Political turmoil moves Clement XIV's suppression of the order in 1773. Concurrently, Hapsburg monarchs begin a state-controlled "reform" of Austrian and Hungarian Catholicism under the inspiration of Febronious (Bishop Joann von Hontheim). Between 1765 and 1789, Emperor Joseph II passes more than six thousand *in publico-ecclesiasticis* decrees abolishing episcopal seminaries, dissolving monasteries, conforming diocesan to state boundaries, and bringing episcopal appointment, religious education, marriage, publication of papal documents, even the length of sermons under state supervision. Joseph's brother, Duke Leopold of Tuscany, adopts the same policy in his Florentine kingdom. In Gerald McCool's analysis, Febronianism "had disastrous consequences for the life of the Austrian Church. The faith and piety of the clergy were impaired. Preaching was reduced to moral instruction in which little reference was made to the Christian mysteries. Religious practice declined."[10]

The second form of state encroachment is the work of violently anticlerical forces unleashed during the French Revolution. After confiscating Church property to replenish an exhausted treasury, the new French National Assembly extends its attack by passing the July 1790 Civil Constitution of the Clergy. Announcing a new state-controlled church with state-elected clergy, the Assembly demands all priests renounce the Roman Church and swear allegiance to the constitution. The clerical rejection of these demands precipitates the September Massacres, during which over 30,000 "nonjuror" bishops and priests are deported and over 200 are killed.

Though large-scale state terrorism ends in France after the creation of the Directory in 1795, ongoing anti-Church attitudes among bourgeois politicians encourage restrictive legislation. This third form of state encroachment gains ground across Europe after the collapse of Metternich's Holy Alliance and the July Revolution of 1830 in France. Joseph Moody observes that "nearly every continental European country in the nineteenth century affords examples of legislative discrimination against Catholicism."[11]

Pre-Leonine period letters persistently protest such expropriation of Church land and property, destruction of Church institutions of charity and education, elimination of religious congregations, and government disregard for Church marriage regulations, Sunday religious observance, and almsgiving.[12] In two cases—France and New Granada (present-day Colombia, Venezuela, and Ecuador)—the popes specifically decry state-enforced loyalty oaths.[13]

It should be noted that the popes' distrust of secular states' motives and actions derives from personal experience. In 1798, Napoleon's General Berthier captures Pius VI during the French occupation of Italy. Stripped of the Fisherman's Ring, spirited out of Italy on a torturous journey, and imprisoned in Valence, the pope dies captive in 1799. With this, writes E. E. Y. Hales, "It was widely supposed that the papacy itself had come to an end."[14] Writing his first encyclical (*Diu satis*) from Venice, Pius VII reminds bishops of the difficulties encountered during the recent conclave: "Cardinals were personally expelled from their sees" and "several of them were imprisoned, some hunted for their lives." Eight years later, the same pope falls into the hands of Napoleon's General Radet. He is whisked out of Rome with "one papetto," driven for weeks throughout Italy and France, and finally imprisoned in Savona for six years. Leo XII, then a papal nuncio, witnesses all these events. In 1808, while bishop of Montalto, Pius VIII undergoes arrest and imprisonment. While abbot of the Monastery of San Gregorio on the Caelian Hill, Gregory XVI is driven out of Rome. During the revolutions of 1848, hostile forces besiege Pius IX in the Quirinal, force his departure, and murder the bishop of Parma in his presence.[15]

These experiences heighten papal concern over state oppression of citizens. In *Quanto conficiamur moerore*, 10, Pius IX decries the misuse of state power by a few, gripped by an "insatiable passion for power and possessions." Specific instances of oppression include unjust state expropriation of private property, violation of "rights of parents over their children . . . especially that of providing for education," and all legislation outlawing Roman Catholic religious practices.[16]

Yet, the popes simultaneously reject civil violence against secular states. After the French Revolution, assorted groups of nationalists, socialists, anarchists, and freemasons seek the overthrow of remaining monarchial states. Succeeding bourgeois states subsequently come under the threat of socialist and anarchist terrorism. The groups promoting civil violence throughout the period include: French *Jacobins* and *Babouvists* (1793), the Italian *Carbonaria* (1811), Philippe Buchez' *Charbonnerie française* (1821), Giuseppe Mazzini's *Giovine Italia* (1831), Auguste Blanqui's "Society of the Seasons" (1838), Karl Marx's "Communist League" (1847), Giuseppe Garibaldi's "Red Shirts" (1848), the Russian *Zemlya i Volya* (1862), and Mikhail Bakunin's "International Brotherhood" (1865).[17]

Family Practices. Several family life problems involving marriage and child education concern the popes. As to the former, pre-Leonine period encyclicals consistently target three troublesome forms of marriage: clandestine, mixed, and civil. A clandestine marriage is a secret arrangement between partners, usually for the purpose of marrying a person of choice as opposed to a prearranged marriage. The practice often leads, however, to abandonment of spouses and family feuds. Though already condemned in the Council of Trent's *Tamesti* decree, the practice survives in Central Europe, precipitating Benedict XIV's warnings in *Nimiam licentiam*, 1.[18] Mixed marriages between Roman Catholics and non-Roman Catholics, though not absolutely condemned in canon law, receive persistent papal criticism. Here, popes fear adult loss of faith and the denial of Roman Catholic upbringing to children. Similar problems attend purely civil arrangements, in which Benedict XIV's *Magnae nobis*, 2, says "the sanctity and duties of matrimony" are disregarded.

Economic Practices. Two economic problems trouble the pre-Leonine popes: immoral business practices and theft. Merchants are indicted for the first problem, socialists for the second, and the new liberal states for both.

Immoral business practices include exorbitant profits from sales, fraud, Sunday labor, and usury.[19] Benedict XIV's *Vix pervenit* offers an extended critique of usury. For the pope, usury is a fee charged for the use of money (understood as "sterile"—unable, of itself, to yield a product) without a justifiable "extrinsic" title (such as *periculum*, or risk). As Matthew Habiger notes, Benedict XIV's antiquated understanding of money prevented him from seeing "that in every loan there was an intrinsic value of time that the borrower gained and the lender lost, and that for this the lender should have compensation."[20] Yet beneath this empirical error lies the encyclical's fundamental moral concern: that lenders not exploit borrowers.

Problems with Jewish merchants receive specific papal attention. In *A quo primum*, Benedict XIV cites complaints from Poland concerning Jewish merchants who "control businesses selling liquor and even wine" and are "therefore allowed to supervise the collection of public revenues." Jews also "gained control of inns, bankrupt estates, villages and public land by means of which they have subjugated poor Christian farmers." When employed by wealthy Christians as "'Superintendent-of-the-Household'," Jews "not only administer domestic and economic matters, but they also ceaselessly exhibit and flaunt authority over the Christians they are living with." "Furthermore," Benedict XIV continues, "by means of their particular practice of commerce, they amass a great store of money and then by an exorbitant rate of interest utterly destroy the wealth and inheritance of Christians."

After the Revolution, several newly constituted liberal states proscribe workless religious holidays and individual almsgiving as deleterious to national economic stability.[21] In *Quanta cura*, 4, Pius IX assails such legislation:

> . . . (these wretches) also impiously declare that permission should be refused to citizens and to the Church, "whereby they may openly give alms for the sake of Christian charity"; and that the law should be abrogated "whereby on certain fixed days servile works are prohibited because of God's worship"; and on the most deceptive pretext that the said permission and law are opposed to the principles of the best public economy.

Both liberal states and socialists are charged with property theft. The state is repeatedly indicted for destroying Church property, particularly that devoted to poor relief.[22] Such indictments also lie at the heart of the popes' attitude toward the developing European socialist movement.

The evolution of European socialism during the pre-Leonine period can be broken down into three phases. The first phase begins after the French Legislative Assembly's 1792 call for a halt to the seizure of ecclesiastical and secular property begun during the French Revolution. A dispute over the goals of the revolution ensues. To stabilize property relations, the Girondists support the halt. The Jacobins support continuance, insisting that the revolution's goal of material equity remains unaccomplished.[23] The latter secure victory in the 1793 National Convention and, in their new constitution, decree all lands common, to be equally divided "per head of every domiciled inhabitant of any age or sex, present or absent."[24] But the program is short-lived. Within a year, Robespierre's Committee of Public Safety abolishes the constitution, sending its captured supporters to the guillotine. The egalitarian escapees from the Reign of Terror are the first modern European socialists. Led by François Babeuf, they consider themselves the true standard-bearers of the French Revolution. Babeuf's manifesto declares:

> Nature has given to every man the right to enjoyment of an equal share in all property. . . . The end of the French Revolution is to destroy inequality. . . . The Revolution is not yet terminated, because the rich absorb all valuable productions, and command exclusively. Whilst the poor toil like real slaves, pine in misery, and count for nothing in the State.[25]

Between 1795 and 1796, Babeuf's 'Société des Egaux' undertakes revolutionary political action in the name of economic equality, making three unsuccessful attempts at overthrowing the French Directorate. At this time, the first indirect reference to socialism appears in papal encyclical literature. In *Diu satis*, 13, Pius VII reprehends "enemies of private property and states who are striving to confound all laws, divine and human."

In their second stage of development between 1800 and 1830, socialists turn to various utopian experiments. Some follow the nonviolent, communal vision of Comte de Saint-Simon. Barthélemy Enfantin, an ardent Saint-Simonian, advocates elimination of monogamous marriage in society and forms a church of free love claiming forty thousand members by 1832. Others pursue Charles Fourier's international system of producer *phalanxes*, each containing four hundred families of no more than four members. Though not explicitly cited in the encyclicals, papal knowledge of these developments is probable—both Enfantin and Fourier's writings appear on the Roman *Index Librorum Prohibitorum* in 1835 and 1837.[26]

The radical phase of the socialist movement develops in three steps, beginning with the 1831 silk weavers' revolt in Lyons, France. Deprived of their fixed minimum wage, the workers rebel and seize control of Lyons. This defiance of merchant-politician collusion in the liberal state is routed in ten days. Nevertheless, the experience galvanizes socialists, encouraging a return to earlier aggressive tactics. Within days, Blanqui calls for a dictatorship of intellectuals representing proletariat interests. In 1836 and 1839, his 'minorité consciente' attempts the overthrow of Louis Philippe. In 1839, Louis Blanc declares, "To each according to his need, from each according to his ability." The following year in his essay "Qu'est ce que la propriété?" Pierre Proudhon repeats Brissot's Jacobin indictment against property.

The second step of the radical socialist movement is taken in December 1847, when the secret German branch of Blanqui's 'Society of the Seasons' publishes Karl Marx's *Communist Manifesto*. "Almost immediately," writes Raymond Postgate, "the revolution of 1848 broke out."[27] Over the following weeks, loose coalitions of anarchists, socialists, and nationalists in France, Hungary, Italy, Germany, Ireland, Belgium, Switzerland, and Naples shatter Europe's Holy Alliance. National unification movements are energized and, for the first time, bourgeoisie and proletariat are at loggerheads. During the violence, Monsignor Affre is killed on the Paris barricades. In *Beneficia Dei*, 4, Pius IX calls the Monsignor's murderers "God-forsaken scum." In addition, Count Pellegrino Rossi, the pope's appointee to head the Papal State's new parliament, is assassinated and Pius IX's personal secretary is murdered during a rebel siege of the papal residence. At this time, the first direct encyclical reference to socialism appears. In Pius IX's *Qui pluribus*, 16, the pope disclaims the "unspeakable doctrine of 'Communism' " in which "men in the clothing of sheep" promote "the complete destruction of everyone's laws, government, property, and even of human society."

The third step in the radical phase of the socialist movement occurs in 1865, when various dissident groups create the First International. Though interminably debating socialist theory and practice, "all were agreed," writes Lillian Wallace, "that no compromise was possible with the Catholic Church."[28] Karl Marx, for example, writes to Engels in 1869:

> ... I have become convinced that the priests, especially in the Catholic districts, must be energetically attacked. I shall work along these lines through the International. The dogs (for example, Bishop Ketteler in Mainz, the priests of the Dusseldorf Congress, etc.) are flirting, where they find it suitable to do so, with the labor question.[29]

The following year the socialist *Communards* seize Paris. During the May 1871 Week of Blood, "the Archbishop of Paris [Georges Darboy] and more than fifty priests were shot as hostages and in reprisals."[30] Observing the concurrent rise of radical socialism in Italy, Pius IX writes in *Levate*, 1:

> ... they seek the unjust gain of their own malice and seize the property of others. Then they sadden the lowly and the poor, making widows of wives and orphans of happy children. They pardon the impious and condemn the just, for there are bribes to take and goods to steal; with a corrupt heart they satisfy every depraved desire, to the detriment of all civil society.

Cultural Practices. Problematic cultural practices also come under papal scrutiny. Of particular concern are writing, speech, alcohol consumption, sexual behavior, and education.

Throughout their letters, the popes repeat an almost formulaic diatribe against the period's "great license" of writing and speech. Typical is Clement XIII's complaint against the "contagious plague of books which almost overwhelms us." "They travel with us, stay at home with us, and," cries the pope, "enter bedrooms which would be shut to their evil and deception." The same protest is registered against "immoderate freedom of opinion" which, among other things, gives rein to "maliciously lying" about the Church.[31]

The popes also identify problems concerning alcohol consumption and sexual behavior. Regarding the former, Leo XII admonishes Catholics who, on religious feastdays, "give themselves up to banquets, to

insobriety, to wantonness, and to all the works of the devil."
Regarding the latter, Pius IX attacks the growing houses of prostitution
"established almost everywhere" and "those who live in concubinage
and sometimes in incest."[32]

The pre-Leonine period popes conduct a running battle against state
secularization of education in Europe. After the French Revolution,
newly secularized state schools "engage evil teachers to lead the
students along the paths of Baal by teaching them un-Christian
doctrines." The culprit is European freemasonry, the "secret society"
whose goal is "to eliminate religion and pull apart the bonds of civil
society and overturn it from the ground up."[33] Similarly, socialists and
communists "not content with removing religion from public society,"
writes Pius IX, ". . . wish to banish it also from private families." They
"aim at this result . . . that the salutary teaching and influence of the
Catholic Church may be entirely banished from the instruction and
education of youth."[34] In Oscar Köhler's view, "even if one were critical of a 'world conspiracy' . . . it must be stated that we are dealing
here with the intellectual leaders of the time who waged a ruthless
war against the Catholic Church."[35]

Problematic Ideas

The popes believe "monstrous and depraved suppositions" underlie
Europe's problematic practices.[36] Some of these suppositions are of a
general theological and philosophical nature, others concern specific
social issues. Both sets of concepts require delineation.

General Theological and Philosophical Concepts. Unlike the caricature
of pre-Leonine period popes as unaware and detached from the currents
of modern thought, their encyclicals evidence a lively—though contentious—engagement with new theological and philosophical ideas.[37]
These problematic ideas can be grouped under three topics: God, world,
and humanity.

God. The popes' primary concern is the eighteenth- and nineteenth-
century "trial of the Christian God."[38] Concepts receiving particular
papal attention include the existence and nature of God and the
divinity of Christ.

Regarding God, the popes identify atheism and deism as foremost
problems. In *Christianae reipublicae*, 1, Clement XIII says atheists "deny

God even though He makes Himself known everywhere." Deists, he adds, "represent God Himself as lazy and indolent," and neither "respect His providence" nor "fear His justice." During Clement XIII's reign, deistic tracts by Thomas Woolston (*Six Discourses on the Miracles of Our Saviour* [1727-30]), Voltaire (*L'évangile de la raison*), and Rousseau (*Emile* [1762]—containing the deistic "Profession de foi du vicaire savoyard") are placed on the Index of Forbidden Books. The most outspoken atheist of the period is Baron d'Holbach. His *Le Christianisme dévoilé* (1761) appears on the Index in 1823.

Though the divinity of Christ receives occasional challenge during the eighteenth century, encyclical attention is not aroused until publication of David Friedrich Strauss' *Leben Jesu* (1835-36) and Ernest Renan's *Vie de Jésus* (1863). Both books attract wide readership for their seeming denial of Christ's divinity.[39] Pius IX reproaches this development in *Quanta cura*, 7, warning:

> In this our age some men are found who, moved and excited by the spirit of Satan, have reached to that degree of impiety, as not to shrink from denying our Ruler and Lord Jesus Christ, and impugning His Divinity with wicked pertinacity.

World. The popes also decry atheistic and materialistic interpretations of the physical world inspired by Isaac Newton's laws of matter and motion.[40] These 'naturalistic' understandings of the world are exemplified in Diderot's observation that "the world is no longer a divine thing; it is a machine which has its wheels, its ropes, its pulleys, its springs, and its weights."[41] Voltaire (*Eléments de la philosophie de Newton* [1737]) and Baron d'Holbach (*Système de la nature* [1770]—placed on the Index in 1775) popularize this worldview on the continent. Without naming anyone, Clement XIII complains in *Christianae reipublicae*, 1: "Whether they think that matter has been created or foolishly imagine that it is eternal and independent of causes, they consider that nothing else exists in the universe."

Humanity. The pre-Leonine popes identify several troublesome ideas regarding modern understandings of humanity. These issues include the existence of the human soul, the relationship between reason and faith, and the structure of morality.

The popes lament materialistic disregard for the human soul. In *Histoire naturelle de l'âme* (1745) and *L'homme-machine* (1747-48), Julien Offray de Lamettrie reduces the Christian notion of the soul to an operation of the brain. "Since all the faculties of the soul depend to such a degree on the proper organization of the brain and the whole body," writes Lamettrie, the soul "is clearly an enlightened machine." Thus, the soul is "but an empty word which an enlightened man should use only to signify the part in us that thinks."[42] In *Christianae reipublicae*, 1, Clement XIII argues against those who "preach . . . that the origin and nature of our soul is mortal although it was created in the image of the creator little lower than angels," thereby excluding "the soul from the spirit's heavenly nature."

Several errors regarding the human mind and its relationship to religious faith are noted in the pre-Leonine period letters. Empiricist, Cartesian, skeptical, and critical idealist philosophies are indirectly admonished under the shibboleth "rationalism."

Etienne Bonnot de Condillac was an eighteenth-century Lockean empiricist.[43] In his *Cours d'études pour l'instruction du prince de Parme* (1775), Condillac considers thought a function of the senses, separate from any imagined operation of a soul. In *Christianae reipublicae*, 1, on the other hand, Clement XIII protests: "They are unwilling to understand that in this very weakness of which we are formed something spiritual and incorruptible abides in us. By its power we know, act, will, look to the future, attend to the present, and remember the past." Condillac's work appears on the Index in 1836.

Jean le Rond d'Alembert holds a Cartesian view of knowledge.[44] Here, truth is attained by eliminating all non-self-evident ideas from the mind. On this ground, D'Alembert (unlike Descartes) considers religious faith irrational because its claims are always open to doubt. Again, without explicitly naming his adversary, Clement XIII admonishes "the bold mind of the enquirer" who "takes everything for itself, examines everything, reserves nothing for faith, and deprives faith of merit by seeking proof in human reason."[45] Jean d'Alembert's essays in Diderot's *Dictionnaire Encyclopédique* are condemned in 1759 and 1767.

As a skeptic, David Hume rejects empiricist and Cartesian claims that the mind can attain objective truth. In *An Enquiry Concerning Human Understanding* (1748), Hume thinks what people call "truths" are generalizations based on feelings elicited by observing repeated events. Hume's skepticism, says Cragg, "gradually dissolved the intellectual and religious patterns of thought which had governed European thought since St. Augustine."[46] In *Inscrutabile*, 2, Pius VI admonishes all those who "attack the very bases of rational nature and attempt to overthrow them." Three years after its 1758 revision, Hume's *Enquiry* appears on the Index. In 1827, Hume's complete works are condemned.

Immanuel Kant responds to these conflicting understandings of human cognition and its relationship to religious faith. On the one

hand, Kant accepts Hume's skepticism over acquiring objective knowledge of a "noumenal" world beyond human experience. On the other
hand, Kant insists that objective truths of the "phenomenal" world can
be acquired through the twelve 'a priori' categories of human self-consciousness. Kant also accepts Hume's claim that religious faith neither
contributes to the mind's internal operations, nor exists as a proper
object of rational enquiry. But unlike Hume, Kant holds that the
experience and social necessity of religious faith may yet be real.
Without directly citing Kant, Pius IX complains that some

> . . . feel as if philosophy, which is wholly concerned with the search for truth in
> nature, ought to reject those truths which God Himself, the supreme and merciful
> creator of nature, has deigned to make plain to men as a special gift.[47]

Kant's 'critical idealism' is publicly condemned in 1836 with the
appearance of his *Kritik der reinen Vernunft* (1781) on the Index of Forbidden Books.

In the popes' view, these theories of human cognition and religious
faith are variations on the error of 'rationalism.' According to McCool,

> . . . 'reason' degenerated to 'rationalism' when it claimed that its philosophical
> conclusions entailed either the rejection of religious belief or the confinement of
> religious teaching within the limits of pure reason.[48]

New ideas concerning morality also alarm the popes. With less
intellectual confidence in religious ethics, philosophers propose
exclusively 'natural' criteria for the moral life. The popes directly
criticize two of these innovations: positivism and utilitarianism.

Eighteenth century ethical positivists hold that human beings, by
virtue of their rationality, are naturally good and slated to progress. In
Esquisse d'un tableau historique des progrès de l'esprit humain (published
posthumously in 1795), Marquis de Condorcet outlines ten stages of
humanity's rational progress from religious ignorance to scientific
maturity. "To Condorcet," writes J. Schapiro, "belief in progress was
diametrically opposed to a belief in revealed religion."[49] Auguste Comte,
the precursor of modern sociology, adopts Condorcet's perspective. In
Cours de philosophie positive (1830-42), Comte reduces the ten stages of
human development to three: the primitive, theological stage; the
middle, metaphysical stage; and the modern, scientific stage. Pius IX
makes a related comment in *Qui pluribus*, 12, where he argues against
those who "attempt to destroy faith on the pretext of human progress,
subjecting it in an impious manner to reason and changing the meaning

of the words of God." Condorcet's work appears on the Index in 1827; Comte's treatise is condemned in 1864.

Jeremy Bentham believes "nature has placed mankind under the governance of two sovereign masters, 'pain' and 'pleasure'." As a result, "it is for them alone to point out what we ought to do, as well as to determine what we shall do." According to the "principle of utility," a human action is morally approved or disapproved "according to the tendency which it appears to have to augment or diminish the happiness of every party whose interest is in question."[50] But in *Mirari vos*, 11, Gregory XVI says "every law condemns deliberately doing evil simply because there is some hope that good may result." Bentham's *Deontology* not only receives condemnation in 1835, but is placed on a special list of books forbidden even to members of the hierarchy.

Specific Social Concepts. Though rarely appearing in pre-Leonine period texts, the word 'liberalism'—considered a product of atheism, naturalism, and rationalism—is used to denote all the troublesome concepts affecting social life. This "erroneous philosophical system," in turn, is thought to encourage those social practices identified as threatening Europe's religious, political, familial, economic, and cultural community.[51]

Religion. In pre-Leonine period encyclicals, three ideas are criticized for promoting problematic religious practices: indifferentism, freedom of conscience, and febronianism. Because the last two are considered outcomes of the first, indifferentism receives much papal attention.

Indifferentism is the idea that all religions are equally truthful and valuable. During the pre-Leonine period, indifferentism is promoted by two groups: one using the concept to attack organized religion in toto, the other to challenge the notion of a uniquely privileged divine revelation, religion, or church.[52] No doubt positively influenced by Félicité Lamennais' three-volume *Essai sur l'indifférence* (1817-23), Leo XII issues the first explicit rejection of religious indifference in *Ubi primum*, 4. "It is impossible for the most true God," he writes, "... to approve all sects who profess false teachings which are often inconsistent with one another and contradictory."[53]

An associated notion is the religious "principle of freedom of conscience," wherein an individual claims "a wide freedom to embrace and adopt without danger to his salvation whatever sect or opinion appeals to him on the basis of his private judgment."[54] In *Inter praecipuas*, 9 and 14, Gregory XVI accuses the New York Protestant "Christian League" of promoting private judgment in scriptural interpretation among Italian immigrants to break their attachment to the Catholic Church. Similarly, Pius IX accuses socialists of trying to "draw the Italian people over to Protestantism," knowing "full well that the chief principle of the Protestant tenets, i.e., that the holy scriptures are to be understood by the personal judgment of the individual, will greatly assist their impious cause." By this tactic, he says in *Nostis et Nobiscum*, 6, socialists eventually "cause men to call into doubt the common principles of justice and honor."

The popes also consider Febronianism a product of religious indifference. Febronianism, proposed by Johann von Hontheim in 1763, asserts that the Roman Catholic Church should be governed not by the papal office, but by general councils in doctrinal matters and national churches in disciplinary matters. Moved by this idea, several groups in the Austro-Hungarian Empire, Italy, France, Germany, and Switzerland propose the jurisdictional independence of national Catholic groups from Rome, a democratic concept of church authority in which the entire congregation makes judgments on faith and morals, and a married clergy. Gregory XVI charges one group, the German Offenberg Reformers, with making a false "distinction between the teaching and the discipline of the Church," in this way holding that "there are many things in the discipline of the Church in the present day ... which are not suited to the character of the time." They seek, he adds, "a revolution in the Church ... spread by an impious and absurd system of indifference toward religious matters."[55]

Politics. For the popes, the practical problems of state encroachment on Church affairs, government oppression of citizens, and civil violence are products of false political ideas. In particular, the popes cite mistaken theories of state authority, law, Church-state relations, political freedom, and rights.

Two troublesome ideas concern state authority. The first is the social contract theory. This theory postulates the origin of state authority in the popular will. In *Quanta cura*, 3-4, Pius IX condemns this "totally false idea of social government." Here, "the people's will, manifested by what is called public opinion or in some other way, constitutes a supreme law, free from all divine and human control."[56]

The second error is the idea that state authority originates in human sinfulness. In his bitter disappointment over Louis Philippe's reign in

France, Lamennais writes in *Paroles d'un croyant* (1834): "C'est le péché qui a fait les princes."[57] In *Singulari Nos*, 4, Gregory XVI condemns Lamennais, saying, "the writer transposes the power of the princes, through a new and wicked idea, to the power of State and an omen of subterfuge, as if it were dangerous to divine law, even a work of sin."[58]

In the social contract theory, the foundation of civil law is either popular opinion or the will of the ruler.[59] For the popes, the former idea means that a successful rebellion or "a ludicrous type of plebiscite" can establish law without appeal to God.[60] The latter idea, says Pius IX in *Quod nunquam*, 6, suggests that rulers can impose law "as if on slaves so that they may extort forced obedience through fear."

In the popes' view, the deleterious separation of law from God is a product of the modern theory of Church-state separation. To the supporters of this theory, "guided by the naturalism and rationalism of the Enlightenment," says McCool, "the Church was a private society which, like every other subordinate society in a modern national state, must be subject to the control of the national government."[61] Gregory XVI predicts increasing problems "for religion and government from the plans of those who desire vehemently to separate the Church from the state."[62]

The popes also decry Enlightenment perspectives on political freedom. In the seventeenth century, Hobbes defines the "Free Man" as "he, that in those things, which by his strength and wit he is able to do, is not hindred to doe [sic] what he has a will to." In the following century, Rousseau proclaims: "Man is born free, and everywhere he is in chains."[63] Pius VI complains in *Inscrutabile*, 7:

> They keep proclaiming that man is born free and subject to no one, that society accordingly is a crowd of foolish men who stupidly yield to priests who deceive them and to kings who oppress them, so that the harmony of priest and ruler is only a monstrous conspiracy against the innate liberty of man.[64]

The new concept of human rights associated with the Enlightenment perspective on political freedom receives similar papal disapproval. Hobbes speaks of the "right of nature" as "the liberty each man hath, to use his own power, as he will for himselfe, for the preservation of his own Nature."[65] R. H. Tawney observes that during the Enlightenment " 'nature' had come to connote not divine ordinance but human appetites, and natural rights were invoked by the individualism of the age as a reason why self-interest should be given free play."[66] The popes reject this notion of human rights as overlooking, on the one hand, "the rights both of the sacred and civil power," and, on the other hand, the duties individuals owe God and the community.[67] In *Quanta cura*, 3, Pius IX laments the idea that "a right resides in the citizens to an absolute liberty." Here, "the genuine notion of justice and human right is darkened and lost."[68]

Family. In the pre-Leonine period letters, family problems are linked with mistaken understandings of the nature and purpose of marriage and child upbringing. The popes reject reducing the marriage bond to a "civil contract" and disavow the general suitability of mixed marriage.[69] Noteworthy too is Pius VIII's criticism of the idea that marriage has "no other purpose than that of bringing children into the world."[70]

Economics. During the pre-Leonine period, mistaken notions of amoral economic laws and narrow self-interest receive papal scrutiny. The popes consider these problems a feature of both capitalism and socialism.

Consistent with eighteenth-century fascination over Newton's physical laws and the burgeoning capitalist market system, the novel concepts of 'natural,' amoral economic laws and functional self-interest are promoted throughout Europe. In France, Gourney says "laissez faire et laissez passer, voilà toute la police du commerce" and Morellet calls for "freedom of conscience in trade." In England, Adam Smith thinks a merchant "will be more likely to prevail if he can interest [others'] self-love in his favor, and show them that it is for their own advantage to do for him what he requires of them."[71]

In the popes' view, these ideas are thin veils for avarice. In *Quanto conficiamur moerore*, 10, Pius IX issues a lengthy diatribe against this "most pernicious error." He writes:

> . . . we are referring to that unbridled and damnable self-love and self-interest that drive many to seek their own advantage and profit with clearly no regard for their neighbor. We mean that thoroughly insatiable passion for power and possessions that overrides all rules of justice and honesty and never ceases by every means possible to amass and greedily heap up wealth. Completely absorbed in the things of earth, forgetful of God, religion and their souls, they wrongfully place all their happiness in procuring riches and money.

It is noteworthy that Pius IX links the social contract theory of political authority with the rise of economic avarice. In *Quanta cura*, 4, he asks:

But who does not clearly perceive that human society, when set loose from the bonds of religion and true justice, can have, in truth, no other end than the purpose of obtaining and amassing wealth, and that (society under such circumstances) follows no other law in its actions, except the unchastened desire of administering to its own pleasure and interests?

In *Qui pluribus*, 16, Pius IX considers this same self-interest the core of "the unspeakable doctrine of 'Communism.' " In *Nostis et Nobiscum*, 18, Pius IX accuses " 'Socialism' and 'Communism' " of mutually "misapplying the terms 'liberty' and 'equality' " while deluding the "lower class" with "the promise of a happier condition." Ironically, liberal states spawn their own nemesis. Pius IX writes in *Quanta cura*, 5:

> . . . the [states'] frequent seizure, robbery and open sale of temporal goods which belong to the Church shows a decrease in the people's respect for property consecrated to the use of religion. Consequently, the men who rashly proclaim 'Socialism' and 'Communism' find many prepared to listen to them when they falsely claim that in other similar cases, the property of others can be taken and divided or in some other way turned to the use of everyone.

On a practical and theoretical level, the pre-Leonine period popes consider socialism and communism a derivation, not an antithesis, of the social contract theory of political liberalism.[72]

Culture. In the realm of cultural life, new notions of communication and education trouble the popes. Concerning communication, Pius IX's *Quanta cura*, 3, rejects the idea that people "may be able openly and publicly to manifest and declare any of their ideas whatever, either by word of mouth, by the press, or in any other way." In section 4, he reproaches "the most fatal error of 'Communism and Socialism' " whereby "on civil law alone depend all rights of parents over their children, and especially that of providing for education." Troublesome too is the "new modern style of teaching, which is based on the freedom—or rather license—of knowledge."[73]

Solutions

The pre-Leonine popes not only identify Europe's problematic practices and ideas, but also offer solutions. These solutions are an amalgam of theological perspectives and social recommendations. Delineating both aspects clarifies the popes' positive encyclical teaching.

Theological Perspectives

In the pre-Leonine period texts, a literary device commonly employed in conveying key themes of Christian faith is the pastoral metaphor of a shepherd and his flock. Drawing on scriptural and patristic sources, the popes use this metaphor to envision the person and work of Christ, the problem of sin, the requirements of salvation, and the nature of the Church. Though other images are also used, the frequency of the sheepfold metaphor gives the pre-Leonine period discussion of God, the world, and humanity a distinct character.

When Pius IX says "all our hopes must be placed in God alone," the typical pre-Leonine period referent is Christ the Good Shepherd. The principal source for this image is Jn 10:1-31, where an analogy is drawn between a shepherd's care for his flock and Christ's readiness to teach and die for humanity.[74]

Correspondingly, the popes represent the world as a pasture. Unlike the Enlightenment's heady optimism over a machine-like, controllable world, the popes' pastoral image imparts a cautionary worldview. Though the pasture provides nourishment and rest for the flock, it also contains "trackless places," "ravening wolves," and evil men "in the clothing of sheep."[75]

The general papal perspective on humanity is also influenced by the sheepfold metaphor. Though meager by philosophical standards, the popes' theological anthropology treats the issues of faith, reason, morality, and religious fellowship in human life.

For the popes, Christian faith centers on the teaching, salvific death, and promised return of the Good Shepherd, Jesus Christ. Characteristic of the pastoral genre in literature, the popes emphasize the role of memory in conveying faith across generations. In *Cum summi*, 4-5, Clement XIV encourages Christians to retain the "magnificient heritage" of Christ's teaching (as preserved in the Roman Catholic Church) and "cling to the footsteps of our ancestors."[76] Not until Pius IX's *Qui pluribus* is the role of reason in bolstering faith explored. There—no doubt through the hand of neo-Thomist Joseph Kleutigen—the pope anticipates the correlation of faith and reason found in the First Vatican Council's *Dei filius* document and in the subsequent Leonine period encyclicals. Pius IX writes:

> . . . although faith is above reason, no real disagreement or opposition can ever be found between them; this is because both of them come from the same greatest source of unchanging and eternal truth, God. They give such reciprocal help to each other that true reason shows, maintains and protects the truth of faith, while faith frees reason from all errors and wondrously enlightens, strengthens and perfects

reason with the knowledge of divine matters.

Also reflecting a pastoral literary orientation, the popes' moral perspective emphasizes conversion, imitation of the shepherd, nostalgia for the past, and the virtues of compassion, simplicity, and obedience. Faith, not reason, is the basis of the moral life. Christian morality begins, says Clement XIII in *A quo die*, 11, when human beings "enter the grave with Christ, in order to leave behind the flesh defiled by sin." By this action, the converted "hand over the old man to the wrath of God" so that "a new man might return to life." The "new man" imitates Christ, "model of true virtue." The foremost virtues are love, humility, obedience, and dutifulness "to God, to the Church, to our country, our fellow citizens, and all other men."[77] The "laws of Christ" (Decalogue, Great Commandment, precepts of the Church) assist the virtuous along what Benedict XIV's *Nimiam licentiam*, 14 calls the "age-old, well-trodden way."

This salvific heritage of faith and morality is available only through participation in the religious fellowship of the Roman Catholic Church. Consistent with the popes' pastoral imagery, the predominant pre-Leonine period metaphor for the Church is a flock. In *Quartus supra*, 12, Pius IX defines the Church as "the people in union with the priest, and the flock following its shepherd."[78] As indicated in Pius IX's *Nostis et Nobiscum*, 10, the popes support the principle of *extra ecclesiam nulla salus*—with the *ecclesia* solely represented by the Roman Catholic Church. In *Singulari quidem*, 7, Pius IX allows that one ignorant of this salvific requirement may be excused from God's punishment (a concession first announced only two years earlier in his *Singulari quadam* allocution).

Social Recommendations

Through these conceptualizations of God, the world, and humanity—largely contoured by the sheepfold metaphor—the popes fashion a positive social teaching. These encyclical teachings can be arranged within the religious, political, familial, economic, and cultural dimensions of social life.

Religious Ideas and Practices. The popes' principal emphasis regarding religious life is ecclesial unity. Jesus' Jn 17:21 prayer "that they may all be one" and Cyprian's *Unitate ecclesiae* are favorite pre-Leonine period sources for this focus. Two aspects of this unity are stressed: the hierarchical organization of ecclesiastical power and authority, and the operation of evangelization, education, and spiritual renewal. Several specific teachings attach to both aspects.

The popes hold three factors essential for the organizational unity of religious life. These include the power and authority of the pope, authority and obedience between clerical ranks, and the willful compliance of the laity. The pope, writes Gregory XVI in *Commissum divinitus*, 11, is the "center of unity." "It is Church dogma," he continues, "that the pope, the successor of St. Peter, possesses not only the primacy of honor but also primacy of authority and jurisdiction over the whole Church." The popes cite Jn 21:15-17 and 1 Pt 5:2-4 as warrants for their leadership. In the first pericope, Jesus asks Peter three times, "Do you love me?" and, after repeated assurances, tells him: "feed my lambs," "tend my sheep," feed my sheep." In the second passage, Peter, in turn, directs Church elders to "tend the flock of God that is in your charge." From both passages, Benedict XIV constructs the opening lines of the first modern encyclical:

> When it first pleased God to raise Us to the supreme See of Saint Peter, He entrusted to Us the power of the Vicar of Christ as governor of his universal Church. We heard the divine voice: "Feed my lambs; feed my sheep." The care of both the lambs of the Lord's flock (who are the people scattered through the entire world) and of the sheep (the bishops who act as tender parents of the lambs) is entrusted to the pope.[79]

Relations between and among Church members follow Benedict XIV's pastoral pattern. Bishops, "joined together in the hierarchy," exercise authority over their assigned portion of the flock. Though not members of the hierarchy, priests exercise authority over their assigned parishes in "ecclesiastical spirit" with their bishop. For their part, laity must "show obedience" to their priest, bishop, and pope, "who by God's ordering leads and rules them."[80]

All levels within the organization of the Church must promote activities augmenting ecclesial unity. Major among these operations are evangelization, education, and spiritual renewal.

The popes consider preaching an essential activity of the Church. Clement XIII cites 1 Cor 9:16, saying, "the principal duty of the bishop is to preach the word of God." Preaching forms the flock, "reveals to the faithful the wolves," and recalls lost sheep.[81] Regarding those outside the flock, Gregory XVI's *Probe nostis*, 6-7, extols missionaries who "bravely enter the woods and caves of savages" and "fight the Lord's battles against heresy and unbelief by private and public speech and writings."

Religious education is the second major pre-Leonine period concern. The popes' broad discussion of this issue can be organized around four topics: seminary education, ongoing clerical education, theological study, and the instruction of the laity.

The encyclicals repeatedly recommend that bishops establish seminaries emphasizing the study of Scripture, patristics, and Church law. In the seminaries, writes Clement XIII in *A quo die*, 12, teachers and students "should go to both testaments of the Bible, to the traditions of the Church, and to the writings of the holy fathers." As in their approach to Christian morality, the pre-Leonine period popes do not recommend a single theologian or theological system as a model for seminary education; instead, focus is placed on the study of Scripture and patristics. Haynes observes that Benedict XIV, when bishop of Bologna, ruled that

> . . . the basis of all clerical education . . . must be the reading of the Bible, and of the Early Fathers of the Church. Theology cut off from its sources, he said, "was only a simulacrum," a lifeless image, and those who learned it thus "understood nothing but words, got to know nothing but a form of scholasticism with as many distinctions as a hedgehog has prickles."[82]

Ongoing clerical education should improve homiletics and confession. The recommended source for homiletic instruction is the Roman Catechism, written by Charles Borromeo in 1564 on request of the Council of Trent and reissued by Clement XIII. "They should read often and reflect upon the Roman Catechism," writes Clement XIII, "the summation of Catholic teaching, which provides holy sermons to give to the faithful."[83] Regarding confessors, Benedict XIV admits in *Apostolica Constitutio*, 21:

> . . . since moral theology deals with so many important questions which depend on a knowledge of the sacred canons and the apostolic constitutions, it is obviously a hard task for anyone to know all these well and immediately to solve every question.

Consequently, in difficult cases confessors should consult theological books (avoiding those which "do not well agree with the simplicity of the Gospel and the teaching of the holy fathers") and follow "the opinion which reason suggests and authority confirms."

Theologians assist religious education by clarifying Church teaching and publishing works "to instruct the people." "In this way," explains Pius IX in *Singulari quidem*, 8, "the precious stones of divine dogma might be worked, adapted exactly and wisely decorated, so that they increase in grace, splendor, and beauty—but always in the same fashion and doctrine, in the same meaning and judgment, so that we can speak of a new manner and not a new substance." In their interpretations and publications, theologians must "avoid extremes," neither judging matters with "severity," nor being too "indulgent."[84] Bishops must be prepared, writes Clement XIII in *In Dominico agro*, 4, to "cut away certain developing ideas" among theologians which could "harm the minds of the faithful." In warning theologians, however, bishops should "beware lest words cut too harshly."[85]

The ultimate purpose of seminary, clerical, and theological education is instruction of the laity. According to Benedict XIV in *Ubi primum*, 3, teachers should communicate "those things which the faithful must know for their salvation and explain the main principles of divine law and Catholic dogma." Here, the Roman Catechism should be used as "the norm of Catholic faith and Christian discipline." By this means, the laity, especially young people and "those who are simple or uncultivated," avoid "peculiar ideas—even those of Catholic scholars."

The protection of the laity from "peculiar ideas" underlies the popes' support for long-standing restrictions against the Jews. The Jewish ghetto and the use of the 'badge' were first encouraged by Pope Paul IV in 1555. In *A quo primum*, Benedict XIV cites Paul IV's constitutions approvingly, paying particular attention to proscriptions against Jewish employment of Christian workers and participation in public office. Egal Feldman observes that Pius VI and Leo XII sustain Benedict's policy. For his part, Pius IX removes the gates to the Roman ghetto in 1846, but later reinstalls them.[86]

The third major activity promoting ecclesial unity is the spiritual renewal of clergy and laity. Concerning the clergy, the popes recommend episcopal synods, retreats, spiritual exercises, and recitation of the daily office.[87] The laity are encouraged to pray and fast, receive the sacraments, go on Jubilee Year pilgrimages, and join pious organizations.[88]

Political Ideas and Practices. The pre-Leonine period encyclicals contain several political recommendations. These proposals treat the origin, purpose and exercise of state authority; citizenship; Church-state relations; political freedom; and rights.

The popes' central political teaching is the divine origin of legitimate state authority. "May all recall, according to the admonition of the apostle," asks Gregory XVI in *Mirari vos*, 17, "that 'there is no authority except from God.'" From this foundation, the purpose of state authority is to "protect public safety and enforce the equity of law." Paraphrasing Rom 13:4-5, Clement XIV's *Cum summi*, 6, says rulers are "ministers of God and not without reason do they carry the sword as vindicators in wrath on him who does wrong." But as God's ministers, rulers must avoid abuse of power under threat of eternal punishment. In *Nostis et Nobiscum*, 23, Pius IX quotes Wis 6:6-7, warning rulers that "princes in Christian times feared 'the stern judgment in store for governors,' and the eternal punishment prepared for sinners, in which 'the strong will suffer strong torments.' "

Because God is the remote source of all legitimate temporal authority, the citizens' primary political obligation is obedience to the just state. Citing Rom 13:1-2 and 1 Pt 2:13, the popes insist that "the obedience which men are obliged to render to the authorities established by God is an absolute precept which no one can violate." However, when a state enactment runs "counter to the laws of God or of the Church," rulers forfeit their claim to authority and citizens must passively disobey the law in question.[89] Quoting Acts 5:29, Pius IX notes in *Quod nunquam*, 10: "'It is better to obey God than to obey men.'" Determining these exceptional circumstances, however, is the prerogative of the Church hierarchy.

Pre-Leonine period teaching on Church-state relations emphasizes close collaboration between both institutions. Gregory XVI's remark in *Commissum divinitus*, 20 is representative: "The tranquility of the citizens and the welfare of the Church; these two things cannot be separated from one another." It should be noted, however, that the popes limit their discussion of this topic to traditionally Roman Catholic countries of the post-Reformation era (France, Italy, Austria, Poland, Hungary, Bavaria) and non-Catholic countries containing long-standing Roman Catholic regions (Switzerland, Prussia, Russia).

From this perspective, the popes address three specific topics: the distinction between Church and state, the areas of joint jurisdiction, and the institutional priority of the Church. According to the popes, a distinction must be drawn between Church and state power. Citing Lk 20:25, Pius IX says in *Etsi multa*, 16:

> ... two kinds of power must be distinguished on earth—one natural that looks to the tranquility and secular business of human society; the other, whose origin is above nature, which is in charge of the Church of Christ, divinely instituted for the salvation and peace of souls.

This arrangement requires state administration of secular law, government bureaucracy, and the police and military forces. The Church retains control over the preaching of the Gospel; the time, place, and practice of sacred rites; the distribution and discipline of ecclesiastical offices; the enactment and administration of canon law; and, the regulation of religious congregations, associations, and institutions. The popes, says Pius IX's *Quartus Supra*, 38, take "great pains to maintain this distinction of powers."

Though distinct in power and authority, Church and state share jurisdiction over certain *res mixtae*. For the popes, any civil activity, state law, or policy can become a 'mixed matter' if it directly confronts Christian faith, morality, or worship. Three issues, however, retain persistent status as matters of joint Church-state jurisdiction: marriage, education, and censorship.

Concerning marriage, the popes acknowledge state control over licensing, residency requirements, rights of succession, and the exchange of dowries and inheritances, but insist that Church law govern the requirements of valid marriage, sacramental celebration, and divorce. "Recalling that matrimony is a sacrament and therefore subject to the Church," Gregory XVI says the state must "consider and observe the laws of the Church concerning it."[90]

Despite the eighteenth- and nineteenth-century transition in Roman Catholic countries from a system of optional, Church-administered education to various systems of compulsory state-operated education, the popes insist on Church control over religious and moral instruction in all schools. In *Maximae quidem*, 4, Pius IX worries that

> . . . if these schools stray from the doctrine, authority, and vigilance of the Church . . . honorable men who are destined for the duties of public government and who can contribute so much to the formation of the common spirit of civil society will be infected with errors and false doctrines.

Consequently, Pius IX advises Sicilian bishops in *Cum nuper*, 7 to "Diligently inspect both private and public schools; see that your young people are free from all danger and that they receive a sound and completely Catholic education."

The popes also expect Church and state cooperation in book censorship. In *Inter praecipuas*, 14, Gregory XVI instructs bishops to banish dangerous books "with the aid of the civil powers." "This affair," insists Pius VI's *Inscrutabile*, 8, "is of the greatest importance since it concerns the Catholic faith, the purity of the Church, the teaching of the saints, the peace of the empire, and the safety of the nations." Owen Chadwick observes that, for the episcopacy, "the prestige or comfort of a single author weighed like a feather compared with what lay in the balance, the eternal salvation of a mass of simple folk."[91]

While Church and state distinction and joint jurisdiction are recognized, the popes give social priority to the Church. As a "perfect society," says Pius IX in *Vix dum a Nobis*, 4, the Church claims absolute, autonomous jurisdiction over its affairs and special insight into the spiritual and moral needs of society. "Jesus Christ conferred on His Church," writes Gregory XVI in *Commissum Divinitus*, 10, "the supreme power of administering religion and governing Christian society." According to the popes, this social priority does not threaten the state, but preserves it. Only under Church tutelage, Gregory XVI continues, do people "learn from the cradle itself to maintain their loyalty to rulers, to obey authority, and to venerate the law not only because of fear, but also because of conscience." In addition, Clement XIV's *Cum summi*, 5-6 notes how states benefit from Church advice concerning "the deplorable evils and changes which affect the people and the princes themselves."

Given the benefits of this patronage, states should assist the Church, respecting its jurisdiction and temporal holdings. In particular, the popes call for international recognition of the papal states. With rapid and multiform state incursions on Church affairs during the pre-Leonine period, the popes fear not only change in Church-state relations, but the outright destruction of the Church. Retention of the papal states is thought necessary lest hostile governments dominate and altogether destroy Roman Catholicism. Moody writes: "Pius IX's remark that he would not become a chaplain to the House of Savoy neatly summed up the papal position."[92]

On the subject of political freedom, the popes believe its true exercise is rooted not in the desires of individual will, but in the law of Christ. "Christian law," says Pius IX in *Nostis et Nobiscum*, 24, "protects true liberty." In *Quartus supra*, 40, the pope quotes 1 Pt. 2:16: "As free men, do not use freedom as a pretext for wrongdoing, but use freedom for your work as servants of God."

In the popes' view, human rights are rooted in the rights of God. "There is a strong bond," says Clement XIV's *Cum summi*, 5, "between divine and human rights." Within these twin categories, four types of rights are cited in the pre-Leonine period encyclicals. Divine rights include God's rights to belief, moral obedience, and worship, as well as the Church's institutional right to exist, exercise episcopal jurisdiction, and receive the obedience of the faithful.[93] Human rights include the institutional right of the state to exist, exercise legitimate authority, and receive the obedience of citizens, as well as the individual citizen's right to educate and care for children, possess property, and receive necessary material goods from the superfluity of society.[94] In addition, "Catholic people have a right not to be impeded in the divinely imposed duty of following the doctrine, discipline, and laws of the Church."[95]

Overall, the popes understand rights not as warrants for the exercise of individual will, but as divine titles grounding the jurisdictional authority of Church and state, as well as the expectations human beings may justifiably possess regarding types of positive treatment in society. This perspective approximates what Richard Tuck calls a 'passive theory.' Here, "all rights were claim rights: they all required other men to act in some way towards the claimant, to grant him something." Also, like the popes' approach, the passive theory locates the rights of the state in the will of God. This approach differs from an 'active theory,' where rights are considered a prerogative located in the human will whereby individuals are morally free to pursue personal desires short of physically injuring others. Unlike the popes' approach, the active theory locates the rights of the state in the popular will.[96]

Family Ideas and Practices. Pre-Leonine period teaching on family life touches three topics. These include the nature and purpose of marriage, the proper relationship between partners, and the responsibilities of spouses and parents.

In the popes' view, marriage is marked by the twin features of sanctity and perpetuity. Drawing on Eph 5:21-6:9, Pius VIII links these characteristics with Christ's relationship to the Church:

> The union of marriage signifies the perpetual and sublime union of Christ with his Church; as a result, the close union of husband and wife is a sacrament, that is, a sacred sign of the immortal love of Christ for His spouse.

The popes emphasize religious education of children as a primary purpose of married life. Here, they borrow Augustine's notion of procreation and nurture as primary goods of marriage, but stress the second good over the first. Since Christ raised marriage "to the dignity of a sacrament," according to Pius VIII, ". . . its purpose is not so much to generate offspring as to educate children for God and for religion."[97]

The popes also use Augustine's interpretation of Eph 5:21- 6:9 as a guide for proper relations between spouses. Quoting Augustine's *De moribus Ecclesiae Catholicae*, Pius IX says in *Nostis et Nobiscum*, 33, that wives should be subject to their husbands, while husbands should rule their wives "not in scorn of the weaker sex but under the law of pure love." Benedict XIV gives a brief example of appropriate spousal behavior in his *Apostolica Constitutio*, 7, announcement of the 1750 Holy Year. According to the pope, husbands should not go on pilgrimage without their wives' permission; a wife may travel to Rome alone, but preferably accompanied by her husband's brother.

Spouses are responsible for educating themselves and their children in the Christian faith. Concerning the former obligation, Pius VIII's

Traditi humilitati, 10, says bishops and priests should assist spouses by explaining "those things which pertain to the essence of the sacrament."[98] As to the latter responsibility, Gregory XVI cites Eph 6:4 in *Summo iugiter studio,* 6, "which enjoins parents to rear their children in the discipline and admonitions of the Lord." In *Cum religiosi,* 1, Benedict XIV emphasizes the father's catechetical role:

> Fathers of families and Lords of houses should be gravely advised of the duty imposed on them of being themselves instructed and of seeing to the instruction in the commandments of Christian doctrine of the sons and of the members of the household.[99]

Economic Ideas and Practices. Papal teaching on economic life concerns the conduct of business in the developing market system, property ownership, relations between the rich and the poor, and the economic role of the Church and the state. Several recommendations are made under each category.

According to the popes, it is fully appropriate for Christians to participate in the modern market system of economic production and distribution. Christians may spend and invest money "either to provide oneself with an annual income or to engage in legitimate trade and business." They may also make a "simple, plain loan," establish contracts "in the realm of business," and practice "money-changing." All these activities should serve the needs of both the individual and the community.[100]

The popes approve individual ownership of personal and productive property. In *Nostis et Nobiscum,* 20, Pius IX indirectly supports individual ownership by citing scriptural condemnations of theft. "They forbid us strictly," he warns, "even to desire the goods of other men, much less seize them." Nevertheless, ownership is not absolute. "It is not justifiable to use it [material goods] for ourselves in such a way that," says Clement XIII in *A quo die,* 9, "nothing remains for those who could rightfully cry out, 'What you spend is ours!' "

Pre-Leonine period teaching on relations between the rich and the poor is contradictory. On the one hand, some texts follow the paternalistic model of complementarity first proposed in the second-century *Shepherd of Hermas.* Here, the rich charitably assist the poor out of love for Christ and fear of eternal punishment; the poor express gratitude and obedience to the rich, confident that their patience will grant them eternal reward. In Pius IX's view, some people will always "surpass others in different endowments of mind or body or in riches and such external goods." As a result, emphasis should be placed not on elimi-

nation of social classes, but on their spiritual and temporal complementarity.[101]

Clement XIII, on the other hand, asks all Christians to forsake
extravagance and "be content with the good things we receive, that is
food and shelter." Citing Jas 2:15 in *A quo die*, 9, the pope claims alms
are not simply the product of Christian charity, but the "most important fruit of justice." The poor "require our generosity," says Clement
XIII, "as their principal right." Recalling the pre-Leonine period
approach toward the moral life, Clement XIII finds the basis of this
right in the "justice which comes from faith."[102]

As social institutions, both Church and state have important economic
roles. Citing Lk 4:18 in *Charitate Christi*, 18, Leo XII commits the Church
to "the care of all classes . . . but especially that of the poor." The Church
must offer its own goods to the poor, "seek the aid of the wealthy," and
encourage a range of nonstate service organizations such as charitable
associations "under the rule of St. Vincent de Paul," banks of "commodities and money lending," homes for orphans, and hospitals. In addition,
"by the secret judgment of God," the popes are "detailed to fight"
socialism and communism. The state is given the general directive to
observe the laws of the Church on economic matters, especially those
regarding almsgiving and Sunday rest.[103]

Cultural Ideas and Practices. The popes offer several recommendations in the cultural spheres of communication, education, and group
relations. In each sphere, the popes seek improvements through
Church-state cooperation and individual moral reform.

In the area of communication, the popes believe the "license of
thinking, speaking, writing, and reading" must be repressed through
joint Church and state censorship of books. "So long as its stock and
seed is not removed and destroyed (I shudder to say it but it must be
said)," writes Pius VII in *Diu satis*, 17, "it will spread abroad and be
strengthened to reach over the whole world."

The Church must also monitor education and seek the eradication
of secret societies. In *Cum nuper*, 7, Pius IX states: "The prosperity of
the spiritual and civil communities depends greatly on the proper
education of youth." Adverting to the sheepfold metaphor, Pius VII
tells clergy in *Diu satis*, 14: "Keep out the ravening wolves who do not
spare the flock of innocent lambs, and expel them if necessary by the
way they entered." To this end, Pius VI's *Inscrutabile*, 8 asks Church
and state authorities to expel the "foul contagion" of masonic and
socialist secret societies from their lands.

Summary Interpretation

By adopting a textually inclusive and topically broad-gauged approach toward the papal encyclicals, a previously unacknowledged body of papal social teaching emerges from the pre-Leonine period. This teaching is an amalgam of theological perspective and social recommendations forged in lively scrutiny of Europe's problematic practices and ideas. The popes' double-pulsed approach combines negative judgments and positive recommendations regarding general concepts of God, humanity, and the world, and specific practices and ideas concerning religious, political, family, economic, and cultural life.

According to the popes, the problem of eighteenth- and nineteenth-century Europe is the erosion of communal unity in traditionally Roman Catholic countries and regions. This erosion appears in religious life (negligent bishops, arrant clergy, torpid laity, contentious theologians), political life (state encroachment and oppression, civil violence), family life (bad marriages), economic life (merchant immorality, state confiscation, socialist destruction), and cultural life (licentious communication and sexuality, secular education).

The popes believe false ideas underlie this social erosion. In particular, Enlightenment notions of God (atheism, deism, and denial of Christ's divinity), the world (naturalism), and humanity (rationalism and positivist or utilitarian morality) generate the destructive spirit of liberalism. This spirit spawns disastrous theories in every sphere of society: religion (religious indifferentism, Febronianism, and freedom of conscience), politics (social contract, separation of Church and state, autonomous freedom and rights), family (civil marriage), economics (self-interest—whether individualistic, as in capitalism, or collective, as in socialism), and culture (freedom of expression and education).

Alternatively, the popes offer what can be called a 'territorial' communitarian ethic. The ethic is territorial in that the popes focus exclusively on reform of ideas and practices in Roman Catholic countries and regions. From a sociological perspective, the popes view community primarily as a "spatial milieu": a "cluster of people living within a specific geographic area" following a specific recipe of religious and moral customs.[104]

The encyclical ethic is 'communitarian' by virtue of the popes' implied understandings of the self and society. For the popes, the human self is embedded in the traditions of the territorial community. This embeddedness provides a person's sense of identity and purpose, defined by one's functions and obligations in the community. From this perspective, people possess what Alan Buchanan calls "special non-voluntary obligations"—duties to family, friends, parish, neighborhood, and country which precede voluntary choice.[105] The popes' distinctive understanding of freedom and human rights flows from this notion of the communally embedded self.

The popes' model of society in Roman Catholic countries and regions is a hierarchically organized community of mutual aid where people with customarily acknowledged roles and powers work together, deferentially, for the preservation of the whole. This is an example of what Raymond Plant describes as

> ... a stratified but organic and interdependent social order, reflecting the necessary but complementary and functional inequalities in human endowment and the whole being bound together by an ethic of mutual service between the ranks of the hierarchy.[106]

With this vision of an interdependent social order, the popes believe not only problems, but also solutions cut across all spheres of social interaction. This "principle of continuity," says Philip Selznick, characterizes the "communitarian perspective"; it "looks to the continuities of life, to how things fit together and are interdependent, and finds in those continuities the primordial sources of obligation and responsibility."[107] Thus, concerning religious ideas and practices, the popes emphasize papal authority, differential authority and obedience between clerical ranks, the obedience of the laity, homiletic and catechismal religious instruction, and deference of theologians on matters of theological substance. In political life, the popes recommend odedience to divinely established authority, passive resistance to immoral laws, functional distinction and close collaboration between Church and state, and recognition of certain human rights (understood 'passively') and the institutional rights of both Church and state. Concerning family life, the popes emphasize the sanctity and perpetuity of marriage vows, the authority of husbands over wives and children, and parental responsibility for child education. In economic life, the popes accept a market system adjusted to the needs of the community: within limits, private property, trade, investment and loans are approved; material inequality between rich and poor is considered as beneficial as it is inevitable (though Clement XIII offers an implied disagreement on this matter); and, both Church and state have a positive economic role through support of various intermediate institutions offering material assistance to the poor. In the realm of culture, the popes support Church-state collaboration on censorship and education.

Finally, it must be recalled that the popes' territorial communitarian approach constitutes a 'theological' social ethic. The source of social morality is God's will, mediated through Scripture, patristics, and Church tradition, and uniquely envisioned through the pastoral metaphor of a shepherd and his flock. The popes' theological foundations (Christ the Good Shepherd, the ambiguity of the pasture, the Shepherd as moral model of wisdom and virtue, the Church as a flock) encourage the model of a "tightly knit" community characteristic of pastoral literature.[108]

The common view that no substantial encyclical social teaching exists in the pre-Leonine period is incorrect. But beyond its mere existence, pre-Leonine social teaching also plays a vital role in understanding the content and coherence of encyclical social teaching as a whole. Establishing this claim requires an investigation of the next generation of papal encyclicals.

NOTES

1.   Richard L. Camp, *The Papal Ideology of Social Reform: A Study in Historical Development 1878-1967* (Leiden: E.J. Brill, 1969), p. 7. Renzo Bianchi makes the same claim in *Liberalism and Its Critics, with Special Attention to the Economic Doctrine of the Roman Catholic Church* (Northfield, Minn.: Carleton College Economics Club, [1958]), p. 53.

2.   John Herman Randall, Jr., *The Making of the Modern Mind: A Survey of the Intellectual Background of the Present Age*, 50th anniversary ed., with a foreword by Jacques Barzun (New York: Columbia University Press, 1976), p. 15.

3.   See Clement XIII, *A quo die*, 6-8, *In Dominico agro*, 5, *Cum primum*, 13; Pius VI, *Inscrutabile*, 5. Sacramental irregularities occur in marriage (Benedict XIV, *Nimiam licentiam*, 4-6, *Apostolica Constitutio*, 16; Pius VIII, *Traditi humilitati*, 10), holy orders (Benedict XIV, *Ubi primum*, 1-2; Clement XIII, *A quo die*, 13; Pius VI, *Inscrutabile*, 3), and penance (Benedict XIV, *Apostolica Constitutio*, 15-23; Leo XII, *Charitate Christi*, 5-11).

4.   On episcopal residence and visitation, see Benedict XIV, *Ubi primum*, 4-5; Clement XIII, *A quo die*, 15; Pius VI, *Charitas*, 28; Leo XII, *Ubi primum*, 6-9. On schismatic bishops, see Pius VI, *Charitas*, 9-27 and Pius IX, *Etsi multa*, 21-26.

5.   On clerical ignorance, see Benedict XIV, *Ubi primum*, 2, *Quanta cura*; Pius VI, *Inscrutabile*, 3; Pius VIII, *Traditi humilitati*, 8; Pius IX, *Qui pluribus*, 25. On clerical avarice, see Benedict XIV, *Quanta cura*; Clement XIII, *Cum primum*; Clement XIV, *Decet quam maxime*, *Cum summi*, 7; Pius VI, *Inscrutabile*, 5.

6.   In *Summa quae*, Clement XIII rejects clerical participation in the 1768 Confederation of Bar uprising. In *Cum primum*, Gregory XVI protests the 1830 revolts. See Bernhard Stasiewski, "State and Church in Poland-Lithuania to the End of the Republic of the Aristocracy," in Wolfgang Müller et al., *The Church in the Age of Absolutism and Enlightenment*, trans. Gunther J. Holst (New York: Crossroad, 1981), p. 490; and Roger Aubert, "The Other European Churches," in Roger Aubert et al., *The Church between Revolution and Restoration*, trans. Peter Becker (New York: Crossroad, 1981), pp. 156-58.

7.   See Benedict XIV, *Nimiam licentiam*, 1, 4, 6, *Cum Religiosi*; Leo XII, *Charitate Christi*, 13, 15; Pius IX, *Nostis et Nobiscum*, 13, *Amantissimi Redemptoris*, 6.

8. According to Pius VIII in *Traditi humilitati*, 5, proponents of Bible societies "skillfully distort the meaning by their own interpretation" and, when printing Bibles, add "perverse little inserts to insure that the reader imbibes their lethal poison." On intermingling with Jews, see Benedict XIV, *A quo primum* 3, 5. Here, the Polish laity are reproved for accepting employment as servants in Jewish households or employing Jews as head servants. On the use of Moslem names, see Benedict XIV, *Quod Provinciale*, 1.

9. On private interpretation, see Clement XIII, *Cum primum*, 8, *In Dominico agro*, 2-3; Gregory XVI, *Singulari Nos*, 5. On public dissent, see Benedict XIV, *Vix pervenit*, 4, 8; Clement XIII, *A quo die*, 2, *In Dominico agro*, 2, 4-5, 7; Gregory XVI, *Singulari Nos*, 8; Pius IX, *Inter multiplices*, 8, *Neminem vestrum*, 3.

10. Gerald A. McCool, *Catholic Theology in the Nineteenth Century: The Quest for a Unitary Method* (New York: Seabury Press, Crossroad Books, 1977), p. 22.

11. Joseph N. Moody, "The Church and the New Forces in Western Europe and Italy," in Joseph N. Moody, ed., *Church and Society: Catholic Social and Political Thought and Movements 1789-1950* (New York: Arts, Inc., 1953), p. 3. States specifically indicted in the papal letters for some or all of these encroachments include: France (Pius VI, *Charitas*), the Kingdom of Sardinia (Pius IX, *Quanto conficiamur moerore*, *Levate*, 1-2, *Respicientes*, 1, *Ubi Nos*), Austria (Pius IX, *Singulari quidem*, *Vix dum a Nobis*), Switzerland (Gregory XVI, *Commissum divinitus*; Pius IX, *Graves ac diuturnae*, *Etsi multa*), Russia and Poland (*Levate*, 3-8), New Granada (Pius IX, *Incredibili*), and the German states of Prussia (Pius IX, *Etsi multa*, *Quod nunquam*), Bavaria (Pius IX, *Maximae quidem*), and Rhineland (Gregory XVI, *Quo graviora*).

12. On property expropriation, see Pius VII, *Diu satis*, 19; Pius IX, *Quanta cura*, 5. On destruction of institutions and religious congregations, see Leo XII, *Charitate Christi*, 18; Gregory XVI, *Commissum divinitus*, 13; Pius IX, *Nostis et Nobiscum*, 31, *Probe noscitis Venerabiles*, 2, *Singulari quidem*, 17, *Cum nuper*, 7, *Quanto conficiamur moerore*, 12, *Maximae quidem*, 14, *Quanta cura*, 4. On government disregard for Church practices, see Leo XII, *Charitate Christi*, 15; Gregory XVI, *Commissum divinitus*, 13; Pius IX, *Quanta cura*, 4.

13. See Pius VI, *Caritas* and Pius IX, *Incredibili*.

14. E. E. Y. Hales, *Revolution and Papacy, 1769-1846* (London: Eyre & Spottiswoode, 1960), p. 129.

15. See E. E. Y. Hales, *Pio Nono: A Study in European Politics and Religion in the Nineteenth Century* (New York: P.J. Kenedy & Sons, 1954), pp. 91-95.

16. See Pius IX, *Nostis et Nobiscum*, 20 and *Quanta Cura*, 4.

17. For general condemnations, see Leo XII, *Quod hoc ineunte*, 5, 12; Pius VIII, *Traditi humilitati*, 6; Gregory XVI, *Cum primum*, 2; Pius IX, *Qui pluribus*, 4, *Nostis et Nobiscum*, 32, *Levate*, 1. For condemnations of the French revolutionaries, see Pius VII, *Diu satis*, 20. On socialism and violence, see Pius VII, *Diu satis*, 13 (here, socialists are unnamed, but the reference is probable owing to use of what becomes an almost formulaic reproach against them as "enemies of private property and states" who corrupt "young minds"). See also Pius IX, *Qui pluribus*, 13, *Nostis et Nobiscum*, 6, 25, *Apostolicae Nostrae caritatis*, 1, *Quanta cura*, 4. Anarchists are reproved in Gregory XVI, *Mirari vos*, 17, 21, *Singulari Nos*, 4-6 and Pius IX, *Exultavit cor Nostrum*, 2, *Qui Nuper*, 1. Pius IX directly indicts freemasons in *Etsi multa*, 28.

18. Theodore Mackin observes that, until the sixteenth century, the Church was reluctant to condemn clandestine marriages, thinking it outside her competence to invent a new condition for the validity of matrimony beyond the consent of the partners. *What Is Marriage?: Marriage in the Catholic Church* (New York: Paulist Press, 1982), pp. 194-98.

19. The popes frequently refer to "turpe lucrum," which John Baldwin identifies as a long-standing technical term in moral theology for "immoral profits derived from sale." "The Medieval Theories of the Just Price: Romanists, Canonists, and Theologians

in the 12th and 13th Centuries," *Transactions of the American Philosophical Society* 49 (1959): 38. See Benedict XIV, *Quanta cura*, 4; Clement XIII, *Cum primum*, 1; Pius IX, *Quanto conficiamur moerore*, 10. On fraud, see Benedict XIV, *Quanta cura*, 2; Clement XIII, *Cum primum*, 6. On Sunday labor, see Pius IX, *Nostis et Nobiscum*, 13.

20.   Matthew Habiger, "Is the Magisterium a Reliable Moral Guide? The Case of Usury," *Social Justice Review* 80 (May-June, 1989): 75. See also Roger Charles, with Drostan MacLaren, *The Social Teaching of Vatican Two: Its Origin and Development* (San Francisco: Ignatius Press, 1982), p. 287; Henry Davis, *Moral and Pastoral Theology*, Heythrop Series 2, 4th ed., rev. and enl., 4 vols. (London: Sheed and Ward, 1945), 2:375-77; Renée Haynes, *Philosopher King: The Humanist Pope Benedict XIV* (London: Weidenfeld & Nicolson, 1970) pp. 175-77; Franz H. Mueller, "The Church and the Social Question," in Joseph N. Moody and Justus George Lawler, eds., *The Challenge of Mater et Magistra* (New York: Herder and Herder, 1963), pp. 45-46; John T. Noonan, Jr., *The Scholastic Analysis of Usury* (Cambridge: Harvard University Press, 1957), pp. 356-57.

21.   Amintore Fanfani says Italian politicians ask Pius VI in 1783 to reduce workless religious holidays from eighty-eight to seventy-one a year. *Le origini dello spirito capitalistico in Italia* (Milan: Societá editrice "Vita e Pensiero," 1933), p. 64, n. 3. According to Carlo Cipolla, almsgiving accounts for immense transfers of personal, business, and royal income to the Church. He also shows the decline in upper class "ordinary charity" from up to five percent consumption expenditure to less than one percent between the sixteenth and nineteenth centuries. *Before the Industrial Revolution: European Society and Economy, 1000-1700*, 2nd ed. (New York: W. W. Norton & Co., 1980), pp. 19- 24.

22.   In *Charitate Christi*, 18, Leo XII complains that the Church-supported "bank of commodities and of money lending" (*montes pietatis*) were "closed by the rapacity of those who had boasted to be the liberators of the popular happiness." Habiger quotes from the Lateran V *Inter multiplices* document, describing the *montes pietatis* as a "sort of municipal, clerical pawnshop 'founded for the purpose of relieving the needs of the poor by loans of this kind and thus protecting them from the avarice of usurers.' " "The Case of Usury," p. 76.

23.   In his 1780 *Sur la propriété*, Brissot de Warville—an ardent Jacobin—writes: "La propriété, c'est le vol." Quoted in Victor Cathrein, *Socialism: Its Theoretical Basis and Practical Application*, trans. Victor F. Gettelmann (New York: Benziger Bros., 1904), p. 24.

24.   "Jacobin Law on Communal Lands, June 10, 1793," in Raymond Postgate, ed., *Revolution from 1789 to 1906* (Gloucester, Mass.: Peter Smith, 1969), p. 47.

25.   Ibid., pp. 56-57.

26.   The pre-Leonine period popes make several references to the *Index Librorum Prohibitorum*. See Leo XII, *Ubi primum*, 19; Pius VIII, *Traditi humilitati*, 5; Gregory XVI, *Inter praecipuas*, 11; Pius IX, *Inter multiplices*, 7. All references to books on the Index are taken from Joseph Hilgers' list in *Der Index der verbotenen Bücher* (Freiburg im Breisgau: Herdersche Verlagshandlung, 1904) and Albert Sleumer's list in *Index Romanus* (Osnabruck, Germany: Jul. Jonscher, 1951). See also Redmond A. Burke, *What Is the Index?* (Milwaukee: Bruce, 1952); Humphrey J.T. Johnson, "The Roman Index of Prohibited Books," *Downside Review* 73 (April 1955): 160-73; National Literary Commission, *Study Guide to the 'Index Librorum Prohibitorum' and the Censorship Regulations* (Detroit: Marygrove College, n.d.); and Owen Chadwick, *Popes and European Revolution* (Oxford: Clarendon Press, 1981), pp. 324-27.

27.   Postgate, *Revolution*, p. 140.

28.   Lillian P. Wallace, *Leo XIII and the Rise of Socialism* ([Durham, N. C.]: Duke University Press, 1966), p. 42.

29.   Karl Marx to Frederick Engels, September 25, 1869, in Saul K. Padover, ed. and trans., *On Religion: Karl Marx*, The Karl Marx Library, vol. 5 (New York: McGraw-Hill Book Co., 1974), p. 253.

30.   John McManners, *Church and State in France, 1870-1914* (New York: Harper & Row, Harper Torchbooks, 1973), p. 33.

31.   Benedict XIV, *Peregrinantes*, 11. According to Daniel-Rops, "the number of anti-religious lampoons published during the eighteenth century is incredible." *The Church in the Eighteenth Century*, trans. John Warrington (New York: E. P. Dutton, 1964), p. 74. Friedrich Heyer notes that "In France, in twenty years prior to the Revolution, there were 400 new anti-religious publications." *The Catholic Church from 1648 to 1870*, trans. D.W.D. Shaw (London: Adam & Charles Black, 1969), p. 87.

32.   On alcohol consumption, see Leo XII, *Charitate Christi*, 13. On sexual behavior, see Pius IX, *Nostis et Nobiscum*, 13 and *Quanto conficiamur moerore*, 3. In *Love, Sex, and Marriage through the Ages* (New York: Springer Publishing Company, 1974), p. 233, Bernard Murstein argues that "As sin became more socially acceptable during the age of reason and enlightenment, prostitution flourished." According to Edward Shorter, "a revolution in eroticism" occurs between the middle of the eighteenth to the end of the nineteenth centuries. Illegitimacy rates soar due to "heightened ego awareness [public education] and . . . weakened superego controls [social dislocations of market-place economy, such as absence of the father due to separation of home and workplace]." "Illegitimacy, Sexual Revolution, and Social Change in Modern Europe," in Theodore K. Rabb and Robert I. Rotberg, eds., *The Family in History* (New York: Harper & Row, Harper Torchbooks, 1971), pp. 48 and 63. See also Owen Chadwick, *The Secularization of the European Mind in the Nineteenth Century* (Cambridge: Cambridge University Press, 1975), p. 3.

33.   Pius IX, *Exultavit cor Nostrum*, 2. Clement XII (1730-1740) issues the first formal condemnation of freemasonry twenty-one years after the group's founding in 1717. See *New Catholic Encyclopedia*, s.v. "Freemasonry," by W. J. Whalen.

34.   On secularized education, see Pius VIII, *Traditi humilitati*, 7, and Leo XII, *Charitate Christi*, 15; Gregory XIV, *Mirari vos*, 5, *Probe nostis*, 1; Pius IX, *Quanta cura*, 4. On socialism, see Pius IX, *Quanta cura* and *Qui pluribus*, 16.

35.   Oscar Köhler, "The Development of Catholicism in Modern Society," in Roger Aubert et al., *The Church in the Industrial Age*, trans. Margit Resch (New York: Crossroad, 1981), pp. 216-17. Conflict between intellectuals and the Catholic Church is also discussed in Margaret M. O'Dwyer, *The Papacy in the Age of Napoleon and the Restoration: Pius VII, 1800-1823* (Lanham, Md: University Press of America, 1985), p. 205; and Anthony Rhodes, *The Power of Rome in the Twentieth Century: The Vatican in the Age of Liberal Democracies, 1870-1922* (London: Sidgwick & Jackson, 1983), p. 193.

36.   Clement XIII, *Christianae reipublicae*, 1.

37.   Few modern biographies of the pre-Leonine popes exist. Of those that do, Benedict XVI (Haynes), Pius VII (O'Dwyer), and Pius IX (Hales) are depicted as remarkably intelligent and socially aware men.

38.   Emmet John Hughes, *The Church and the Liberal Society* (Notre Dame, Ind.: University of Notre Dame Press, 1961), p. 56.

39.   Discussing Renan's work, Daniel-Rops says "Fifty thousand copies were sold in six months and within a year the work had been translated into six languages." H. Daniel-Rops, *The Church in the Age of Revolution: 1789-1870*, trans. John Warrington (New York: E. P. Dutton, 1965), p. 267. Strauss' book is placed on the Index two years after publication; Renan's appears after two weeks.

40.   Newton himself, however, was neither an atheist nor a materialist. Margaret C. Jacob explains the difference between Newtonianism and later materialists in "Newtonianism and the Origins of the Enlightenment: A Reassessment," *Eighteenth Century Studies* 11 (Fall 1977):1-25.

41.   Quoted in Hughes, *Church and Liberal Society*, p. 62. For proponents of naturalism, writes W. D. Niven, nature "was self-contained and self-explanatory.

Postulating only atoms in motion, the philosopher could explain all phenomena." *Encyclopaedia of Religion and Ethics*, s.v. "Naturalism," by W. D. Niven. Diderot's work is placed on the Index in 1758.

42.   Julien Offray de la Mettrie, *Man a Machine*, notes and translation by Gertrude Bussey (LaSalle, Ill.: Open Court, 1912), p. 128. This work appears on the Index in 1757. Materialists and naturalists agreed, says Niven, that "the soul of man was only rarified matter." "Naturalism." A related claim rejected by the popes is the view that "the holy mysteries of our religion are fictions of human invention." See Pius IX, *Qui pluribus*, 4. This is held by D'Holbach (*System of Nature*), Ludwig Feuerbach (*Essence of Christianity* [1841]), and Karl Marx (*German Ideology* [1846]). The idea goes back to Hobbes' seventeenth-century definition of religion as "Feare of things invisible." Thomas Hobbes, *Leviathan*, ed. and intro. C. B. MacPherson (Harmondsworth, England: Penguin Books, 1968), p. 168.

43.   According to Locke, "external and internal sensation" are the sole "windows by which light is let into this 'dark room.' For, methinks, the understanding is not much unlike a closet wholly shut from light, with only some little openings left, to let in external visible resemblances, or ideas of things." John Locke, *An Essay Concerning Human Understanding*, ed. Alexander Campbell Fraser, 2 vols. (New York: Dover Publishing, 1959), 1:211-12. Locke's essay is placed on the Index in 1734.

44.   In his *Discourse* (1637) and *Meditation on First Philosophy* (1642), Descartes holds that truth comes only through methodical doubt ('dubito ergo sum') and the first truth achieved is knowledge of one's mental activities ('cogito ergo sum'). Though he took Aquinas' *Summa Theologiae* on all his travels, Descartes "broke rather significantly with medieval philosophical thought in his program and proposed method." Richard Schacht, *Classical Modern Philosophy: Descartes to Kant* (London: Routledge and Kegan Paul, 1984), p. 19. Descartes' works appear on the Index in 1663.

45.   Clement XIII, *Christianae reipublicae*, 1. See also Pius VIII, *Traditi humilitati*, 3; Gregory XVI, *Mirari vos*, 22; Pius IX, *Qui pluribus*, 5. By the mid-nineteenth century, French 'traditionalist' theologians (Louis de Bonald, Félicite de Lamennais, Auguste Bonnetty, and Louis Bautain) are condemned for accepting Cartesianism and thereby removing the credibility of God's revelation from reason to tradition. See McCool, *Theology in the Nineteenth Century*, pp. 37-58, and J. Neuner and J. Dupuis, *The Christian Faith in the Doctrinal Documents of the Catholic Church*, rev. ed. (New York: Alba House, 1982), p. 35. In *Ubi primum*, 13, Leo XII rejects the "mad theory that faith should not be investigated, but that each man should persevere in the faith that he was raised in."

46.   Gerald R. Cragg, *The Church and the Age of Reason: 1648-1789* (Harmondsworth, England: Penguin Books, 1970), p. 234.

47.   Pius IX, *Qui pluribus*, 15. Pius IX writes *Qui pluribus* in response to Catholic theological adoption of Kant's ideas, notably by Georg Hermes (works condemned in 1836) and Anton Gunther (works condemned in 1857). See McCool, *Theology in the Nineteenth Century*, pp. 59-67, 88-112 and Neuner and Dupuis, *Christian Faith*, p. 35.

48.   McCool, *Theology in the Nineteenth Century*, pp. 17-18. Rationalism is related to naturalism (and materialism) in that both either deny religious truth (atheism) or derive it entirely from the physical world (deism). Pius IX devotes significant portions of *Qui pluribus* and *Singulari quidem* to this problem.

49.   J. Salwyn Schapiro, *Condorcet and the Rise of Liberalism* (New York: Octagon Books, 1963), p. 179.

50.   Jeremy Bentham, *An Introduction to the Principles of Morals and Legislation*, excerpts in D. D. Raphael, ed., *British Moralists 1650-1800*, 2 vols. (Oxford: Oxford University Press, 1969), 1:313 and 314.

51.   According to Goetz Briefs, "The term 'liberalism' was coined in 1812 when, during a debate in the *Cortes* of Madrid, a conservative delegate addressed the members

of the Constitutional Party as *vosotros liberales.*" "Catholic Social Doctrine, *Laissez-Faire* Liberalism, and Social Market Economy," *Review of Social Economy* 41 (December 1983): 246. The most notorious use of the term in encyclical literature occurs in Pius IX's appendix to *Quanta cura*, where he rejects the idea that "the Roman Pontiff can, and ought to, reconcile himself, and come to terms with progress, liberalism and modern civilization." Quoted in Anne Fremantle, ed., *The Papal Encyclicals in the Historical Context*, with an introduction by Gustave Weigel (New York: New American Library, Mentor Books, 1956), p. 152.

52.   Jacques Sommet notes that the period's religious indifference is "characterized by the establishment of atheism as the struggle against every religious ideology." Jacques Sommet, "Religious Indifference Today: A Draft Diagnosis," in Jean-Pierre Jossua and Claude Geffré, eds., *Indifference to Religion, Concilium*, vol. 165 (Edinburgh: T. & T. Clark, 1983), p. 4. See also Neuner and Dupuis, *Christian Faith*, pp. 279-80.

53.   According to Daniel-Rops, Leo XII so admired Lamennais' early work that he "kept a portrait of La Mannais in his room." *Age of Revolution*, p. 175. On indifferentism, see also Pius VIII, *Traditi humilitati*, 4; Gregory XVI, *Summo iugiter studio*, 2, *Mirari vos*, 13-14; Pius IX, *Qui pluribus*, 15, *Singulari quidem*, 3, *Quanta conficiamur moerore*, 3.

54.   Benedict XIV, *A quo primum*, 1. See also, Leo XII, *Ubi primum*, 12.

55.   Gregory XVI, *Quo graviora*, 4; and *Commissum divinitus*, 2-16. See also Pius VI, *Charitas*, 16; Gregory XVI, *Mirari vos*, 8; Pius IX, *Nostis et Nobiscum*, 16, *Singulari quidem*, 8, *Etsi multa*, 4-28, *Vix dum a Nobis*, 2-11, *Quod nunquam*, 1-7, *Graves ac diuturnae*, 4-7. In *Quartus supra*, 26, Pius IX acknowledges that "testimony of the people concerning faith and morals" was critical during the fourth century Arian crisis and that "the custom indeed lasted for some time in the Church." But, he concludes, "when recurrent discord, disturbance, and other abuses resulted from it, it was necessary to remove the people from the process." The word 'democratic' is first used (disparagingly) in encyclical literature within the context of these ecclesiological problems.

56.   According to Hales, when the popes "looked into the philosophy of the matter they always found the disquieting fact that the sovereignty was held by the liberal to belong in one way or another, with the people. And that struck them as absurd because they were quite sure it belonged to God and that under Him it rested with the Church, in matters spiritual, and with legitimate rulers in matters temporal." E. E. Y. Hales, *Revolution and Papacy*, p. 280. The popes do not differentiate the social contract theories of Hobbes, Locke, and Rousseau.

57.   F. Lamennais, *Paroles d'un croyant* (Paris: Anciennne Maison Michel Lévy Frères, 1877), p. 76.

58.   According to McCool, "Gregory XVI did not wish to condemn a man who had rendered outstanding service to the Church," but, "on the other hand he wished to express his disapproval of the political liberalism which he feared and hated." *Theology in the Nineteenth Century*, p. 46.

59.   Locke's contract theory emphasizes the role of public opinion in formulating law; Hobbes' theory emphasizes the role of the 'leviathan.' Rousseau's approach is a mixture of both: law resides in the will of the people (*volonté générale*), but the 'true' will of all (*volonté de tous*) can only be expressed by an elite.

60.   Pius IX, *Respicientes*, 11; and *Nullis certe verbis*, 8, *Quanta cura*, 4. In his commentary on the *Syllabus of Errors*, Bishop Dupanloup writes, "Le Pape, de sa voix souveraine, proclame et revêt de l'autorité la plus haute, la grande vérité sociale et morale, que des sophistes comme J.-J. Rousseau ont pu méconnaître, mais que les sages de tous les temps ont saluée: le nombre seul ne fait pas le droit." Félix Dupanloup, *La convention du 15. septembre et l'encyclique du 8. décembre* (Paris: Charles Douniol, 1865), p. 137.

61. McCool, *Theology in the Nineteenth Century*, pp. 23-24.

62. Gregory XVI, *Mirari vos*, 20. See also Pius IX, *Quanta cura*, 3. Lamennais thinks separation would free the spiritual work of the Church from political entanglements. But, says Hales, "it didn't seem to Rome that it necessarily would. The Reign of Freedom had been ushered in by a prostitute on the altar of Notre Dame. It had despoiled the Church, closed the monasteries, persecuted priests, abducted two popes, secularised education." E. E. Y. Hales, *Pio Nono*, p. 45.

63. Hobbes' quote is from *Leviathan*, p. 262. Rousseau's remark is from *The Social Contract*, trans. and intro., M. Cranston (Harmondsworth, England: Penguin Books, 1968), p. 49. *Leviathan* appears on the Index in 1701; *The Social Contract* is condemned in 1766.

64. See also Gregory XVI, *Mirari vos*, 17-19 and Pius IX, *Quanta cura*, 8. In *Inter praecipuas*, 14 Gregory XVI traces the notion of absolute individual liberty to the idea of freedom of conscience fostered by religious indifference.

65. Hobbes, *Leviathan*, p. 189.

66. R. H. Tawney, *Religion and the Rise of Capitalism: A Historical Study* (New York: New American Library, 1954), p. 153.

67. Pius IX, *Qui pluribus*, 13 and *Singulari quidem*, 3.

68. Pius IX, *Quanta cura*, 4; and *Apostolicae Nostrae caritatis*, 1. Elsbernd notes that Pius VI already condemned "absolute individual liberty as the foundation of rights" in the 1791 bull *Quod aliquantum*. Mary Elsbernd, "Papal Statements on Rights: A Historical Contextual Study of Papal Teaching from Pius VI-Pius XI (1791-1939)" (Ph.D. dissertation, Catholic University of Louvain, 1985), p. 142.

69. Leo XII, *Charitate Christi*, 15. See also Pius IX, *Graves ac diuturnae*, 5. The idea of marriage as strictly a civil contract permits states to enact laws—especially regarding divorce—which oppose Church teaching. "Nothing, in the Roman view, so symbolized all that was reprehensible about the Enlightenment and the Revolution as did the divorce laws." Hales, *Revolution and Papacy*, p. 174.

70. Pius VIII, *Traditi humilitati*, 10. Murstein observes that "such liberals as Voltaire and Diderot" held this view of the purpose of marriage. "Love, Sex, and Marriage," p. 209.

71. Gourney's remark appears in Georges Weulersse, ed., *Le mouvement physiocratique en France (de 1756 à 1770)*, 2 vols. (Paris: Felix Alcan, 1910; reprint ed., Paris: Editions Mouton, 1968), 2:17, n. 4. Morellet's quote is from Hughes, *Church and Liberal Society*, p. 92. Smith's comment is from *The Wealth of Nations: Books I-III*, intro., Andrew Skinner (Harmondsworth, England: Penguin Books, Pelican Classics, 1974), pp. 118-19.

72. In an 1871 sermon, the influential Bishop Wilhelm Ketteler of Mainz says: "If the principles of Liberalism are valid, then socialism, which is in fact one of the most perverse aberrations of the human spirit, is fully justified." Quoted in Rupert J. Ederer, ed. and trans., *The Social Teachings of Wilhelm Emmanuel von Ketteler* (Washington, D.C.: University Press of America, 1981), p. 506. In Hughes' view, "having accepted the same basic ideal as the Liberal Society, the Marxist crusade appealed to the same instrument and criterion of progress—material accumulation." Hughes, *Church and Liberal Society*, p. 247.

73. Pius IX, *Maximae quidem*, 4 and *Qui pluribus*, 16. See also Clement XIII, *In Dominico agro*, 3, *Christianae reipublicae*, 1; Gregory XVI, *Singulari Nos*, 8.

74. Pius IX, *Exultavit cor Nostrum*, 3 and *Singulari quidem*, 22, *Quartus supra*, 14. See also Benedict XIV, *Ubi primum*, 4; Leo XII, *Ubi primum*, 8; Pius VIII, *Traditi humilitati*, 2. In addition to direct scriptural references, the popes also cite use of the sheepfold metaphor in Cyprian's third century *De catholicae ecclesiae unitate*, Leo the Great's fifth-century sermons, and Gregory the Great's sixth century *Liber regulae pastoralis*.

75.   See Benedict XIV, *Ubi primum, Quanta cura*; Clement XIII, *Appente sacro, In Dominico agro*, 3, *Christianae reipublicae*, 2; Pius VI, *Charitas*, 28; Pius VII, *Diu satis*, 14; Leo XII, *Ubi primum*, 19, *Charitate Christi*, 20; Gregory XVI, *Mirari vos*, 6, *Quo graviora*, 13; Pius IX, *Qui pluribus*, 17, 31, *Nostis et Nobiscum*, 7, *Singulari quidem*, 2, 4, 7, *Levate*, 21, *Etsi multa*, 10, *Graves ac diuturnae*, 4. Noting the distinctions between mechanical and pastoral metaphors, Andrew Ettin relays how Voltaire despised the latter, once exclaiming, "Ah! Le bon temps que ce siècle de fer!" Andrew V. Ettin, *Literature and the Pastoral* (New Haven: Yale University Press, 1984), p. 35. Pope Gregory XVI, on the other hand, thought dimly of the grand implement of the new iron age, remarking: "chemin de fer—chemin enfer." Quoted in Rhodes, *Power of Rome*, p. 53.

76.   On the role of memory in pastoral literature, see Peter V. Marinelli, *Pastoral* (London: Methuen & Co., 1971), pp. 1-14.

77.   On the characteristics of pastoral morality, see Helen Cooper, *Pastoral: Mediaeval to Renaissance* (Totowa, N.J.: D.S. Brewer, Rowman, and Littlefield, 1977), pp. 71-79; Ettin, *Literature and the Pastoral*, pp. 146-78; and Renato Poggioli, *The Oaten Flute: Essay on Pastoral Poetry and the Pastoral Ideal* (Cambridge: Harvard University Press, 1975), pp. 213-19. One indication of the increased general interest in the "imitatio Christi" approach toward Christian morality during the pre-Leonine period is the fact that Thomas à Kempis' *Imitatio Christi* went through nineteen French editions between 1735 and 1789. Noted in Heyer, *The Catholic Church*, p. 87.

78.   See also Clement XIII, *Summa quae*; Clement XIV, *Cum summi*, 2; Gregory XVI, *Commissum divinitus*, 1.

79.   Benedict XIV, *Ubi primum*, 1. Cooper observes that a characteristic theme of pastoral literature is the flock's dependence on the shepherd's wisdom and the shepherd's role as social critic. *Pastoral: Mediaeval to Renaissance*, pp. 72-73 and 76.

80.   On the role of bishops, see Pius VI, *Inscrutabile*, 8. See also Gregory XVI, *Commissum divinitus*, 10. In *Singulari quidem*, 22, Pius IX advises bishops to wield authority "not as exercising a power of dominion," but as "loving fathers who desire to become models for the flock." The popes repeatedly emphasize the necessity of leadership through good example. See Benedict XIV, *Peregrinantes*, 13, *A quo primum*, 7; Clement XIII, *A quo die*, 6, 16; Clement XIV, *Cum summi*, 7; Leo XII, *Ubi primum*, 3, *Charitate Christi*, 17. On the role of the clergy, see Benedict XIV, *Ubi primum*, 2. See also Pius IX, *Singulari quidem*, 14. Members of religious institutes—clerics or laity dedicated to the evangelical counsels—must observe the same spirit of unity under the authority of their superior who, in turn, defers either to the local bishop or directly to the pope. See Gregory XVI, *Probe nostis*, 9; Pius IX, *Nostis et Nobiscum*, 27, *Cum nuper*, 10. On the role of the laity, see Pius VI, *Inscrutabile*, 8 and *Charitas*, 32. See also Pius VII, *Diu satis*, 15; and Pius IX, *Quartus supra*, 11.

81.   Clement XIII, *A quo die*, 14 and *Christianae reipublicae*, 2.

82.   Haynes, *Philosopher King*, p. 56. On establishing seminaries, see Benedict XIV, *Ubi primum*, 2; Clement XIII, *A quo die*, 12; Pius VI, *Inscrutabile*, 3; Pius VII, *Diu satis*, 12; Leo XII, *Ubi primum*, 5, *Charitate Christi*, 16, 18; Pius VIII, *Traditi humilitati*, 8; Pius IX, *Qui pluribus*, 22-23, 28, *Nostis et Nobiscum*, 26, *Probe noscitis venerabiles*, 2, *Inter multiplices*, 4, *Singulari quidem*, 15, *Cum nuper*, 5, *Amantissimus*, 15. In *Meridionali americae*, Pius IX encourages seminaries for native clergy in South America. In *Nemo certe ignorat* and *Optime noscitis*, the pope supports establishment of the Catholic University of Ireland. On the popes' emphasis on Scripture and patristics, see Benedict XIV, *Vix pervenit*, 7; Clement XIII, *A quo die*, 12; Pius VI, *Inscrutabile*, 1, 8, *Charitas*, 2; Pius IX, *Qui pluribus*, 28, *Singulari quidem*, 15, *Amantissimus*, 16.

83.   Clement XIII, *A quo die*, 12; and *In Dominico agro*, 5. The Roman Catechism presents the typical catechetical structure of creed, code, and cult in four parts. Part 1

outlines the twelve articles of the Apostles' Creed; part 2, the seven sacraments; part 3, the Ten Commandments; and part 4, the seven petitions of the Lord's Prayer. Aubert observes that, during the eighteenth century, catechetical instruction "became the object of several revival efforts," especially in France and Germany. Roger Aubert, "Old and New in Pastoral Care and Theology," in Roger Aubert et al., *The Church in the Age of Liberalism*, trans. Peter Becker (New York: Crossroad, 1981), p. 16.

84.   Benedict XIV, *Vix pervenit*, 8. Renée Haynes notes that one of Benedict XIV's favorite sayings was that "fanaticism 'is the most dangerous of the demons to be exorcized.' " Haynes, *Philosopher King*, p. 177.

85.   Clement XIII, *A quo die*, 7. On the subject of reproving theologians, Clement XIII cites 2 Thes 3:15. See also Pius VI, *Charitas*, 1. On the general episcopal duty of book censorship, see Clement XIII, *Christianae reipublicae*, 2; Pius VI, *Inscrutabile*, 8; Pius VII, *Diu satis*, 15; Leo XII, *Ubi primum*, 19; Gregory XVI, *Inter praecipuas*, 14.

86.   *Encyclopaedia Judaica*, s.v. "Church, Catholic," by Egal Feldman.

87.   See Benedict XIV, *Ubi primum*, 3; Leo XII, *Charitate Christi*, 18; Pius IX, *Qui pluribus*, 27, 29, *Optime noscitis*, 4, 12, *Singulari quidem*, 10, 14, 18-19, 22.

88.   On prayer and fasting, see Clement XIII, *A quo die*, 10; Leo XII, *Charitate Christi*, 14; and Pius IX, *Nostis et Nobiscum*, 13. On reception of sacraments, see Pius IX, *Nostis et Nobiscum*, 10, *Nemo certe ignorat*, 6, *Probe noscitis venerabiles*, 2, *Singulari quidem*, 17. As a change in custom, Pius IX recommends frequent reception of the Eucharist. Pilgrimages are encouraged during Holy Years announced for 1750, 1775, 1825, 1850, 1851, 1864, and 1875. See Benedict XIV, *Peregrinantes, Apostolica Constitutio*; Clement XIV, *Inscrutabili divinae sapientiae*; Leo XII, *Quod hoc ineunte, Charitate Christi*; Pius IX, *Exultavit cor nostrum*. On pious organizations, see Gregory XVI, *Probe nostis*, 14.

89.   On political obedience, see Gregory XVI, *Cum primum*, 3, *Mirari vos*, 17, *Commissum divinitus*, 20. See also Clement XIV, *Cum summi*, 5-6; Pius IX, *Qui pluribus*, 22, *Nostis et Nobiscum*, 19, *Singulari quidem*, 19. On passive political disobedience, see Gregory XVI, *Cum primum*, 3 and *Commissum divinitus*, 20. See also Pius IX, *Qui pluribus*, 22, *Singulari quidem*, 19, *Etsi multa*, 17, *Quod nunquam*, 7.

90.   Gregory XVI, *Mirari vos*, 12. See also Pius VIII, *Traditi humilitati*, 10. A valid marriage is a monogamous union between a man and a woman free from impediments of age, impotence, earlier marriage, religion, holy orders, consent, consanguinity, and prior public concubinage.

91.   Owen Chadwick, *Popes and European Revolution*, p. 330. Chadwick also observes that during the eighteenth century, "all governments including the Protestants' regarded consorship of books as necessary." Ibid., p. 324. In the nineteenth century, liberal states disregard the Church's *Index Liborum Prohibitorum*, but retain and exercise their own power of book censorship.

92.   Moody, "New Forces," p. 29. On international recognition of the papal states, see Pius IX, *Optime noscitis*, 1, *Nullis certe verbis*, 2, *Respicientes*, 12, *Ubi Nos*, 7, *Quod nunquam*, 1.

93.   See Gregory XVI, *Mirari vos*, 19; Pius IX, *Qui pluribus*, 13, *Quartus supra*, 48.

94.   On state's rights, see Gregory XVI, *Mirari Vos*, 19; Pius IX, *Qui pluribus*, 13, *Quartus supra*, 47, *Etsi multa*, 17. On parental rights, see Pius IX, *Quanta cura*, 4. On property rights, see Pius IX, *Nostis et Nobiscum*, 20. The right to necessary goods is explicitly recognized in Clement XIII, *A quo die*, 9.

95.   Pius IX, *Vix dum a nobis*, 4. See also Pius IX, *Qui nuper*, 6-7, 10. In "Papal Statements on Rights," p. 411, Elsbernd incorrectly states that the issue of a citizens' right to practice religion "had not been addressed" before Pius X's 1906 encyclical *Vehementer Nos*.

96.   Richard Tuck, *Natural Rights Theories: Their Origin and Development* (Cambridge:

Cambridge University Press, 1979), p. 15. Elsbernd argues that Pius IX's appeal to parental rights in *Quanta cura*, 4 (in addition to his reference to a "genuine notion" of rights) constitutes a "subtle shift" toward "an initial accommodation to subjective [or, active] modern rights." Elsbernd, "Papal Statements on Rights," pp. 170, 179. This interpretation is based on two gratuitous assumptions. First, that Grotius, Hobbes, and Locke's subjective rights theory is the 'genuine notion' of human rights. Second, that Pius IX had the subjective rights theory in mind when he used the phrase. Pius IX more likely understood the 'genuine notion' of rights as the approach recognizing God, not humanity, as the source of divine and human rights. He would no doubt have agreed with Clement XIV's comment in *Cum summi*, 5: "From no other source than these laws of true religion do we recognize more clearly the established rights of citizens and society."

97.   Pius VIII, *Traditi humilitati*, 10. See also Benedict XIV, *Nimiam licentiam*, 8. In *Mirari vos*, 12, Gregory XVI supports both features of marriage with reference to Heb 13:4. Because sanctity and perpetuity are also marks of marriage between heretics (baptized Christians who doubt one or more truths of Catholic faith), a Catholic seeking dispensation to marry a divorced heretic must insure that the partner's first marriage is "declared invalid by an ecclesiastical judgment made according to canonical standards." See Gregory XVI, *Summo iugiter studio*, 8.

98.   Pius VIII directs priests and bishops to consult the Roman Catechism on questions of marriage. Two aspects of the Catechism discussion are noteworthy. First, "mutual aid" between spouses—as opposed to procreation or control of concupiscence—is listed as the first of the three 'ends' of marriage. Second, procreation is given greater prominence as an end of marriage than in Pius VIII's letter. These points indicate the looseness and flexibility of the pre-Leonine period encyclical discussion of the purpose of marriage. See the *Catechism of the Council of Trent*, trans. J. Donovan (Dublin: James Duffy, 1906), pp. 295-97. See also Macklin, *What Is Marriage?*, pp. 198-99.

99.   Sarah C. Maza notes that the eighteenth-century concept of a household included the master, his family, and his servants. In standard handbooks on Christian morals, says Maza, "masters were enjoined to provide catechism lessons for their employees, to conduct daily services within the household, to supply their servants with prayerbooks, and to make sure that they took communion at least four times a year." "An Anatomy of Paternalism: Masters and Servants in Eighteenth-Century French Households," *Eighteenth Century Life* 7 (October 1981): 12.

100.   On trade, see Benedict XIV, *Vix pervenit*, 5. According to Mueller, "Benedict XIV pointed out that the Church did not consider the institution of investment credit and the return from capital as violating justice." Mueller, "Church and the Social Question," p. 45. O'Dwyer notes that Pius VII introduced monetary reform and free trade into the papal states in accord with "the liberal doctrines of the day." Benedict XIV and Pius VII had attempted these changes earlier, but "in face of privileges, ecclesiastical and lay" and "opposition from noble landowners and local provinces," the reforms failed. *Papacy in the Age of Napoleon*, p. 65. On loans, Benedict XIV's *Vix pervenit*, 3, quotes Jesus' approval in Lk 6:34-35. These exchanges, the pope warns, must be governed by "the commutative bond of justice" which ensures "the equality of what is given and returned." If equality is breached, the business person "must make restitution." On contracts, Benedict XIV advises in *Vix pervenit*, 9: ". . . those who desire to keep themselves free and untouched by the contamination of usury and to give their money to another in such a manner that they may receive only legitimate gain should be admonished to make a contract beforehand. In that contract they should explain the conditions and what gain they expect from their money." On money-changing, see Clement XIII, *Cum primum*, 9. On service to the common good, see Benedict XIV, *Vix pervenit*, 3.

101.   Pius IX encourages the rich to love the needy by citing Christ's identification with the poor in Mt 25:45. He cites Mt 25:41 as evidence for the judgment awaiting wealthy people who disregard the poor. To encourage patience on the part of the poor, the pope quotes Mt 5:3. Pius IX, *Nostis et Nobiscum*, 22. Bernard Groethuysen argues that because this two-class model dominated religious thinking in the eighteenth century, clergy were slow in apprehending the significance of the rising bourgeoisie and the modern capitalist system they introduced. "The clergy," he writes, "was at a complete loss in the face of the pretensions of this [bourgeois] man." It is true the pre-Leonine period texts make no mention of the bourgeoisie class phenomenon. However, the popes do acknowledge and accept key features of the emerging market system. Bernard Groethuysen, *The Bourgeois: Catholicism and Capitalism in Eighteenth-Century France*, trans. Mary Ilford, intro. Benjamin Nelson (New York: Holt, Rinehart and Winston, 1969), p. 7. On Christian paternalism in the eighteenth century, see Maza, "An Anatomy of Paternalism," pp. 1-24.

102.   Clement XIII, *A quo die*, 9. Tuck says "it is not surprising that a theory about rights as claims [the 'passive' approach] should have evolved from within an institution [the Roman Catholic Church] which was so concerned with the claims made on other men by the needy or deserving." *Natural Rights Theories*, p. 15.

103.   On the goods of the Church, see Leo XII, *Charitate Christi*, 18-19; Gregory XVI, *Probe nostis*, 9; and Pius IX, *Nostis et Nobiscum*, 22. "We hold the goods of the Church," says Clement XIII in *A quo die*, 9, ". . . as if in trust." During severe droughts in Italy between 1763 and 1766, Clement XIII provided food, oil, and shelter to peasants pouring into Rome. At one point he appealed to Louis XV of France for corn. When the King refused, the pope turned to the grain market, where merchants charged him double the market rate. Clement XIII divested papal treasures "so that grain might be bought at any price." When the drought was over, fourteen thousand peasants had been sheltered, clothed and fed. Ludwig Freiherr Von Pastor, *The History of the Popes*, trans. E. F. Peeler, 39 vols. (St. Louis: Herder, 1956), 36:171. On socialism and communism, see Pius IX, *Nostis et Nobiscum*, 8. On the duties of the state, see Benedict XIV, *Vix pervenit*, 10.

104.   Dennis E. Poplin, *Communities: A Survey of Theories and Methods of Research*, 2nd ed. (New York: Macmillan Co., 1979), p. 9.

105.   Allen E. Buchanan, "Assessing the Communitarian Critique of Liberalism," *Ethics* 99 (July 1989): 872.

106.   Raymond Plant, "Community: Concept, Conception, and Ideology," *Politics & Society* 8 (1978): 98.

107.   Philip Selznick, "The Idea of a Communitarian Morality," *California Law Review* 75 (1987): 449.

108.   Ettin, *Literature and the Pastoral*, p. 152.

2

THE LEONINE PERIOD: 1878–1958

Most scholars locate the origin of encyclical social teaching in the writings of Leo XIII. From this beginning it is generally held—with allowance for nonobtrusive shifts due to changing historical circumstance—that a body of papal social thought with "great coherency" evolved.[1] However, if encyclical social thought begins not with Leo XIII, but with the theological perspective and social recommendations of the pre-Leonine period popes, does papal teaching still cohere? John Coleman broached this question in his 1981 speech commemorating *Rerum novarum*: "including these [pre-Leonine period letters] will complicate our question about the authority and unity of papal social encyclicals as a corpus."[2]

This chapter argues that significant differences exist not only between pre-Leonine and Leonine period social teachings, but within the latter period itself. Yet, commonalities also perdure. As a result, neither the placid developmental approach to encyclical change, nor the view that papal teaching is fundamentally incoherent satisfactorily answers the question of the content and coherence of encyclical social teaching.

As in the previous chapter, examination of the encyclicals begins with a brief overview. Two following sections indicate the problems cited in the letters and the solutions offered. The chapter concludes with a summary interpretation of Leonine period social teaching and its relationship to pre-Leonine period thought.

Overview

The Leonine period corpus contains 185 letters written by five popes between 1878 and 1958. As in the preceding period, the encyclicals are primarily addressed to bishops (exceptions include one letter to missionaries, one to professors and students of fine arts, and one to the people of Italy). Proportionately more letters are addressed to all the bishops than to specific bishops during the Leonine period. Similarly, more letters address doctrinal (six) and moral (152) issues than in the previous period.

The encyclicals can be arranged in three chronological clusters, called here the "prewar," "World War I," and "World War II" groups. The first group of one hundred prewar encyclicals is the work of Leo XIII (1878-1903) and Pius X (1903-14). During this period, the popes encourage a revival of Thomistic studies and discourage theological 'modernism.' In external relations, the Church confronts the German, Swiss, Belgian, Italian, and Hungarian *Kulturkampf*, the Austrian *Los-von-Rom* movement, and truculent Church-state separations in France and Portugal. Parliamentary democracies initiate aggressive African and Asian colonization policies. The third stage of the Industrial Revolution, or 'high capitalism,' ushers in closely monitored assembly-line production, increased foreign trade and investment, and a wave of inventions, including electrical power (1882), the gasoline engine (1884), automobile (1885), wireless telegraph (1897), and airplane (1903). The field of political economy is replaced in 1890 by Alfred Marshall's mathematical economics. In philosophy, Friedrich Nietzsche inaugurates penetrating criticism of bourgeois culture, Ernst Haeckel and Herbert Spencer advance materialist evolutionary theories, and William James introduces pragmatism. Dégas, Monet, and Renoir, then Seurat and Cézanne, develop artistic impressionism and postimpressionism. Paul Gauguin's rejection of European civilization and his emigration to Tahiti, as well as the brooding subjectivism of Toulouse-Lautrec, Vincent Van Gogh, and Edvard Munch signal a decisive shift in the period's artistic expression. Tchaikovsky, Bruckner, Débussy, and Puccini capture these movements in music, while Ibsen, Tolstoy, Zola, and Chekhov communicate these 'natural' and 'psychological' concerns in literature.

The forty-two letters of Benedict XV (1914-22) and Pius XI (1922-39) represent the World War I group of encyclicals. A robust neo-Thomist philosophical and theological movement continues within Roman Catholicism, while relief efforts during and after the war mark the Church's external mission. A split between the *entente* and 'central power' governments triggers Europe's first modern world war. When the war is over, newly self-conscious ethnic groups clamor for self-rule, laboring classes are energized by the Russian Revolution, and the bourgeoisie seek means of political stabilization. Europe's parliamentary democracies successively collapse under this collective turmoil, ushering in totalitarian regimes of right-wing fascist or left-wing communist ideologies. After a brief period of postwar economic growth, Europe and the Americas enter a period of deep depression. In 1936, John Maynard Keynes frames a theory of economic stimulation through government adjustment of interest rates, taxes, and deficit financing. In philosophy, new systems emerge: Edmund Husserl's phenomenology, the Vienna Circle's logical positivism, Martin Heidegger's existentialism, Henri Bergson's vitalism, and Jacques Maritain's neo-Scholasticism. New movements in art include Picasso's cubism, Duchamp's dadaism, and Dali, Klee, and Miro's surrealism. T. S. Eliot, D. H. Lawrence, F. Scott Fitzgerald, Eugene O'Neill, and Ernest Hemingway are the period's influential authors, while Bartok, Ravel, and Stravinsky prevail in music. Just as literacy rates begin rising within the European and North American working class, 'high' culture is supplanted by 'popular' culture in the forms of radio broadcasting and motion pictures.

The last cluster of Leonine period encyclicals is the World War II group, containing the forty-two letters of Pius XII (1939-58). During this period, neo-Thomist theology is challenged by *nouvelle théologie*. Externally, the Church faces a new wave of oppression in Russia and its satellite states. Governments around the world are locked in the century's second major war. After the war, Western Europe returns to pre-World War I patterns of parliamentary democracy, but its political power is eclipsed by the two 'superpowers.' In philosophy, Sartre and Marcel expand existentialism, while Merleau-Ponty continues phenomenology. The posthumous appearance of Ludwig Wittgenstein's writings enlivens analytic philosophy. In the fine arts, Jackson Pollock and William de Kooning introduce abstract expressionism. Camus and Becket employ new 'existentialist' literary styles. Britten, Copland, and Shostakovich predominate in music. By the 1950s, television emerges as the dominant force in popular culture.

Problems

As with the pre-Leonine period letters, it is useful to begin investigating the popes' social teaching with a description of problems they identify. As earlier, these can be divided into problematic practices (religious, political, familial, economic, and cultural) and ideas (general theological and philosophical concepts and specific social concepts).

Problematic Practices

Religious Practices. The Leonine period popes sustain their predecessors' warnings over lapses in episcopal leadership, clerical discipline, lay religiosity, and theological study. New areas of concern include Roman Catholic religious journalism and intercreedal relations.

On episcopal leadership, Leo XIII reproves Italian and Hungarian bishops for apathetic responses to freemasonry (*Inimica vis*, 7) and the *Kulturkampf* (*Constanti Hungarorum*, 8). In addition, Pius XI's *Rerum Ecclesiae*, 31 warns bishops in missionary lands against "building churches or edifices that are too sumptuous and costly."

The political behavior of lower clergy receives ambivalent treatment in the Leonine period texts. Direct clerical participation in European politics is reproved, while priests in Latin America involved in "legislative assemblies" and the "administration of the state" are merely warned against imprudent conduct in office.[3] Clergy are also chided for insubordination toward bishops and participation in condemned sects and schismatic religious movements.[4]

Problems in lay religiosity include lack of vocations and inappropriate political behavior. In *Ad catholici sacerdotii*, 83, Pius XI complains that modern "seductions . . . prematurely awaken the passions of youth," thus decreasing religious vocations among upper and middle class families. Regarding politics, Leo XIII admonishes the faithful for neglecting religious identity in public life and permitting political differences to split their confessional unity.[5]

The modernist movement and *nouvelle théologie* intensify papal concerns over the research methods and public comportment of theologians. "Modernism" is a term given by Pius X in *Pascendi dominici gregis* to a multiform trend in certain theological circles at the turn of the century stressing the subjective and historical dimensions of religious experience and expression. Names associated with this movement include Müller, Schell, Ehrhard, and Merkle (Germany); Blondel, Loisy, Laberthonnière, and Le Roy (France); von Hügel and Tyrrell (England); Minocchi, Buonaiuti, and Semeria (Italy). Relating theology to contemporary philosophy, *Nouvelle théologie* carries the modernist orientation forward after World War II. Representatives of this movement include de Chardin, Chenu, Congar, Daniélou, Leclerq, de Lubac, and Montcheuil. As in the pre-Leonine period, the popes fear that these movements encourage private interpretation of Scripture and doctrine and contentious public dissent from Church teaching.[6]

New papal complaints are aroused regarding religious journalism and intercreedal relations. Concerning the former, Leo XIII's *Cum multa*, 15 decries acrimony and disloyalty in the Roman Catholic press. Regarding the latter, Pius XI explains in *Mortalium animos*, 10 that the Church "has never allowed its subjects to take part in the assemblies of non-Catholics." This remark is precipitated by the desire of some Roman Catholics to attend the first meeting of the intercreedal World Conference for Faith and Life in Lausanne.[7]

Political Practices. The popes scrutinize the extraordinary political upheavals between 1878 and 1958. As in the pre-Leonine period, the encyclicals rebuke state encroachment on Church affairs, government oppression of the population, and civil violence. In addition, the popes address the problems of nationalism and war.

The Church experiences four stages of state encroachment during the Leonine period. In the first stage, from 1878 to 1914, liberal states continue the pattern of restrictive, anticlerical legislation begun during the pre-Leonine period. Specific countries admonished include Italy (Leo XIII, *Dall'Alto dell'Apostolico seggio, Inimica vis, Custodi di quella fede, Spesse volte*), France (Leo XIII, *Nobilissima gallorum gens*; Pius X, *Vehementer nos, Gravissimo officii munere, Une fois encore*), Prussia (Leo XIII, *Iampridem*), Hungary (Leo XIII, *Quod multum, Constanti Hungarorum, Insignes*), Manitoba, Canada (Leo XIII, *Affari vos*), Peru (Leo XIII, *Quam religiosa*), Portugal (Leo XIII, *Gravissimas*; Pius X, *Iamdudum*), and Ecuador (Leo XIII, *Dum multa*).

In the second stage, spanning 1914 to 1939, the popes face incursions by communist and leftist states. Specific countries cited are Russia (Pius XI, *Acerbi animi*, 12, *Divini Redemptoris*, 18-19, 23), Mexico (Pius XI, *Iniquis afflictisque, Acerba animi, Divini Redemptoris*, 18-19, *Nos es muy conocida*), and Spain (Pius XI, *Dilectissima nobis, Divini Redemptoris*, 18-19). Like the French Reign of Terror, communist and leftist suppression frequently involves torture and murder.[8]

During the third stage, between 1939 and 1945, the popes criticize fascist encroachment in Italy (Pius XI, *Non abbiamo bisogno*) and Germany (Pius XI, *Mit brennender Sorge*). This encroachment vacillates between propaganda, restrictive legislation, and outright violence against the Church.[9]

Finally, from 1945 to 1958, Pius XII decries post-World War II communist persecution. In *Orientales Ecclesias*, he addresses communist incursion in Bulgaria, Rumania, and the Ukraine. He treats the same problem in Hungary (*Luctuosissimi eventus, Laetamur admodum, Datis nuperrime*), Poland (*Laetamur admodum*, 2), and China (*Ad sinarum gentem, Ad Apostolorum Principis*).

The experience of communist and fascist totalitarianism increases papal concern over state oppression of the population. As in the pre-Leonine period, the popes warn against rule of an unjust few over the many and rule by force. Consequently, state loyalty oaths, violations of an individual's right to own property, and the parental right to educate their children are proscribed.[10] New forms of what Pius XI's *Divini Redemptoris*, 33 calls "collective terrorism" include: state suppression of worker associations; forced labor; unjust imprisonment; propaganda; legalized euthanasia, eugenics, and abortion.[11]

The Leonine period popes, like their predecessors, reject unjust civil disobedience and violence. The late nineteenth century rise in anarchistic violence receives particular papal attention.[12] In addition, Leo XIII's *Saepe nos*, 2 rejects the "methods of warfare known as Boycotting and the Plan of Campaign" used by Irish Catholics in their struggle against the British; this despite the fact that Pius IX approved the idea of boycotting against the schismatic Old Catholics in Prussia thirteen years earlier.[13]

The popes give new attention to excessive nationalism and war. They accuse freemasonry and fascism of encouraging warfare by fomenting an exaggerated nationalism. The "hideous slaughter" of war is first condemned in Benedict XV's *Ad Beatissimi Apostolorum*, 3. During and after both world wars the popes reject the proliferation of conventional weapons. After World War II, Pius XII decries nuclear weapons and the cold war "armaments race." He also criticizes international violation of a state's rights to independence, life, and cultural development.[14]

Family Practices. Family problems receive significant attention in Leonine period texts. Earlier papal complaints over irregularities in marriage, state control of adolescent education, and socialist influence over youth are repeated. New concerns include 'experimental' marriage, divorce, sexual immorality, women's emancipation, and the impact of war on family life.

Marriage irregularities are a constant concern. As in pre-Leonine period, mixed and civil marriages receive papal opprobrium. New is Pius XI's criticism of "'temporary,' 'experimental,' and 'companionate marriages.'" Divorce receives its first encyclical discussion in the Leonine period letters. In the popes' view, this practice weakens kindness between partners, induces unfaithfulness, harms children, breaks up homes, and causes desertion of women, family rivalries, and jealousy. "Divorces," writes Leo XIII in *Arcanum*, 29, "are in the highest degree hostile to the prosperity of families and states."[15]

Regarding marital sexuality, Pius XI's *Casti connubii* prohibits contra-ception, abortion, and sterilization, as well as adultery, polygamy, and polyandry.[16] John Noonan suggests three reasons why Pius XI first raised these issues: the August 1930 Lambeth Conference in which Anglicans were permitted to follow their own consciences on contra-ception; the controversy surrounding the June 1930 article "Revolution-izing of Marriage" in the German Catholic periodical *Hochland*; and the concern of Arthur Vermeersch (the encyclical's principal author) that priests "were not enforcing the [Church] teaching" on marital sexuality.[17]

In *Casti connubii*, 21 and 73-74, Pius XI also rejects the "false" notion of women's emancipation. In his view, this encourages neglect of "domestic society," "administration of family affairs," and proper "rearing of children."

Finally, the Leonine period encyclicals note the destructive impact of war on family life. "We behold," writes Pius XI in *Ubi arcano Dei consilio*, 13, "sons alienated from their fathers, brothers quarreling with brothers, masters with servants, servants with masters." War not only creates orphans, widows, refugees, but also increases domestic immorality through the "absence of fathers and sons from the family fireside."

Economic Practices. The Leonine period popes show great concern over economic problems. As in earlier encyclicals, individual merchants, liberal states, and socialists are indicted for immoral business practices and theft. Consistent with the period's industrial growth, new focus is placed on the behavior of manufacturing employers and employees, the economic activity of nation states, and slavery.

Leo XIII inaugurates encyclical criticism of inappropriate intrafirm relations between industrial employers and employees. Throughout the Leonine period letters, employers are reproached for permitting poor working conditions, demanding long hours, paying unfair wages, abusing women and children, neglecting employee illness and old age compensation, disregarding the workers' spiritual needs, and denying workers the right to organize.[18] In these ways, writes Leo XIII in *Rerum novarum*, 20, some employers "misuse men as though they were things."

Despite the "misery of the working class, employees err if they press demands which destroy businesses or "resort to violence in defending their own cause." Workers, warns Leo XIII in *Rerum novarum*, 3, must not "injure the property," nor "outrage the person, of an employer." Though he recognizes that motivations behind labor strikes are frequently justified, the pope warns that strikes constitute a "grave inconvenience" and can be "extremely injurious to trade and to the general interests of the public."[19]

Problems attending interfirm employer behavior can be arranged in four groups. First, Leo XIII's *Rerum novarum*, 20, decries "unchecked competition" based on a false theory of "the survival of those only who are strongest." This exaggerated competition promotes not only greed, usury, speculation, and fraud, but also the accumulation of wealth in the hands of a few. According to Pius XI's *Quadragesimo anno*, 107, such monopolies—the second papal bane—"hold and control money" through "despotic economic domination." This creates a third problem: the "fierce battle" among industrialists "to acquire control of the State." Through these means government becomes "a slave, bound over to the service of human passion and greed." Finally, to obfuscate social responsibility, some business owners delegate management to non-owning "directors" who commit injustices and frauds "beneath the obscurity of the common name of the corporate firm."[20] In section 109, Pius XI notes the irony that, by these practices, "free competition has committed suicide; economic dictatorship has replaced a free market."

State economic practices also come under papal scrutiny. As in pre-Leonine period letters, Leo XIII's *Rerum novarum*, 30 rebukes liberal capitalistic states for suppressing religious holidays and almsgiving. New concerns are raised over unjust distribution, neglect of the agricultural sector, international imperialism, "artificial barriers" in "international trade relations," overtaxing, elimination of workers' associations, unemployment, and the manufacture of armaments.[21] The popes also criticize the Soviet system of "collective labor" which so dragoons "the recalcitrant against their wills" that the people "groan beneath the yoke imposed on them."[22]

Though Leo XIII criticizes "any precipitate action in securing the manumission and liberation of the slaves," he opposes slavery itself. In *In plurimus*, 9, he rejects the "system" wherein humans hold others as "cattle born for the yoke." Such "shameful trading in men" particularly affects Africa, where "new roads are being made, and new commercial enterprises undertaken" by European imperialists.

Cultural Practices. The Leonine period encyclicals expand the list of cultural grievances. As in earlier letters, these problems concern communication, lifestyle, and education. New warnings surface regarding science, technology, and group relations.

Old and new forms of communication attract papal attention. The popes rebuke "journals and pamphlets with neither moderation nor shame" and sensationalist newspapers (*stampa perversa*) which form "the ideas of the inexperienced masses."[23] Among the new forms of mass communication, motion pictures and television receive papal scrutiny. In section 20 of the first encyclical devoted to social communications (*Vigilanti cura*), Pius XI complains that immoral films are "exhibited to spectators who are sitting in darkened theatres." He continues:

> All men know how much harm is done by bad films; they sing the praises of lust and desire, and at the same time provide occasions of sin; they seduce the young from the right path; they present life in a false light; they obscure and weaken the wise counsels of attaining perfection; they destroy pure love, the sanctity of matrimony and the intimate needs of family life. They seek moreover to inculcate prejudiced and false opinions among individuals, classes of society and the different nations and peoples.

Regarding television, Pius XII says in *Miranda prorsus*, 64, that unless people view it discriminately, "all can inhale, even within the home, the poisoned air of those 'materialistic' doctrines which diffuse empty pleasures and desires of all kinds."

The popes identify several problems affecting modern life-styles. Warnings against "the vice of drunkenness" and sexual licentiousness reappear in Leonine period letters. New alarms are issued against stage presentations "remarkable for license," "shameful dances," immodest attire, and dueling. Plagued by these inducements, people increasingly "take their lives with cowardly suicide."[24]

The popes also continue staunch opposition to exclusive control of education by liberal states. New problems attending liberal state instruction include coeducation and sex education. According to Pius XI's *Rappresentanti in terra*, 66 and 68, the former encourages "promiscuity" and equality "in the training of the two sexes," whereas the latter forgets that sexual problems are "the effect not so much of ignorance of intellect, as of weakness of the will exposed to dangerous situations."

The challenge of liberal secularization pales, however, in comparison with fascist and communist educational practices. Though ideologically distinct, both remove Christianity from adolescent education. In *Rappresentanti in terra*, 49, Pius XI complains of the "military turn" given the "so-called physical training" of boys and girls in fascist schools. Troublesome too is the "exaltation of athleticism," "which even in pagan times marked the decline and downfall of genuine physical training." In section 73, Pius XI cites the Soviet Union, where "children are actually being torn from the bosom of the family, to be formed (or, to speak more accurately, to be deformed and depraved), in godless schools."

The Leonine period popes register the first explicit encyclic warnings over modern developments in science and technology. After World War II, Pius XII's *Mirabile illud*, 2, decries "the mechanical equipment and instruments of modern warfare." In the late 1950s, Pius XII adds in *Miranda prorsus*, 18, that "during the past century the technological progress made by industry has often had the result, that the machines which men intended to serve man have actually reduced him to serfdom."

Racism receives encyclical attention for the first time in the Leonine period texts. In *Lacrimabili statu*, 1, Pius X attacks race hatred in Latin America, where European colonists "scourge men [native Indians] and brand them with hot iron, often for most trivial causes, often for mere lust of cruelty." At the outset of World War I, Benedict XV's *Ad Beatissimi Apostolorum*, 7, laments that "race hatred has reached its climax."

Women also receive papal attention for the first time. On the one hand, the popes support women by warning employers not to abuse them in the workplace. On the other hand, they criticize the new women's emancipation movement on two grounds. First, the popes link the perceived rise in sexual immorality to women's participation in the industrial workforce, indecent dance and fashion, and coeducation. Second, Pius XI worries in *Casti connubii*, 74, that families will suffer as women seek "physiological" freedom from the duties of companionship and motherhood, "social" freedom for careers in business and public affairs, and economic freedom so as to "be at liberty to conduct and administer her own affairs."

Finally, Pius XII condemns social disregard for the handicapped. With Hitler's euthanasia program in mind, the pope writes in *Mystici Corporis Christi*, 94: "To Our profound grief We see at times the deformed, the insane, and those suffering from hereditary disease deprived of their lives, as though they were a burden to Society [sic]."

Problematic Ideas

General Theological and Philosophical Concepts. Like his predecessors, Leo XIII states in *Etsi nos*, 8, that "vicious and shameful doctrines" lie behind society's destructive practices. These problematic ideas include general theological and philosophical concepts concerning God, the world, and humanity, as well as specific social concepts treating religious, political, family, economic, and cultural life.

God. "The first and principal cause of every form of disturbance and rebellion," says Pius XI in *Caritate Christi compulsi*, 28, is "the revolt of man against God." While both atheism and denial of Christ's divinity continue as central elements in this revolt, the popes raise new concerns over agnosticism, pantheism, and misinterpretations of revelation, grace, the Kingdom of God, and the meaning of religious dogma.

Atheism acquires three new carriers during the Leonine period: independent French freemasonry, Soviet communism, and Sartre's existentialism. Much of Leo XIII's attack on freemasonry is fueled by fears of atheism. In *Humanum genus*, 12, he argues that freemasons consider human nature (or, reason) their sole "mistress and guide." They deny, says the pope, that "anything has been taught by God." Though Leo XIII recognizes that deistic freemasons profess God "in a general way," others "who obstinately contend that there is no God are as easily initiated as those who contend that God exists."[25]

Communism is first identified as a standard-bearer of atheism in the letters of Pius XI. By this time the Russian Revolution is accomplished, the Soviet Union is established, and official denunciation of God and persecution of believers is under way. From the outset, Marx and Engels' atheistic theory of 'dialectical materialism' is the movement's self-proclaimed ideology. Vladimir Ilyich Lenin, architect of the Revolution and the Soviet Union's first premier, insists: "a Marxist must be a materialist, i.e., an enemy of religion." According to Pius XI's *Divini Redemptoris*, 9, "Bolshevistic and Atheistic Communism" holds the view that "there is in the world only one reality, matter . . . there is no room for the idea of God." Communist expansion and religious persecution in Eastern Europe and China after World War II spurs Pius XII's ongoing condemnation of "atheistic communism."[26]

After World War II, Pius XII also confronts atheistic existentialism. According to Jean-Paul Sartre, the movement's leading spokesperson, "there is no human nature, because there is no God to have a conception of it." This philosophy, complains Pius XII, is atheistic in that it "concerns itself only with the existence of individual things and neglects all consideration of their immutable essences."[27] Sartre's complete works are placed on the Index in 1948.

New papal concern is raised over religious agnosticism. Pius X considers agnosticism a serious problem among 'modernist' theologians. In the pope's view, modernists confine human reason "entirely within the field of 'phenomena' " such that the mind "is incapable of lifting itself up to God." "From this it is inferred," continues Pius X, "that God can never be the direct object of science, and that, as regards history, He must not be considered as an historical subject."[28]

Pantheism also affronts the popes. Pius X considers pantheism the logical consequence of modernistic religious agnosticism. If God is divorced from reason, denied objectivity, evacuated from history, and reduced to an expression of human sentiment, "the rigorous conclusion from this is the identity of man with God, which means Pantheism." On his part, Pius XI decries the "pantheistic confusion" of German fascism. Fascists use the word 'God' "as though it were a meaningless label," identifying divinity "within the narrow limits of a single race."[29]

The popes continue their predecessors' admonitions against denial of Christ's divinity. Pius X accuses modernist Scripture scholars of reopening this issue. "According to what they call their 'real' history," complains Pius X, Christ "was not God and never did anything divine, and that as man He did and said only what they, judging from the time in which He lived, can admit Him to have said or done."[30]

The popes also denounce misinterpretations of four theological concepts. The first problem concerns the idea of revelation. Here, Pius X says in *Pascendi dominici gregis*, 8 that modernists "make consciousness and revelation synonymous," while Pius XI's *Mit brennender Sorge*, 23 accuses fascists of loading the term with " 'suggestions' of race and blood," equating revelation with "the irradiations of a people's history." The second problem involves the idea of grace. Pius X's *Pascendi dominici gregis*, 19 accuses modernists of thinking that "divine action is one with the action of nature," while Pius XI's *Mit brennender Sorge*, 28 assails fascists who believe grace refers to natural gifts possessed by people "of a German type." Third, in *Divini Redemptoris*, 8, Pius XI accuses communists of propounding a "false messianic idea" wherein the Christian notion of God's kingdom is equated with a future state of material equality on earth. Finally, the popes reject the claim that religious dogmas are simply "'secondary' propositions" amenable to change.[31] According to Pius X's *Pascendi dominici gregis*, 13, this idea perverts "the eternal concept of truth" and leads to dogmatic relativism.

World. The Leonine period popes successively decry several troublesome concepts regarding the origin and operation of the visible world. Like their predecessors, Pius X (*Pascendi dominici gregis*, 16) and Pius

XII (*Humani generis*, 18) condemn philosophical naturalism. Two new challenges emerge from the studies of Charles Darwin and Karl Marx.

The popes are not consistent in their treatment of the biological theory of evolution. In *On the Origin of Species by Means of Natural Selection, or the Preservation of Favoured Races in the Struggle for Life* (1859), Darwin argued that plant and animal evolution is a function of natural selection in death rates favoring those most successful in the struggle for physical survival. The implication that divine activity is needless to explain change and variety in organic life sparked immediate theological controversy. Leo XIII broaches the topic in *Exeunte iam anno*, 6, denying that "men and beasts have the same origin and nature." Sixty-two years later, Pius XII overturns Leo XIII's view, acknowledging the possibility of human evolution from other life forms. The pope warns, however, that the theory cannot be held as irrevocably proven and should not be used to imply that nothing exists in the world which is "absolute, firm and immutable."[32] Additionally, Pius XII's *Humani generis*, 37, condemns polygenism, the theory that existing human races have evolved not from one pair of ancestors (i.e. Adam and Eve) but from two or more distinct ancestral types.

The popes consistently reject the philosophical theory of dialectical materialism. This theory is first formulated by Marx and Engels through a combination of Hegel's dialectical method and Feuerbach's materialism. Dialectical materialism construes the world "not as a complex of ready-made things, but as a complex of [material] processes." These processes are not "smooth, continuous, and unbroken," as in the mechanical world model suggested by Newton, but "interrupted by breaks" as matter makes "the sudden leap from one state to another" caused by an internal struggle between its opposing tendencies.[33] This "world picture," writes Lenin, "is a picture of how matter moves and of how 'matter thinks.'"[34] In *Divini Redemptoris*, 12, Pius XI denounces the "principles of dialectical and historical materialism." Pius XII sustains this condemnation noting dialectical materialism's affinity to Darwin's evolutionary theory.[35]

Humanity. The Leonine period popes repeat and expand earlier warnings against errors regarding the existence of the human soul, the operation of the mind, the relationship between faith and reason, and the criteria of the moral life. New attention focuses on mistaken notions of sin and free will.

As during the pre-Leonine period, Leo XIII's *Humanum genus*, 17, accuses freemasons of denying the immateriality and immortality of the soul. In *Mit brennender Sorge*, 23, Pius XI admonishes fascists for equating the soul's immortality with "the collective survival of his [God's] people for an indefinite length of time."

The popes likewise continue their predecessors' condemnation of rationalism. This doctrine, says Leo XIII, claims "the supremacy of the human reason, which, refusing due submission to the divine and eternal reason, proclaims its own independence, and constitutes itself the supreme principle and source and judge of truth." As a result, the notion of religious faith is either denied or entirely relegated to human sentiment.[36] In *Immortale Dei*, 47, Leo XIII states: "The integrity of Catholic faith cannot be reconciled with opinions verging on naturalism or rationalism."

Concerning the moral life, the popes combine new complaints over ethical subjectivism with their predecessors' rejection of utilitarianism. In *Mit brennender Sorge*, 29-30, Pius XI disapproves those who "hand over the moral law to subjective opinion," committing a "dereliction of the eternal principles of an objective morality." Subjectivism bares the moral vacuity of utilitarianism, where "right is common utility" independent of God's law. Unlike the earlier popes, Leo XIII (*Libertas*, 15) and Pius XII (*Summi Pontificatus*, 28) associate both problems with "forgetfulness of the natural law."

The popes also decry distorted interpretations of virtue in moral life. Modernists, says Pius X, "adopt the principle of the Americanists, that the active virtues are more important than the passive, both in the estimation in which they must be held and in the exercise of them."[37] Similarly, Pius XI's *Mit brennender Sorge*, 27, criticizes fascist ideology which "rails at Christian humility as though it were but a cowardly pose of self-degradation."

Undergirding these distorted moral concepts are problematic interpretations of sin and free will. In *Humanum genus*, 20, Leo XIII argues that

> . . . naturalists and Freemasons, having no faith in those things which we have learned by the revelation of God, deny that our first parents sinned, and consequently think that free will is not at all weakened and inclined to evil.

Pius XI expresses the view in *Ad salutem*, 32, that the denial of sin leads to Rousseau's "pernicious error" that "the inborn impulses of the will should neither be feared nor curbed, since all of them are right and sound." Protestants err in the other direction "by teaching that free will in man, once his original justice was lost, is but a name and no more."

Specific Social Concepts

Religion. The Leonine period popes adopt and extend their predecessors' warnings against religious indifferentism, freedom of conscience, and febronian theories of Church reform. In addition, new attention is given the incompatibility of Roman Catholicism with socialism and communism.

Concerning indifferentism, Pius XII's *Humani generis,* 27, criticizes those who consider "the necessity of belonging to the true Church in order to gain salvation" a "meaningless formula." In *Octobri mense,* 2, Leo XIII says indifferentism causes people to neglect "all forms of religion" and finally "become estranged from faith."

The Leonine period popes identify the concept of religious freedom of conscience as causing the first of three movements in the decline of Western civilization. As Leo XIII explains in *Immortale Dei,* 23, the decline began in the sixteenth century when, on the basis of individual religious freedom, "the so-called Reformation . . . attacked at the very foundation religious and civil authority." "From this heresy," says Leo XIII, "there arose in the last century a false philosophy [rationalism and naturalism]." "Hence we have reached the limit of horrors, to wit, communism, socialism, nihilism, hideous deformities of the civil society of men and almost its ruin."

Revised febronian theories of ecclesiology also arouse papal attention. The modernists, says Pius X in *Pascendi dominici gregis,* 25, hold that "the magisterium springs, in the last analysis, from the individual consciences [of the faithful] and possesses its mandate of public utility for their benefit" and that "the ecclesiastical magisterium must be subordinate to them, and should therefore take democratic forms." From another perspective, Pius XII's *Mortalium animos,* 6, argues that the 'Pan-Christians' "understand a visible Church as nothing else than a federation, composed of various communities of Christians, even though they adhere to different doctrines." In *Mit brennender Sorge,* 22, Pius XI rejects the fascist notion of a "national German Church." Similarly, Pius XII's *Ad sinarum gentem,* 21 condemns the communist National Chinese Church governed by the 'three autonomies' of self-rule, self-support, self-propagation.

In *Quadragesimo anno,* 117, Pius XI addresses a "question which holds many minds in suspense": Can a Catholic be a socialist or communist? Though he notes some similarities between Church teaching on care for the poor and moderate (noncommunist) socialism, Pius XI concludes in *Quadragesimo anno,* 117 and 120, that "if it really remain socialism [i.e. committed to the theories of class struggle and dialectical materialism], it cannot be brought into harmony with the dogmas of the Catholic Church." As a result, "'religious socialism,' 'Christian socialism' are expressions implying a contradition in terms." "No one," the pope concludes, "can be at the same time a sincere Catholic and a true socialist." Lenin would have agreed: a true socialist is a communist; "only Communism and Catholicism [offer] two diverse, complete and 'inconfusible' conceptions of human life."[38]

Politics. Mistaken concepts regarding political life are a major papal concern. Earlier problems involving the origin and exercise of state authority, Church-state relations, and the meaning of law, freedom, and rights reappear. Communist and fascist political theory add new dimensions to these problems.

The Leonine period popes continue the encyclical condemnation of the social contract theory of state authority. This theory promotes two dangerous ideologies: majoritarianism and authoritarianism. Concerning the former, Leo XIII's *Humanum genus*, 22, rejects the idea that "power is held by the command or permission of the people, so that, when the popular will changes, rulers may lawfully be deposed." Under such complete majoritarianism, the pope writes in *Immortale Dei*, 35, the "risk of public disturbance is ever hanging over our heads." Elsewhere, Leo XIII explains how social contract theories court authoritarianism. Alluding to Hobbes' contract theory, the pope writes in *Diuturnum*, 12:

> Those who believe civil society to have risen from the free consent of men, looking for the origin of its authority from the same source, say that each individual has given up something of his right, and that voluntarily every person has put himself into the power of the one man in whose person the whole of those rights has been centered.

Though Leo XIII argues against the social contract theory in two different ways, the central problem is the same: the "unwillingness," he writes in *Humanum genus*, 22, "to attribute the right of ruling to God." This, he thinks, results in violent political rebellion by either the masses or elite. In a canny observation, Pius XII says in *Summi Pontificatus*, 53, that if these false ideas "do not always exercise their full influence" in liberal society, it is only because "age-old Christian traditions, on which the peoples have been nurtured, remain still deeply, even if unconsciously, rooted in their hearts."

The popes also discuss mistaken views on Church-state relations. For clarity, this discussion can be broken down into three topics: religion and the state, churches and the state, and the Roman Catholic Church and the state. According to Leo XIII's *Immortale Dei*, 6, "it is a sin for the State not to have care for religion." In *Vehementer nos*, 3, Pius X cites four problems attending this error: first, "a great injustice to God" is committed; second, "this thesis is an obvious negation of the supernatural order"; third, it "upsets the order providentially established by God in the world"; and fourth, it "inflicts great injury on society itself."

On the question of relations between churches and the state, Leo XIII's *Humanum genus*, 22, rejects the claim that the state should allow all churches "to occupy the same place" in society. In *Immortale Dei*, 25, he says this erroneous belief holds that the state

> . . . is not obliged to make public profession of any religion; or to inquire which of the very many religions is the only one true; or to prefer one religion to all the rest; or to show to any form of religion special favor; but, on the contrary, is bound to grant equal rights to every creed, so that the public order may not be disturbed by any particular form of religious belief.

In *Libertas*, 35, he adds the wry remark that

> . . . in spite of all this show of tolerance, it very often happens that, while they [liberals] profess themselves ready to lavish liberty on all in the greatest profusion, they are utterly intolerant toward the Catholic Church, by refusing to allow her the liberty of being herself free.

Finally, the popes condemn the separation of the Roman Catholic Church from the state. "This teaching," explains Leo XIII in *Libertas*, 39, "is understood in two ways." One way opposes the very existence of the Roman Catholic Church, seeking its outright elimination. The other way opposes "not the existence of the Church," but reduces it to a status "like any voluntary association of citizens." Though acknowledging that the latter condition exists "in certain countries" and "offers some advantages," the pope insists in *Au milieu des sollicitudes*, 28, that practical considerations "cannot justify the false principle of separation nor authorize its defense." In both ways, "order is disturbed, for things natural are put above things supernatural . . . and a way is prepared for enmities and contentions between the two powers."[39]

In *Arcanum*, 28, Leo XIII likewise rejects any "principles of jurisprudence" which abandon God's will. Later, in *Au milieu des sollicitudes*, 28, he scorns "the separation of human legislation from Christian and divine legislation." When "the divine is denied," writes Pius XII in *Summi Pontificatus*, 55,

...an autonomy is claimed which rests only upon a utilitarian morality, there human law itself justly forfeits in its more weighty application the moral force which is the essential condition for its acknowledgement and also for its demand of sacrifices.

The foundation of utilitarianism's positivistic theory of law, says Leo XIII's *Libertas*, 15, is the faulty notion that "every man is the law unto himself." The idea that "each one is naturally free; that no one has a right to command another," is absurd.[40]

Finally, Pius XI's *Mit brennender Sorge*, 30, warns against a theory of human rights which "severs from the divine foundation of Revelation, not only morality, but also the theoretical and practical rights." "The world," protests Leo XIII in *Tametsi futura prospicientibus*, 13, "has heard enough of the so-called 'rights of man.' " "Let it hear something of the rights of God."

Family. The popes expand earlier encyclic condemnations of trouble-some ideas regarding the nature of marriage and parental education of children. As in the pre-Leonine period letters, the popes' primary complaint concerning the nature of marriage is the modern notion that "marriage belongs to the genus of commercial contracts."[41] The "basic principle," says Pius XI in *Casti connubii*, 49, "lies in this, that matrimony is repeatedly declared to be not instituted by the Author of nature nor raised by Christ the Lord to the dignity of a true sacrament, but invented by man."

For the popes, the contract theory of marriage generates several problems. Pius XI treats four of these in *Casti connubii*. In section 74, he rejects the idea that "a subjection of one party to the other is unworthy of human dignity, that the rights of husband and wife are equal." This does away with "the honorable and trusting obedience which the woman owes to the man." Second, in section 78 he disapproves the notion that marriage is solely based on "a certain vague compatibility of temperament," such that "when it ceases the marriage is completely dissolved." Third, in sections 65 and 73 the pope deplores the idea that

. . . a great freedom of feeling and action in [third party] external relations should be allowed to man and wife, particularly as many (so they consider) are possessed of an inborn sexual tendency which cannot be satisfied within the narrow limits of monogamous marriage.

Finally, he condemns those who

. . . state that marriage, being a private contract, is, like other private contracts, to be left to the consent and good pleasure of both parties, and so can be dissolved for any reason whatsoever.[42]

A second series of errors associated with the contract theory of marriage concerns offspring. Here, Pius XI discusses three problems. At the outset, the pope rejects arguments favoring contraception. He writes in *Casti connubii*, 53:

> Some justify this criminal abuse on the ground that they are weary of children and wish to gratify their desires without their consequent burden. Others say that they cannot on the one hand remain continent nor on the other can they have children because of the difficulties whether on the part of the mother or on the part of family circumstances.

In sections 63-64 he condemns arguments justifying abortion on grounds of self-defense and "extreme necessity." This would leave the question of abortion to "the will of the father or the mother," permit abortion in cases of serious "medical, social, or eugenic 'indications,'" and allow public authorities to "provide aid for these death-dealing operations." In section 68 the pope spurns justifications for sterilization for the purpose of either public health or private birth control. Regarding the former argument, the pope says supporters "wish the civil authority to arrogate to itself a power over a faculty [sexual reproduction] which it never had and can never legitimately possess. In section 71, he thinks it wrong for people to "render themselves unfit for their natural functions."

In *Humanum genus*, 21, Leo XIII accuses both philosophical naturalists and socialists of promoting the view that "civil government should at its option intrude into and exercise intimate control over the family." According to Pius XI, socialism and communism "logically make of marriage and the family a purely artificial and civil institution." Consequently, "the notion of an indissoluble marriage-tie is scouted," the emancipation of women "is proclaimed as a basic principle," the care of children "devolves upon the collectivity," and "the right of education is denied to parents, for it is conceived as the exclusive prerogative of the community."[43]

Economics. The Leonine period popes highlight several troublesome concepts associated with both capitalism and socialism. Concerning capitalism, the popes expand on two problematic ideas already identified in the pre-Leonine period: economic individualism and market self-regulation. Each idea includes a number of attendant fallacies.

Regarding economic individualism, Pius XI's *Quadragesimo anno*, 50, decries the view that an individual's "superfluous income" should be "left entirely to his own discretion." In sections 4, 46, and 109 the pope says this notion denies the "social and public aspect of ownership" and mistakenly abandons "to charity alone the full care of relieving the unfortunate, as though it were the task of charity to make amends for the open violation of justice." On the international plane, economic individualism promotes the false notion that "where a man's fortune is, there is his country."

In sections 42, 54, 57, and 88 of *Quadragesimo anno*, Pius XI also condemns the capitalist "principle of self-direction" wherein economic affairs are left to "the free play of rugged competition." Here, it is held as "an inexorable economic law" that "all accumulation of riches must fall to the share of the wealthy, while the workingman must remain perpetually in indigence or reduced to the minimum needed for existence." Associated with this idea is the faulty belief that economics and morality are "distinct and alien" and that "the former in no way depends on the latter." As a result, some capitalists mistakenly contend that the determination of wages is entirely a function of the laws of supply and demand, independent of the actual needs of the worker, or that they should be "free from any intervention by public authority." Though insisting that the market system "is not vicious of its very nature," Pius XI believes it has become so, in practice, through the promotion of these erroneous ideas.[44]

The encyclical diatribe against socialist and communist economic thought focuses on two mistaken concepts: the socialist community of goods theory and the theory of class struggle. As with capitalism, these concepts include additional errors.

From the many criticisms of the socialist community of goods theory in the papal letters, four basic arguments can be distilled. First, the popes believe this theory precludes private property. "The socialists," writes Leo XIII, ". . . destroy the 'right' of property, alleging it to be a human invention opposed to the inborn equality of man."[45]

Second, the popes consider the socialist community of goods as anchored in Marx's theory of surplus value wherein the market system of wages is condemned.[46] In *Quadragesimo anno*, 68, Pius XI disapproves Marx's notion that "the worth of labor and therefore the return to be made for it, should equal the entire value added." As a result, in sections 55 and 64 the pope neither agrees that "all products and profits, excepting those required to repair and replace invested capital, belong by every right to the workingman," nor that "the wage contract is essentially unjust."

Third, the popes believe the socialist community of goods theory mistakenly expands the power of the state. For the sake of this theory,

the state could claim a right to acquire, own, and ad
productive property, as well as control distribution of a...
goods. In *Rerum novarum*, 4, Leo XIII calls this "emphatically unjust," for
it would "rob the lawful possessor, distort the functions of the state, and
create utter confusion in the community."[47]

Finally, the popes reject the idea of material egalitarianism underlying the socialist theory. In *Rerum novarum*, 15, Leo XIII explains that
in a completely socialist society "no one would have any interest in
exerting his talents and industry"; in such a system it "would be in
reality the leveling down of all to a like condition of misery and degra-
dation."

The second overall socialist teaching rejected by the popes is the
theory of class struggle. Two problems are cited. First, the popes
denounce the theory of dialectical materialism which undergirds
Marx's notion of class conflict. Second, Pius XI's *Divini Redemptoris*, 9,
criticizes the socialist notion that class struggle, though inevitable,
should be "accelerated by man." On the basis of the atheistic theory
of dialectical materialism, its historical application in the theory of
class struggle, and the community of goods doctrine, Pius XI deems
communism and socialism "intrinsically wrong."

Like their predecessors, the popes believe capitalist and socialist
errors flow from the same source: the Enlightenment association of
freedom with the satisfaction of material desires. According to Oswald
Nell-Breuning (principal author of *Quadragesimo anno*), "Socialism is
nothing but the heir of Liberalism." The difference is that the former
applies the ideals of freedom and material goods to the masses, while
the latter applies them to the bourgeosie.[48]

Culture. In *Rite expiatis*, 29, Pius XI says a "false spirit of secularism"
threatens Western culture. The deleterious effects of this separation of
religion from morality and the substitution of "naturalism for Christianity" shows in modern theories of communication, education, and
science.[49]

The popes repeat earlier papal disdain for the principle of unbridled
"'liberty of speech,' and liberty of press." In *Miranda prorsus*, 32, Pius
XII applies this principle to film: "We cannot approve the stand of
those who claim and defend their freedom to depict and display whatever they please."

Modern art theory receives critical attention for the first time in the
Leonine period letters. Leo XIII opens this discussion by condemning
artistic "verism." Later, Pius XII rejects the theory of "art for art's

sake" on grounds that it neglects "the end for which every creation is made."[50] In *Musicae sacrae*, 22, Pius XII also disapproves the view "that artistic inspiration is free and that it is wrong to impose upon it laws and standards."

Leo XIII's *Libertas*, 24 continues his forerunners' attack against "liberty of teaching" which "claims for itself the right of teaching whatever it pleases." The crux of papal concern is the theory of "pedagogic naturalism," an educational method "founded wholly or in part, on the denial or forgetfulness of original sin and of grace, and relying on the sole powers of human nature." According to Pius XI, this theory encourages

> ... modern systems bearing various names which appeal to a pretended self-govern-ment and unrestrained freedom on the part of the child, and which diminish or even suppress the teacher's authority and action, attributing to the child an exclusive primacy of initiative, and an activity independent of any higher law, natural or divine, in the work of education.[51]

On this basis, the popes condemn 'neutral' schools (state institutions proscribing religious instruction) and 'mixed' schools (state institutions permitting separate religious instruction).

Finally, Leo XIII's *Officio sanctissimo*, 11, warns against "a tendency of human science to fall into most grievous errors especially those of materialism and rationalism." The consequence, he continues in section 7, is a "prostitution of the highest things" under the "false name of scientific and social progress." In *Ad salutem*, 12, Pius XI explains at length:

> ... today, we repeat, when the creations of art and industry, products of mind or mechanical toil are being multiplied and with incredible speed are carried to every corner of the earth, our spirit, absorbed in creatures, grows too forgetful of its Creator, makes fleeting goods its goal to the neglect of eternal ones, and turns to personal and public harm, aye, to its own ruin, those gifts which it has received from the bountiful God for the purpose of extending the kingdom of Christ and of promoting its own salvation.

Solutions

As with the pre-Leonine period encyclicals, the Leonine period letters not only point out problematic practices and ideas, but also offer solutions. Again, delineating these solutions into theological perspectives and social recommendations helps clarify the popes' encyclical teaching.

Theological Perspectives

The Leonine period popes change the dominant interpretive image of Christian faith employed by their predecessors. By retrieving medieval theologian-philosopher Thomas Aquinas and his architectonic vision of all things emanating from God, sustained by God, and returning to God through Jesus Christ, the popes shift the principal interpretive image of Christianity from the pre-Leonine period pastoral metaphor of shepherd and sheepfold to the metaphor of cosmological design. This shift alters the popes' perspective on Christianity's key themes, giving the Leonine period discussion of God, the world, and humanity a distinctive cast.[52]

The basis of this metaphor shift lies in the popes' new representation of God. Rather than portraying God through the pastoral image of Christ the Good Shepherd, the Leonine period popes emphasize a cosmological image of God as designer of the universe. Here, the popes incorporate Aquinas' emphasis on God as rational creator, sustainer, and fulfiller of all things.[53]

Linked with this representation of God, the popes adopt Aquinas' model of the natural world as a hierarchy of created entities moving through space and time by virtue of ordered causes.[54] In this view, entities do not move randomly; rather, they strive toward the greatest possible expression of their God-embedded purposes.[55] "For God, the Maker of all things," says Leo XIII in *Arcanum*, 25, "well knowing what was good for the institution and presentation of each of His creatures, so ordered them by His will and mind that each might adequately attain the end for which it was made." Buoyed by what Pius XI's *Quadragesimo anno*, 43, calls a "universal teleological order," the popes drop their predecessors' more cautious attitude toward environs beyond the flock's provincial boundaries and acquire confidence in the fundamental intelligibility and goodness of the entire natural world.

Human beings—as natural, created entities—participate in the world's "curve of destiny."[56] Like all creatures, writes Leo XIII in *Libertas*, 20, "we are ever in the power of God, are ever guided by His will and providence, and, having come forth from Him, must return to Him." Unlike other creatures, however, human beings possess a soul whereupon "the likeness of God," he says in *In plurimus*, 4, "is stamped on us all." This "naturally Christian soul" empowers two characteristics unique to the human species: rational knowledge and moral freedom.

Concerning rational knowledge, the popes follow Aquinas' view that only the nonmaterial soul, through the 'agent intellect,' can move the mind from simple apprehension of objects and events to complex understanding and judgment. "Man judges," contends Leo XIII, "only because he has a soul that is simple, spiritual, and intellectual."[57]

Moral freedom depends upon the soul's rational power. Like Aquinas, the popes consider reason's judgment of the proper ends or purposes of human action prior to the will's free choice of means. "The will cannot proceed to act," says Leo XIII in *Libertas*, 5, "until it is enlightened by the knowledge possessed by the intellect." Reason's proposition to the will is the natural law. This law, "written and engraved in the mind of every man," says the pope, "is nothing but our reason, commanding us to do right and forbidding sin." Natural law possesses this power of command because it represents God's soul-inscribed intentions for human moral life. This "law of nature," continues Leo XIII, "is the same thing as the 'eternal law,' implanted in rational creatures, and inclining them 'to their right action and end': and can be nothing else but the eternal reason of God, the Creator and Ruler of the world." As a result, the popes construe moral freedom as an expression of humanity's inborn movement toward God in which the will, guided by sound reason, follows the natural law.

The popes realize that humanity's natural movement toward God is impaired by sin. With "the unhappy fall of Adam," not only did pain and death enter human existence, but also reason and will became imperfect.[58] Challenged by irascible and concupiscent appetites, reason often proposes to the will "something which is not really good, but which has the appearance of good."[59]

God gratuitously repaired Adam's fault through the death and resurrection of His son, Jesus Christ. In *Tametsi futura prospicientibus*, 3, Leo XIII says Christ "made abundant satisfaction in His Blood to the outraged majesty of His Father and by this infinite power He redeemed man from his ruin." From God's standpoint, "wrath was appeased, the primeval fetters of slavery were struck off from unhappy and erring man, God's favour was won back, grace restored, the gates of Heaven opened, the right to enter them revived, and the means afforded of doing so." For its part, humanity "beheld at length the light of truth" which teaches "that we come from God and must return to Him." "From this first principle," Leo XIII continues, "the consciousness of human dignity was revived."

Though Christ's death and resurrection erased Adam's fault, the penalty of sin still afflicts human life. "By Our Redeemer's grace human nature hath been regenerated," writes Leo XIII, but "still there remains in each individual a certain debility and tendency to evil."[60] This exists, according to A. Tanquerey, because "it is fitting that we cooperate in our own salvation by carrying our cross after Christ."[61]

Because of the lingering effects of sin, the popes believe that clear exercise of rational knowledge, full appreciation of moral freedom, and complete reunion with God can come only through personal faith in Jesus Christ. But rather than appealing to the pre-Leonine period image of Christ the Good Shepherd, the Leonine period popes commonly cite Eph 1:9-10, where emphasis is placed on Christ as the source of knowledge and restorer of God's cosmic order.[62]

Sustaining an intellectual development begun by Thomistic scholars late in the pre-Leonine period, the popes admit no necessary conflict between God's revelation through Jesus Christ and human reason. Faith in Christ fortifies reason's partial apprehension of God and, through revealed truths unavailable to reason, makes possible a fuller comprehension of God. Faith and reason cannot conflict, writes Pius XI, in *Rappresentanti in terra*, 28, because "both come from God, who cannot contradict Himself."

For the popes, faith in Christ also makes possible complete moral freedom. While God's natural law provides humanity the lower rungs of morality, only Christ's divine law—the Ten Commandments and the two precepts of charity—furnishes the higher footholds needed for full moral freedom.[63] Stressing this point, Pius XI says in *Mit brennender Sorge*, 29: "It is on faith in God, preserved pure and stainless, that man's morality is based." Unlike ethical formalism, subjectivism, and utilitarianism, Christ's divine law offers "eternal principles of an objective morality."

Like their predecessors, the Leonine period popes believe access to Christ—and, ultimately, the Father in Heaven—comes through participation in the faith, moral life, and worship of the Church. Though "it was possible for Him of Himself to impart these graces to mankind directly," writes Pius XII in *Mystici Corporis Christi*, 12, ". . . He willed to do so only through a visible Church made up of men." This visible body is the Roman Catholic Church, wherein "the Pontiffs who succeed Peter in the Roman Episcopate receive the supreme power."[64] Coextensive with the metaphor shift in Leonine period letters, the popes deemphasize the earlier papal representation of the Church as a 'flock' and introduce the image of the 'Mystical Body of Christ.' According to Leo XIII:

> The Son of God decreed that the Church should be His mystical body, with which He should be united as the Head, after the manner of the human body which He assumed, to which the natural head is physiologically united.[65]

Social Recommendations

The cosmological design metaphor gives the Leonine period theological perspective a distinct character. This distinctiveness is apparent in the popes' positive teaching on human relations in the various spheres of social life.

Religious Ideas and Practices. The popes sustain their predecessors' emphasis on unity in religious life, but modify its organizational and operational requisites. In particular, the Leonine period letters enhance the role of the papacy and place new emphasis on Thomistic studies, missionary activity, social action, lay associations, and devotional piety.

Organizationally, the Leonine period encyclicals show several signs of the papacy's growing role in religious life: a heightened programmatic self-consciousness, a broadening sense of pastoral responsibility for the whole of Western civilization, a greater preoccupation with specific moral issues, and a stronger claim to religious and moral authority. These developments reflect the political context of the time and the period's new theological perspective wherein the pope, as the temporal representative of Jesus Christ, is imaged as the head of the earthly mystical body. Like the head, the pope—and the hierarchy in union with him—receives the "Spirit of Truth" by which he must "guard Christian doctrine" and "propagate it in all integrity and purity."[66]

Unlike their forerunners, the popes formulate overall themes for their pontificates, announcing them for the entire Church. In *Divinum illud munus*, 2, Leo XIII writes:

> We have endeavoured to direct all that We have attempted and persistently carried out during a long pontificate towards two chief ends: in the first place, towards the restoration, both in rulers and peoples, of the principles of Christian life in civil and domestic society [and] . . . secondly, to promote the reunion of those who have fallen away from the Catholic Church.

Citing Eph 1:10, Pius X announces his theme in *E supremi*, 4: "We proclaim that We have no other programme in the Supreme Pontificate but that of 'restoring all things in Christ.'" According to Benedict XV's *Ad beatissimi apostolorum*, 8, the "keynote of Our Pontificate is to strive in every possible way that the charity of Jesus Christ should once more rule supreme amongst men." These "two programs of Our Predecessors," writes Pius XI in *Ubi arcano Dei consilio*, 49, "We desire to unite in

one—the reestablishment of the Kingdom of Christ by peace in Christ."
For his part, Pius XII announces in *Summi Pontificatus*, 2, "the spread of
the Kingdom of Christ" as "the alpha and omega of Our aims."

Consistent with the cosmological design metaphor, the popes expand
the pastoral responsibility of their office. Unlike their forerunners, the
Leonine period popes perceive their task as not only overseeing the
needs of Roman Catholic countries and regions, but also defending and
restoring what Pius XI calls, in *Caritate Christi compulsi* 25, "the moral
order in the universe." In *Casti connubii*, 4, for example, Pius XI speaks
to "the whole Church of Christ and indeed to the whole human race."

Linked to their new role as mobilizers and directors of society's
Christian restoration, the popes draw a greater array of religious and
moral questions under their immediate purview. Because "the deposit
of truth" is "entrusted to Us by God," says Pius XI in *Quadragesimo
anno*, 41, popes hold the "weighty office of propagating, interpreting
and urging in season and out of season the entire moral law." When
new, perplexing social situations arise, Pius XI recommends in
Singulari quadam, 8, that the faithful "first turn to their Bishops for
counsel, and then submit the matter to the Apostolic See for its
decision." In these cases, writes Leo XIII in *Grave de communi re*, 4, the
popes must "define what Catholics are to think."

This enlargement of papal responsibility increases the degree to
which all members of the Church must look to the pope as artificer,
administrator, and adjudicator of religious life. "Whatever the Roman
Pontiffs have hitherto taught, or shall hereafter teach," asserts Leo
XIII's *Immortale Dei*, 41, "must be held with a firm grasp of mind, and,
so often as occasion requires, must be openly professed."

Concerning the operation of the Church, the popes encourage the
faithful to engage in activities preserving and promoting ecclesial
unity. The pontiffs continue, for example, their predecessors' stress on
religious education, but replace the earlier popes' emphasis on
instruction in Scripture and patristics with training in the philosophy
and theology of Thomas Aquinas.

In principle, the popes' position on theological study mirrors the
pre-Leonine period view. "In the profession of doctrines taught by the
Church all shall be of one mind," writes Leo XIII in *Immortale Dei*, 46,
but "in mere matters of opinion it is permissible to discuss things with
moderation." In practice, however, the popes' support for a single,
Thomistic system of theology, the increased frequency of their encyclical teaching, and their claim of direct authority over an expanded
range of issues shrinks the category of "matters of opinion." In *Humani
generis*, 19, Pius XII acknowledges that "many matters that were

formerly open to discussion, no longer now admit of discussion." In section 20, he continues:

> Nor must it be thought that what is expounded in Encyclical Letters does not of itself demand consent, since in writing such Letters the Popes do not exercise the supreme power of their Teaching Authority . . . if the Supreme Pontiffs in the official documents purposely pass judgment on a matter up to that time under dispute, it is obvious that that matter, according to the mind and will of the same Pontiffs, cannot be any longer considered a question open to discussion among theologians.

For the popes, greater episcopal control over education ensures that the laity receive a "correct education and intellectual preparation, supported by Christian philosophy—that is the philosophy which was truthfully called perennial philosophy."[67] "The true Christian, product of Christian education," writes Pius XI

> is the supernatural man who thinks, judges, and acts constantly and consistently in accordance with right reason illuminated by the supreme light of the example and teachings of Christ; in other words, to use the common terms, the true and finished man of character.[68]

Consistent with their sense of worldwide pastoral responsibility, the Leonine period popes assume a larger role stimulating and directing foreign missions. "The object of missionary activity," writes Pius XII in *Evangelii praecones*, 22, ". . . is to bring the light of the Gospel to new races and to form new Christians," as well as "to establish the Church on sound foundations among non-Christian peoples, and place it under its own native Hierarchy."

During the period, however, two changes occur in the papal perception of missionary activity. First, the popes shift from the pre-Leonine period emphasis on homiletic evangelization to the more implicit method of providing for the peoples' medical, educational, and social needs.[69] Second, the popes stop referring—as Leo XIII does in *Sancta Dei civitas*, 10—to foreign non-Christians as 'savages' and 'barbarians' requiring introduction to "civilized life." Instead, Pius XII's *Evangelii praecones*, 56 instructs missionaries not to "destroy or extinguish" whatever native people possess "that is naturally good, just or beautiful." In section 20, the pope says that a missionary must "consider the country he is going to evangelize as a second fatherland and love it with due charity," seeking no "earthly advantage for his own country or religious Institute." The popes' growing concern over protecting native culture from untoward European ideas and practices retains, however, an identifiably Thomistic perspective: "The Church is no obstacle to the native talent of any nation," writes Pius XII, "but rather perfects it in the highest degree."[70]

In *Il fermo proposito*, 7, Pius X also calls upon lay members of the Church to participate in the restoration of "Jesus Christ to the family, the school and society." The recommended method of participation is membership in one or more of the burgeoning Catholic associations established to promote everything from religious education, missionary activity, charity, and prayer, to morality in art and cinema, family life, and political and economic change. The title given this associational movement is 'Catholic Action.'[71]

Catholic Action has two central features. In *Il fermo proposito*, 8 and 17, Pius X says it involves "works, sustained and promoted chiefly by lay Catholics and whose form varies according to the needs of each country." The emphasis should be on serving humanity's spiritual and material needs through "practical means." Second, lay associations must operate under the authority of the bishop. In *Non abbiamo bisogno*, 5, Pius XI gives the "solemn and authentic definition" of Catholic Action: "The participation and the collaboration of the laity with the Apostolic Hierarchy." Consistent with Leonine period ecclesiology, the popes view lay participation in social restoration "almost exclusively as an expansion and extension of the action of the clergy."[72]

Concern over the spiritual renewal of clergy and laity reappears in the papal letters, though the popes emphasize different forms of spirituality than those recommended in the pre-Leonine period. Four developments distinguish the Leonine period approach to spiritual renewal. First, the popes place great stress on the intellectual and spiritual example of the saints. Whereas no letters focused on the lives or thoughts of the saints during the pre-Leonine period, Leonine period encyclicals commemorate the births, deaths, and canonizations of twenty major saints.[73] Second, greater devotion to the Virgin Mary is emphasized through recitation of the Rosary. The single most repeated topic of Leo XIII's encyclical corpus is the rosary, to which he devoted eleven letters.[74] Third, the popes promote veneration of the Sacred Heart of Jesus. Initiated in the seventeenth century, this practice focuses piety on the love and suffering of Christ for humanity. Finally, lay membership in paraclerical Third Orders is encouraged. Here, lay people observe special rules in their daily lives under the auspices of a religious order. Typically, these rules include frequent reception of the sacraments, simplicity in life-style, recitation of the daily office, routine pursuit of an assigned apostolate, and wearing a scapular and cord beneath the outer clothing.[75]

Alongside their intrinsic spiritual function, all these devotions assist the organizational and operational developments of religious life during the Leonine period. They unite Catholics of different nationalities around common practices of piety, draw Catholics closer to clerical life, and provide an element of affectivity and spontaneity in a religious life otherwise directed toward the exercise of reason and observance of order.

Political Ideas and Practices. The popes' teaching on the origin and exercise of state authority, Church-state relations, the duties of citizenship, political freedom, and rights follows much of the pre-Leonine period instruction. With their new theological perspective, however, the popes expand their predecessors' political thought and, in some cases, alter it.

While concurring with their forerunners that God is the foundation of state authority, the popes present new discussion of the citizens' role in the derivation of God's power to rulers. This issue, in turn, generates the first encyclical deliberation on the moral status of democratic government.

Leo XIII thinks it appropriate for citizens to participate in the selection of rulers. "Those who may be placed over the State," he writes in *Diuturnum*, 6, "may in certain cases be chosen by the will and decision of the multitude." But the pope adds that by this selection, citizens are not 'transferring' a power of authority exclusively theirs, but 'designating' the person to whom God grants power. Because "no man has in himself or of himself the power of constraining the free will of others," reminds Leo XIII, "this power resides solely in God . . . and it is necessary that those who exercise it should do it as having received it from God."[76]

By acknowledging elective government, Leo XIII accepts the participatory democratic state. "It is not of itself wrong," he says in *Libertas*, 44, "to prefer a democratic form of government." In his 'ralliement' policy toward the democratic French Republic, for example, Leo XIII suggests in *Au milieu des sollicitudes*, 21 that the "distinction between 'constituted power' and 'legislation'" be "carefully kept in view." Thus, one could reject the Republic's anticlerical legislation and still accept the government's constituted power. The acceptance of democracy, however, does not grant it moral priority over other governmental arrangements. Rather, says the pope, "no one of the several forms of government is in itself condemned inasmuch as none of them contain anything contrary to Catholic doctrine."[77]

Regardless of form, all governments have one naturally assigned purpose: to serve the common good. Human beings create states "so that what was wanting to his [humanity's] nature, and beyond his attainment if left to his own resources, he might obtain by association with others." As a result, writes Leo XIII in *Libertas*, 21, "public authority exists for the welfare of those whom it governs." In addition, Pius XII's *Summi Pontificatus*, 59 insists that states care for the "good of all nations." In section 74, the pope says that "It is indispensable for the existence of harmonious and lasting contacts and of fruitful relations that the peoples recognize and observe these principles of international natural law."

In *Rerum novarum*, 35, Leo XIII says states must exercise "fatherly solicitude" over their citizens. This requires, he explains in *Libertas*, 18, care for not only the people's "external well-being" but also "the welfare of men's souls." In section 21, the pope refers to these twin concerns as the 'proximate' and 'remote' ends of government. Adopting this terminology in *Vehementer nos*, 3, Pius X says the "proximate object of political societies" is "public prosperity during this life." This object entails protection and improvement of the citizenry. Regarding protection, states must make just laws, "defend the lives of the innocent," "punish malefactors," and ensure the "harmony and co-ordination of all social forces." Regarding temporal improvement, states must oversee "public morals," "promote to the utmost the interests of the poor," and insure the education of "the masses."[78]

The state's remote object, writes Pius X in *Vehementer nos*, 3, is "man's eternal happiness." As a result, "one of their chief duties," according to Leo XIII in *Immortale Dei*, 6, "must be to favor religion, to protect it, to shield it under the credit and sanction of laws" and ensure the "public profession of religion." "Justice therefore forbids, and reason itself forbids," insists Leo XIII, "the State to be godless."[79]

To this end, the Leonine period popes emphasize Church-state collaboration. "The principle of civil and religious power," says Leo XIII in *Officio sanctissimo*, 13, "is one and the same, namely, God." "Therefore," he continues, "there can be no discord between them . . . for God cannot be at variance with Himself." Like their predecessors, the popes discuss the distinction between Church and state, areas of joint jurisdiction, and the institutional priority of the Church. Unlike their predecessors, the popes expand their discussion to include Church-state relations in traditionally non-Catholic countries.

According to the popes, Church and state constitute two distinct powers. "The Almighty," says Leo XIII in *Immortale Dei*, 13, ". . . has given the charge of the human race to two powers," one "set over divine, the other over human things." Between the administration and regulation of Church and state, he continues, an orbit is "traced out within which the action of each is brought into play by its own native right."

Because Church and state concerns meet in the same subject (the human person) their institutional orbits frequently overlap. As in the pre-Leonine period letters, the popes believe any human action of moral import can become a matter of joint jurisdiction. Marriage, education, and censorship, however, occupy permanent status as issues of joint concern. Like their forerunners, the Leonine period popes think state practice should follow Church teaching in these matters.[80]

Though the popes recognize Church and state as 'perfect societies,' they affirm the earlier papal position emphasizing the institutional priority of the Church. Consistent with the design metaphor, the popes speak of this priority as analogous to the soul's preeminence over the body. "There must, accordingly, exist between these two powers a certain orderly connection," explains Leo XIII, "which may be compared to the union of soul and body in man."[81] As the soul of society, the Church has the "direct and proximate purpose to lead the world to peace and holiness." As society's body, the state must assist "the interests of Catholicism," since "the profession of one religion is necessary in the state" and the religion professed must be that "which alone is true."[82]

Despite their teaching on the institutional priority of the Church, the popes recognize two facts. First, the likelihood of institutional priority being granted the Roman Catholic Church in traditionally non-Catholic states is remote. Second, Church insistence that Catholic citizens press for such institutional status in non-Catholic states could cause more harm than good. As a result, the Leonine period popes approve situations of less than optimal Church status out of considerations of expedience. Leo XIII says,

> ... while not conceding any right to anything save what is true and honest, she [the Church] does not forbid public authority to tolerate what is at variance with truth and justice, for the sake of avoiding some greater evil, or of obtaining or preserving some greater good.[83]

In this spirit, Leo XIII's *Licet multa*, 3, advises "all Catholics" to "have before their eyes and faithfully imitate the prudent conduct which the Church herself adopts in matters of this nature."

Papal teaching on citizenship expands and changes during the Leonine period. While the popes—like Leo XIII in *Libertas*, 13—accept their predecessor's view that "the highest duty is to respect authority, and obediently to submit to just law," they add new discussion on participation in government and political dissent.

Consistent with their new teaching on ruler selection and demo-cratic government, the popes encourage citizen participation in politi-cal affairs. "At certain times," writes Leo XIII in *Immortale Dei*, 36, ".
. . participation may not only be of benefit to the citizens, but may even be of obligation." For, "to take no share in public matters would be as wrong as to have no concern for, or to bestow no labor upon, the common good." Catholics, in particular, "have just reasons for taking part in the conduct of public affairs" because they can "infuse, as it were, into all the veins of the State the healthy sap and blood of Christian wisdom and virtue."[84]

Papal teaching on political dissent is ambiguous in the Leonine period. Though Leo XIII accepts the pre-Leonine period theory of passive, Church-directed disobedience to specific laws contradicting God's will, his acknowledgment of democracy and citizen participation encourages active citizen resistance against bad law. This resistance, however, can only take the form of advocacy within the legislative processes of government. "Upright men," says Leo XIII's *Au milieu des sollicitudes*, 24, should "unite as one" to oppose "abuses of legislation" by "all lawful and honest means." In *Libertas*, 43, Leo XIII adds that

. . . wherever there exists, or there is reason to fear, an unjust oppression of the people on the one hand, or a deprivation of the liberty of the Church on the other, it is lawful to seek for a change of government as will bring about due liberty of action.

Yet, in *Au milieu des sollicitudes*, 16, he writes: "All individuals are bound to accept these governments and not attempt to overthrow or change their form." Neither linguistic nor contextual analysis resolves these contradictory statements. While Leo XIII stresses the Christian duty to assist in building new governments from the ashes of the old, he offers no moral criterion to determine either when a government is irrevocably corrupt or how a Christian may participate in its over-throw. In his study of Leo XIII, Dorr concludes that

. . . if criticism cannot obtain justice within the existing system they may not take the further step of trying to topple it by means declared illegal by the regime itself. At that point the limit has been reached; injustice must then be endured.

"It would appear," says Dorr, "that according to the teaching of Leo XIII there can be no such thing as a justified revolution."[85]

Pius XI and Pius XII alter Leo XIII's teaching. During the National Revolutionary Party's control of Mexico, Pius XI instructs Catholics not to "resign themselves passively" to state violation of their "religious and civil liberties."[86] Rather, citizens should engage in active resistance against not only unjust laws, but the state itself. While the Church "condemns every unjust rebellion or act of violence against the properly constituted civil power," writes Pius XI,

> . . . there would appear no reason to condemn citizens for uniting to defend the nation and themselves by lawful and appropriate means against those who make use of the power of the State to drag the nation to ruin.[87]

The pope cites five principles governing such resistance: (1) retribution must not be the "absolute end" of revolt, (2) the means of revolt cannot be "intrinsically evil," (3) the means of revolt must be "proportionate to the end," (4) the means, including "violent defense," cannot "enter in any manner in the task of the clergy or of Catholic Action as such," (5) clergy and Catholic Action must "contribute to the prosperity of the nation." Later, Pius XII supports the 1956 Hungarian revolt against the communist government of Ernö Gerö and decries the subsequent arrival of Soviet troops in Budapest. The pope praises the Hungarians "who long with all their hearts for their rightful freedom."[88]

Concerning political liberty, the popes continue the pre-Leonine period emphasis on the necessary relationship between freedom and moral law. In characteristically Thomistic language, Leo XIII describes liberty in *Immortale Dei*, 32 as "a power perfecting man, and hence should have truth and goodness for its object." In an apparent reversal, Pius XI declares himself "happy and proud to wage the good fight for the liberty of consciences" in *Non abbiamo bisogno*, 41. But, he quickly adds, this does not imply support for the notion of "'the liberty of conscience,' which is an equivocal expression too often distorted to mean the absolute independence of conscience."

The popes place new emphasis on human nature as the proximate source of rights. But unlike liberal theories, the natural basis of rights is not individual desire, but divinely created laws internal to all human beings. Habiger points out that Cardinal Zigliara (author of the second and third drafts of *Rerum novarum*) made a "very strong connection . . . between *jus naturae* and *lex naturalis*." Here, "Rights stem from our duties to move toward our appropriate end."[89] Thus, Pius XI writes in *Non abbiamo bisogno*, 27: "The first right is to do one's duty"; and in *Mit brennender Sorge* 30: "The basic fact [is] that man as a person possesses rights he holds from God."

It is from this perspective that the popes discuss various individual rights. All rights mentioned in the pre-Leonine letters are repeated, including the rights of God, Church, and State.[90] Individual rights stated for the first time include: life, bodily integrity, language, association, marriage, resistance to unjust law, voting, providing for sustenance, freedom to "live according to law and right reason" and publicly communicate truth, the right of children to education, and the "civil rights of the wife."[91]

Family Ideas and Practices. Papal teaching concerning family life increases during the Leonine period. Like their predecessors, the popes discuss the nature and purpose of marriage, proper relations between spouses and children, and the responsibilities of parents. New efforts are made to depict ideal family life and discuss the social role of family.

Sanctity and perpetuity continue as central traits of matrimony in the Leonine period encyclicals. Consistent with their theological perspective, the popes derive these traits not only from the Eph 5:21-6:9 analogy between marriage and Christ's relationship to the Church, but also from the natural "innate holiness" of matrimony established by God at the creation of the world. According to Leo XIII's *Arcanum*, 19, marriage was "holy by its own power, in its own nature," prior to the coming of Christ.

The new focus on nature shifts papal teaching regarding the purpose of marriage. In *Arcanum*, 10, Leo XIII sustains pre-Leonine period emphasis on religious education of children as the "higher and nobler purpose" of marriage. But later, in *Rerum novarum*, 12, Leo XIII isolates procreation and education as "the chief and principal purpose of marriage," basing this on God's Gen 1:28 command to "increase and multiply." Pius XI continues this transition in *Casti connubii*, 17. Here, quoting canon 1013 of the new Code of Canon Law, the pope writes: "The primary end of marriage is the procreation and education of children." According to Mackin, Thomistic philosophers and theologians (like Cardinal Pietro Gasparri, author of the new canons on marriage) rearranged the priority of Augustine's three 'goods' of marriage, identifying the 'natural' act of procreation as the *finis operis* of marriage.[92]

While supporting earlier encyclical teaching on the husband's preeminent authority over family affairs, the Leonine period popes give new attention to affective relations between spouses and the status of wives. Marriage begins, says Pius XI in *Casti connubii*, 6, with the "free consent of each of the spouses." As marriage proceeds, love must grow into a "deep attachment of the heart" looking not only to external needs, but also

... that man and wife help each other day by day in forming and perfecting themselves in the interior life, so that through their partnership in life they may advance
ever more and more in virtue, and above all that they may grow in true love toward
God and their neighbor.[93]

With this in mind, Pius XI's *Casti connubii*, 27 says husbands should
not exercise authority as to "deny or take away the liberty which fully
belongs to the woman both in view of her dignity as a human person,
and in view of her most noble office as wife and mother and companion." Women should not be "put on a level with those persons who in
law are called minors." For her part, a wife should refuse to "obey her
husband's every request if not in harmony with right reason or with the
dignity due to the wife." Indeed, "if the husband neglects his duty,"
adds Pius XI in section 28, "it falls to the wife to take his place in
directing the family." The pope concludes that while "a certain inequality and due accommodation" between spouses is necessary for "the good
of the family and the right ordering and unity and stability of home life,"
"both parties enjoy the same rights" of marital consent and a loving,
spiritual relationship consistent with the "dignity of the human soul."

Spouses have responsibilities not only to each other, but also to their
children. If state-run schools do not support Roman Catholic religious
education, writes Leo XIII in *Officio sanctissimo*, 11, Catholics must
build "establishments of their own." In addition to religious education,
Pius XI introduces three obligations concerning sexuality and procreation. First, because "the conjugal act is destined primarily by nature for
the begetting of children," couples may not "deliberately frustrate its
natural power" through artificial birth control. However, couples
may—in consideration of "mutual aid, the cultivating of mutual love,
and the quieting of concupiscence"—"use their right [of conjugal
union] in the proper manner, although on account of natural reasons
either of time or of certain defects, new life cannot be brought forth."
Second, couples must "preserve the life of offspring" inside and
outside the womb. Third, couples may not undergo sterilization, "or
in any other way render themselves unfit for their natural functions."[94]

The Leonine period popes also offer a portrait of the model
Christian family. The "ideal home," writes Pius XI, in *Ad catholici
sacerdotii*, 81, abounds in parental love, industriousness, family
devotions to Jesus, Mary, and Joseph, "respect for holy places and
persons," compassion for others, sharing with the poor "the much or
little they possess," and "numerous posterity." In *Magni nobis*, 5, Leo
XIII promotes devotional attachment to the "Holy Family of Nazareth."

Finally, the Leonine period letters emphasize the centrality of family
life for social order. The family, says Pius XII in *Summi pontificatus*, 61,

is the "primary and essential cell of society" and, as such, is "anterior to the state." As a result, governments should "supply for the insufficient forces of individual effort" and help needy families with housing, employment, food and clothing at reasonable prices, and child care.[95]

Economic Ideas and Practices. The Leonine period popes adopt, expand, and—in some cases—change their predecessors' teachings concerning business activity, property ownership and use, relations between rich and poor, and the roles of Church and state in economic life. New terminology concerning justice and government intervention is introduced, as well as a new theory of economic organization.

Like their forerunners, the popes find nothing intrinsically wrong with market system trade, contracts, profit, investment, loans, banking, and property ownership. As in the pre-Leonine period letters, the moral test of these economic activities is their contribution to the community.

Property ownership in market systems receives particular encyclical attention. Here, papal thought moves through two stages during the Leonine period. According to Leo XIII's *Rerum novarum*, 5-7, the "sacred and inviolable" right of property is "sanctioned by the natural law," though its historical form is "fixed by man's own industry and the laws of individual peoples." Habiger identifies four arguments in *Rerum novarum* for the right to private property: an "argument from justice" drawing on the workers' right to dispose wages as they see fit; an argument "based upon reason" such that humans require possessions "not only for temporary use, but in stable and permanent possession"; an argument from causality in that human beings impress their personalities on their work; and an argument based on the "obligations of a father to the family."[96]

In *Rerum novarum*, 22, the pope notes that the natural 'right of possession' must be distinguished from 'right of use.' Regarding the latter, he quotes Aquinas: "Man should not consider his material possessions his own, but as common to all, so as to share them without hesitation when others are in need." But unlike the teaching of Clement XIII in the pre-Leonine period, Leo XIII contends such sharing "is a duty, not of justice (save in extreme cases), but of Christian charity."[97]

In *Quadragesimo anno*, Pius XI accepts Leo XIII's arguments on property, but places greater emphasis on the "two-fold aspect of ownership" and expands discussion of the person's moral title to property.[98] "While saving the essence of the primary and fundamental rights, such as the right of ownership," writes the pope in *Nos es muy conocida*, 15, people must "remember that at times the common good imposes restrictions on such rights as a recourse more frequent than in the past." Yet, he insists in *Quadragesimo anno*, 47 that "the very misuse or even the non-use of ownership" neither "destroys" nor "forfeits the right itself." Pius XI recognizes "first occupancy" as a title to property and warns that labor constitutes a "title to its fruits" only when human beings work as their "own master," not when one labors "on the property of another."[99]

The popes provide ample teaching on economic relations between individuals. On one level, the popes' general instruction remains influenced by the Hermasian model of interaction between rich and poor used in the pre-Leonine period letters. In *Auspicato concessum*, 24, for example, Leo XIII writes:

> . . . the question that politicians so laboriously aim at solving, viz., the relations which exist between the rich and the poor, would be thoroughly solved if they held this as a fixed principle, viz., that poverty is not wanting in dignity; that the rich should be merciful and munificent, and the poor content with their lot and labour; and since neither was born for these changeable goods, the one is to attain heaven by patience the other by liberality.

Consequently, inequality between rich and poor is natural and functional. Drawing on the cosmological design metaphor, Leo XIII adds in *Rerum novarum*, 19:

> Just as the symmetry of the human frame is the result of the suitable arrangement of the different parts of the body, so in a State is it ordained by nature that these two classes should dwell in harmony and agreement, so as to maintain the balance of the body politic.

In section 24, however, he adds that God "seems inclined rather to those who suffer misfortune."

The distinctive Leonine period addendum regarding economic relations lies in the popes' recognition that the rich and poor occupy multiple roles in the economy. Throughout their letters, the popes identify the poor as both employees and laborers, and the rich as both employers and capitalists. By considering these roles, two things happen in the Leonine period encyclicals. First, the popes develop a substantial teaching on micro- and macroeconomic human relations. Second, they move away from the Hermasian model of relations between economic actors.

Relations between rich and poor in the business firm come under the topic of employer-employee affairs. According to the popes, employers may rightfully own productive property, receive a "due share of the profit," and expect honest work from employees. On the other hand, they must respect the worker's "dignity as a person," allow the worker "time for his religious duties," ensure "that he be not led away to neglect his home and family," avoid taxing workers "beyond their strength, or employ them in work unsuited to their sex and age," and see that "wages are fair."[100]

Employees have a corresponding set of expectations and obligations. Workers may rightfully expect working conditions that are physically, morally, and religiously safe, an opportunity to issue grievances and negotiate for workplace improvements, and a fair wage. "The wage earner is not to receive as alms," insists Pius XI in *Divini Redemptoris*, 49, "what is his due in justice." A just wage is one sufficient for the support of the worker and his family without "ruin" to the firm or the public welfare. In *Quadragesimo anno*, 65, the pope adds that wage contracts "should, when possible, be modified somewhat by a contract of partnership"; thus "the workers and executives become sharers in the ownership or management, or else participate in some way in the profits." As participants in the enterprise, workers must "fully and faithfully" "perform the work which has been freely and equitably agreed upon," never "injure the property" nor "outrage the person, of an employer," and never "resort to violence in defending their own cause."[101]

On the macroeconomic level, rich and poor interrelate as capitalists and laborers. Concerning the former group, Pius XI's *Quadragesimo anno*, 88, regards competition between entrepreneurs as "justified and quite useful" if kept "within certain limits." With funds gained in just competition, capitalists provide an essential economic service by investing in productive enterprises.[102] In section 136, the pope says that an entrepreneur or investor who "renders service to society and develops its wealth should himself have his proportionate share of the increased public riches." All must recognize, however, the "double character, individual and social, of capital." While individuals may rightfully own capital, their investment practices must satisfy social "standards of equity and just distribution." In addition, capitalists must monitor "trustees and directors of invested funds," accept accountability "for corporations, with their divided responsibility and limited liability," make credit available on reasonable terms, and resist untoward influence over the state.[103] "The fundamental point," writes Pius XII in *Sertum laetitiae*, 34, "is that the goods created by God for all men should in the same way reach all, justice guiding and charity helping."

Similarly, laborers have prerogatives and obligations in the economic system. Because work possesses a natural and spiritual dignity, laborers deserve social respect. Such respect is concretized when workers are given a chance to "rise above poverty and wretchedness, and better their condition of life." This advancement is possible when society acknowledges the laborers' natural right to property, "equal opportunity for work," and association.[104]

During the Leonine period, vigorous debate occurs over two issues touching economic associations: (1) composition (must associations include employees and employers, or are separate associations permissible?); (2) confession (must Catholics establish and join only Catholic associations, or may they participate in either non-Catholic Christian associations, or secular groups?). Leo XIII leaves the composition and confession question open, with the exception of proscribing Catholic participation in nonreligious, secular associations. Pius X approves Catholic membership in non-Catholic Christian associations in Germany, but requires that Catholics maintain simultaneous membership in Catholic groups. Pius XI neither condemns Catholic participation in nonreligious, secular associations, nor refers to any Catholic obligation of dual membership.

Like capitalists, laborers also have moral responsibilities. They must neither associate with "men of evil principle," nor press demands which harm society. A scale of wages "excessively high," says Pius XI, "causes unemployment" which "ruins the prosperity of the nation and endangers public order." Nor is a "strike of workers or concerted interruption of work" appropriate if "there should be imminent danger of disturbance to the public peace."[105] According to Leo XIII's *Rerum novarum*, 19, "mutual agreement results in the beauty of good order," with order in the economy requiring that "capital cannot do without labor, nor labor without capital."

Like their forerunners, the Leonine period popes consider Church activity necessary to both the care of the poor and maintenance of a healthy economy. The Church must promote economic morality through hortatory, educational, and institutional means. "There is no intermediary more powerful than religion (whereof the Church is the interpreter and guardian)," asserts Leo XIII's *Rerum novarum*, 9, "in drawing the rich and the working class together, by reminding each of its duties to the other." Beyond exhortation, the Church must ensure that the laity and "candidates for the priesthood" are "suitably instructed in the pontifical documents relating to the social question."[106] On a practical level, the popes encourage bishops and clergy, religious congregations, and Catholic Action groups to organize and maintain hospitals, orphanages, homes for the aged, night shelters, rural banks, low-cost bakeries, recreation clubs, information bureaus, labor unions, and aid for emigrés. In *Divini Redemptoris*, 61, Pius XI recommends that priests " 'Go to the workingman, especially where he is poor; and in general, go to the poor.'"

The Leonine period popes give substantial attention to the state's role in economic life. In *Rerum novarum*, 32, Leo XIII argues that states have a special obligation to oversee the "interests of the poor." In section 37, he continues:

> The richer classes have many ways of shielding themselves, and stand less in need of help from the state; whereas the mass of the poor have no resources of their own to fall back upon, and must chiefly depend upon the assistance of the state.

Such assistance should include housing, clothing, health care, and employment. Regarding relations between employers and employees, states should monitor workplace conditions, wages, and Sunday rest. From the broader standpoint of capital and labor relations, states must oversee business competition and distribution of goods. By these means, governments can "forestall and prevent" labor strikes.[107]

When describing the economic role of the state, the Leonine period popes introduce new terminology concerning justice and a new principle regulating government action. The term 'social justice' is systematically inserted in encyclical literature for the first time by Pius XI.[108] Though never clearly defined, Pius XI uses the term when emphasizing both government and citizen responsibility for constructing a social order which expedites human compliance with the economic requirements of the common good. As several commentators recognize, social justice in papal letters closely resembles Aquinas' notion of general justice. Here, fairness in the overall structure of society is stressed, as distinct from commutative and distributive concerns over equity between society's parts.[109]

In a related move, Pius XI explicitly identifies, for the first time, the "principle of subsidiarity" as a "fundamental principle of social philosophy, fixed and unchangeable," directing state activity in economic life.[110] According to this principle, "it is an injustice . . . to transfer to the larger and higher collectivity functions which can be performed and provided for by lesser and subordinate bodies." Though the state should "prove a help to members of the social body," writes Pius XI in *Quadragesimo anno*, 79, "it should never destroy or absorb them."

Pius XI also introduces the vocational group, or 'corporative,' theory of economic organization into papal encyclical literature.[111] In *Quadragesimo anno* and *Divini Redemptoris*, the pope encourages building "the whole structure of economic life" on a two-tiered frame of "professional and inter-professional" groups. On the first tier, employees and employers in the same trade would mutually regulate working conditions, wages, and production within a given territory. On the second tier, vocational groups representing different professions would meet and mutually regulate trade relations and production for the common good of society as a whole. "All the occupational groups," says Pius XI's *Divini Redemptoris*, 54, "should be fused into a harmonious unity inspired by the principle of the common good." These groups would be noncompulsory and possess juridical autonomy distinct from the state.[112] Using the cosmological design metaphor, Pius XI writes:

> If then the members of the social body be thus reformed . . . it will be possible to say, in a sense, of this body what the Apostle said of the Mystical Body of Christ: "The whole body [being closely joined and knit together through every joint of the system according to the functioning in due measure of each single part] derives its increase to the building up of itself in love."

The criterion of social justice, subsidiarity, and corporatism is the common good. In Habiger's analysis, Pius XI believed that human groups at various levels (family, neighborhood, occupation, city, nation) have "a goal which transcends their immediate purpose." This goal is "the overall well-being of the larger society," or the common good. And, as is true throughout the Leonine period encyclicals, the common good must "coincide with God's design for His creation."[113]

Cultural Ideas and Practices. Though dramatic changes in social communication, lifestyle, and education occur during the Leonine period, the popes maintain several of their forerunners' cultural recommendations. New, however, are papal instructions concerning art theory, the purpose of science and technology, race relations, the status of women, and the meaning of civilization.

The popes support censorship of false and obscene communications, though suggested methods of suppression differ from pre-Leonine period teaching.[114] In Leo XIII's view, "men have a right freely and prudently to propagate throughout the State what things soever are true and honorable," but "lying opinions . . . should be diligently repressed by public authority."[115] Later, with the rise of radio, motion pictures, and television, papal emphasis shifts from government censorship to local boycott directed by Church-sponsored watchdog organizations. In *Vigilanti cura*, Pius XI praises the United States Legion of Decency, which publishes lists of approved and condemned motion pictures and encourages yearly pledges from Catholics "never to frequent such cinema entertainments as offend the truth and principles of Christian doctrine."[116]

The popes believe the purpose of factual and artistic social communication is dissemination of truth and encouragement of virtue. Accordingly, Pius XII writes in *Miranda prorsus*, 44 that informational and educational media must report the truth and inspire humanity

> . . . so that the bonds between peoples will be made closer, so that men will have better mutual understanding and will assist one another in time of crisis, and finally so that there will be genuine cooperation between public authority and individual citizens.

In section 14, he says artistic media should observe the "true principles of art." These principles require that "every art and work of art . . . be judged in the light of their conformity and concord with man's last end."[117]

As God is humanity's last end, artists should "make full use of that superabundance of material in the storehouse of Christian civilization." Christian actresses and actors should "not lend their talents to parts in plays, or to be connected with the making of films, which are contrary to sound morals." Nor should they "accept from their audience expressions of praise which savor of idolatry." One who has "won great fame" "should remember to give others a notable example of virtue by his private life."[118]

The popes support radio, motions pictures, and television to the extent that their factual and artistic presentations reflect the intrinsic purposes for which these media exist. "Everyone knows," writes Pius XII in *Miranda prorsus*, 123, "what a great contribution good radio programs can make to sound education." In *Vigilanti cura*, 17, Pius XI thinks "cinema is of great importance" because "it is available to all men," "not only for the rich." Regarding television, Pius XII says in *Miranda prorsus*, 157: "it is one of television's advantages that it induces both old and young to remain at home." Yet, over against these media, Pius XI prefers reading. "For to read, or to listen to another reading aloud," he observes in *Vigilanti cura*, 18, "demands a certain concentration and mental effort."

Two areas of cultural life-style treated by the popes are nonmarital sexual relations and leisure. Regarding the first topic, Pius XI insists in *Casti connubii*, 18: "every use of the faculty given by God for the procreation of new life is the right and the privilege of the married state alone, by the law of God and of nature, and must be confined absolutely within the sacred limits of that state." As for leisure, the pope thinks in *Vigilanti cura*, 16 that "recreation of body and soul, in the various forms in which this age has made it available, is a necessity . . . but it must be consonant with the dignity of man and the innocence of morals."

The popes provide ample teaching on the purpose and proper organization of education in society, as well as the social obligations of teachers. In their view, the purpose of education is to assist humanity in meeting the temporal and spiritual requirements of life. Because God is the source, sustenance, and summit of life, "there can be no ideally perfect education which is not Christian education." Pius XI continues in *Rappresentanti in terra*, 7:

> Since education consists essentially in preparing man for what he must do here below, in order to attain the sublime end for which he was created, it is clear that there can be no true education which is not directed to man's last end.

In this task, he adds in section 98, Christian education does not "renounce the activities of this life . . . but develops and perfects them."

To ensure that education achieves its purposes, three institutions must monitor its activity in descending, cooperative degrees of authority. As recipient of Christ's command to instruct all nations (Mt 28:18-20), the Church possesses a supernatural first right of educational oversight. According to Pius XI, this responsibility extends "over all the Faithful" and "equally to those outside the Fold, seeing that all men are called to enter the kingdom of God and reach eternal salvation."[119]

The second institution governing education is the family. Because marriage is created "directly by God" for "the generation and formation of offspring," parents possess the "inviolable natural right to educate the children." The exercise of this right, however, must be "subordinated to the last end and to natural and divine law."[120]

Finally, the state must "protect in its legislation, the prior rights . . . of the family as regards the Christian education of its offspring, and consequently also to respect the supernatural rights of the Church." In pursuing this task, the state possesses a natural right to "take measures to secure that all its citizens have the necessary knowledge of their civic and political duties, and a certain degree of physical, intellectual and moral culture." Because education "is concerned with man as a whole, in the order of nature and in the order of grace," all three institutions must achieve a "co-ordination of their respective ends."[121]

Teachers must observe Church, family, and state prerogatives over education. As a result, a teacher "has no absolute right of his own" in the classroom, but must respect the child's "strict right to instruction in harmony with the teaching of the Church, the pillar and ground of truth." If teachers consider it "necessary to have students read authors propounding false doctrine," this can only be done "for the purpose of refuting it." "Education," writes Pius XI in *Rappresentanti in terra,* 11, "is essentially a social and not a mere individual activity."

The Leonine period encyclicals assign science and technology a cultural responsibility mirroring that of art and education. When properly conducted, writes Pius XI, "the pursuit of science, of methods of science" enhances faith and morals because "the supernatural order . . . not only does not in the least destroy the natural order . . . but elevates the natural and perfects it." With this in mind, Pius XII says that the products of "this age of progress," though the "result of human talent and and toil," are "gifts of God" for the perfection of humanity.[122]

The popes offer several teachings regarding group relations in society. Though he resolutely condemns the secret societies of freemasonry, Leo XIII notes that individuals and local associations may be unaware of the larger body's underlying principles. In *Humanum genus,* 11, he observes that individuals, "although not free from the guilt of having entangled themselves in such associations," may be neither "partners in their criminal acts nor aware of the ultimate object which they are endeavoring to attain." Similarly, though not to be "reckoned as alien to the masonic federation," "affiliated societies, perhaps, by no means approve of the extreme conclusions which they would, if consistent, embrace as necessarily following from their [the parent body's] common principles."

The Leonine period letters make no reference to pre-Leonine period instructions concerning the control of Jewish social life in Europe. On the other hand, no encyclical explicitly addresses the period's oppression and extermination of the Jews. After the Second World War, Pius XII's letters neither approve nor disapprove the newly created State of Israel; instead, the pope asks that Jerusalem be granted international status to guarantee free access to the city's holy places.[123]

The popes inaugurate encyclical teaching on race relations and the social status of women. In *Divini Redemptoris,* 36, Pius XI insists that Christianity affirms "the real and universal brotherhood of all men of whatever race and condition." Pius XII reminds United States bishops in *Sertum Laetitiae,* 9, that "the Negro people dwelling among you . . . need special care and comfort and are very deserving of it."

With respect to women, Pius XI acknowledges the "equality of rights" of women in "those rights which belong to the dignity of the human soul." The possession of rights does not, however, fully express the "noble office of a Christian woman." This office is best expressed in either the life of celibacy and service in a religious order or the life of a wife and mother in marriage. With these functions in mind, and supported by the notion that "nature itself" fashions male and female "different in organism, in temperament, in abilities," the popes argue that women should be protected in schools and workplaces. In the "training of the two sexes," says Pius XI, nothing suggests that there should exist "promiscuity, much less equality" in the "mixing of the sexes." Likewise, women should be protected from work "unsuited" to their sex. "Women," says Leo XIII in *Rerum novarum*, 42, ". . . are not suited for certain occupations; a woman is by nature fitted for home-work."[124]

According to the popes, the authentic cultural values of Western civilization are not only synonymous with, but a patrimony of Roman Catholic Christianity. "The expected Saviour," notes Pius XI in *Divini Redemptoris*, 1, "came to begin a new universal civilization, the Christian civilization." This civilization gradually took root in medieval Europe, after which the "history of Christianity and its institutions . . . is nothing else but the history of true civilization and progress up to the present day." Though the papal letters reflect a growing appreciation for the "peculiar gifts" of non-Western "native art and culture," the popes retain the notion that exposure to Western civilization brings them to what Pius XII's *Evangelii praecones*, 58 calls "a point of aesthetic perfection."[125]

Summary Interpretation

Close analysis of the Leonine period encyclicals challenges the conventional view that encyclical social teaching remains "essentially the same, as the seed developing into the tree."[126] Substantial changes occur in papal letters both across the pre-Leonine and Leonine period and within the periods themselves. Yet, at the same time, important emphases perdure.

In the Leonine period, the prevailing metaphor representing God, the world, and humanity shifts from the earlier sheepfold metaphor to the metaphor of cosmological design. Thus, the idea of God is communicated more through the model of a universal creator, sustainer, and fulfiller than the more parochial image of Christ the Good Shepherd.

Similarly, the earlier model of the world as an ambiguous pasture of sustenance and threat is replaced by the image of a system wherein nature's existence and movement reflects God's beneficent intentions. Human beings, too, are characterized more by common possession of a propitious, rational nature than by their shared territorial traditions. Concomitantly, the divinely established natural law gives humanity a more apparent universal moral standard than that provided by the earlier morality based on personal conversion to faith in Jesus Christ.

Paralleling this shift in theological perspective, several antecedent papal teachings are changed. In the area of religious ideas and practices, educational emphasis shifts from homiletics, Scripture study, and patristics to the philosophical and theological premises of neo-Thomism. Concerning politics, the implication of papal teaching on state authority and Church-state relations is extended beyond traditionally Roman Catholic territories to the world at large. In family life, the primary purpose of marriage is redefined, shifting from the historical transmission of Christian faith to the biological generation of offspring. In economic life, almsgiving moves from a concern of justice (now understood as a 'natural' virtue) to one of charity (a 'supernatural' virtue). In cultural life, the Church undertakes oversight of moral standards for not only traditionally Roman Catholic regions, but Western civilization as a whole.

Nor are the Leonine period encyclicals always internally consistent. The popes are equivocal concerning clerical participation in politics, the theory of evolution, the cultural status of non-Westerners, civil disobedience, and relations between the economically powerful and unpowerful.

Yet vital commonalities between and within the two periods also exist. Stylistically, the Leonine period popes continue their predecessors' double-pulsed method of social instruction, paralleling negative judgments with positive recommendations. In terms of content, the popes still identify communal erosion as the central social problem. Corrosive social practices identified in the pre-Leonine period letters are repeated, with new ones added: episcopal apathy, declining vocations, ecumenical contact, nationalism, weapons production, divorce, contraception, abortion, euthanasia, sterilization, economic exploitation, monopoly, slavery, artistic licentiousness, sex education, racism, and the women's movement.

The popes also sustain the idea that faulty concepts underlie social erosion. Enlightenment atheism, naturalism, and rationalism still receive attention; their modern variants are located in agnosticism, pantheism, existentialism, polygenism, dialectical materialism, subjectivism, and

Americanism. Likewise, pre-Leonine period warnings against indifferentism, freedom of conscience, Febronianism, contractarianism, separation of Church and state, legal positivism, autonomous rights and freedom, secularized education, economic individualism, and socialism are repeated. Other troublesome concepts are new, but indirectly related to earlier problems: ecumenism, fascism, experimental marriage, market self-regulation, scientific socialism (or, communism), secularism, artistic verism and relativism, pedagogic naturalism, and the idea of untrammeled scientific progress.

Positively, the popes sustain their predecessors' communitarian orientation toward social ethics. But unlike the territorial communitarianism of the pre-Leonine period letters, the Leonine period popes offer what can be called a 'cosmological' communitarianism. Here, the communal character of self and society is retained, but grounded in the universal design of nature, not in the exigencies of living in a localized sheepfold.

Thus, human identity and purpose are still understood as embedded in communal functions and obligations. However, one's "constitutive" identity is now understood not by an appeal to territorial customs, but to a universal nature.[127] Similarly, society is still viewed as a hierarchically organized community of mutual service. But now it is justified on universal, not local, grounds. This constitutes what Ken Anderson calls a "precontractual, precategorical, 'natural' (or, more correctly, 'second natural')" view of community.[128]

It should be noted that this approach is qualitatively distinct from both the communist and fascist communitarian theories of the period. Unlike communism, the popes' theological communitarianism is based neither on the socialist community of goods theory (which incorporated a denial of private ownership of productive property and approval of the theory of surplus value, the omnipotent state, and material egalitarianism), nor on the theory of class struggle (which incorporated the philosophy of dialectical materialism and the idea of accelerating social change through revolution). Compared to fascism, or what George Mosse calls the "rightist ideal of community," papal communitarianism is not based on nationalism, racism, or the *Bund* glorification of sport and aggression.[129]

Several specific pre-Leonine period social recommendations reappear in the Leonine period letters; other recommendations are new, but not inconsistent with earlier teachings. In many cases the implications of teachings borrowed from the pre-Leonine period are widened, again reflecting the popes' cosmological design metaphor.

In the practice of religion, ecclesial unity requires a wider exercise of papal power and authority, necessitating a greater degree of episcopal, clerical, lay, and theological deference. New ideas include support for Catholic Action and emphasis on spiritual devotion to Mary and the saints. In political life, obedience is required toward just states; though Church and state are functionally distinct, a close collaboration between them is encouraged; and an expanded list of human rights and freedoms (grounded in the theonomous natural law) is acknowledged. New ideas include the approval of democratic government, the pragmatic recognition of Church-state separation in traditionally non-Roman Catholic countries, and the international common good. In family life, emphasis on the sanctity and perpetuity of marriage, the husband's authority over wife and children, and parental responsibility for adolescent education is maintained. New ideas include the importance of affectivity in spousal relations, the model of the Holy Family, and the family as the essential cell of society. In economic life, the popes accept a regulated market system, expand Church and state involvement in the economy, and demand that the poor be given special consideration. New ideas include the social dimension of individual property; the rights and duties of employers, employees, capitalists, and laborers; the concepts of social justice and subsidiarity; and the theory of vocational groups (or corporatism). In cultural life, Church and state must collaborate on censorship and education. New ideas include Christian theories of art, sex, leisure, teaching, and justice between races.

This chapter provides critical data for analyzing the content and coherence of papal thought within the Leonine period and in relation to the pre-Leonine period. Before moving to an assessment of encyclical social teaching as a whole, the final group of post-Leonine period letters must be investigated.

NOTES

1. Congregation for Catholic Education, "Guidelines for the Study and Teaching of the Church's Social Doctrine in the Formation of Priests," *Origins* 19 (August 1989): 174.

2. Coleman, "Church Social Teaching," p. 175.

3. Leo XIII, *Cum multa*, 12-13, *Constanti Hungarorum*, 16-17; Pius X, *Il fermo proposito*, 24. Pius XI forbids priests to belong to political parties in Italy (priest Don Sturzo, leader of the Italian Popular Party, resigns and goes into exile), Germany (Monsignor Kaas quits the Center Party), Poland (the Bishop of Cracow and the Archbishop of Lwov are forced to resign their elected Senate seats), and France (Pius X condemns Charles Maurras' 'Action Française'). See Anthony Rhodes, *The Vatican in the Age of Dictators: 1922-1945* (New York: Holt, Rinehart and Winston, 1973), pp. 14-15, 31-32, 103-11, 163-65.

4.   On clerical insubordination, see Leo XIII, *Inimica vis*, 5, *Depuis le jour*, 33, *Fin dal principio*, 6; Pius X, *Pieni l'animo*, 2, 14. On clerical schism, Leo XIII's *Iampridem*, 3 continues the pre-Leonine period reproval of the Old Catholics and Pius X's *Tribus circiter* condemns the Polish Mariavites. On the latter group, see Bernhard Stasiewski, "Catholicism in the Slavic World until 1914," in Roger Aubert et al., *Industrial Age*, pp. 174-75.

5.   Leo XIII writes in *Immortale Dei*, 47: "It is unlawful to follow one line of conduct in private life and another in public." In *Affari vos*, he scolds Canadian Catholics for passivity in the face of harmful Manitoba school laws. See also his *Licet multa*, 2, *Cum multa*, 14, *Iampridem*, 15, *Exeunte iam anno*, 11, *Octobri mense*, 2, and *Pergrata*, 7. H. Daniel-Rops describes this problem as distinguishing "the politics of Catholics" from "Catholic politics." The former refers to actual political behavior of individual Catholics. In this case, uniformity is not required. The latter refers to Catholic political principles grounded in hierarchical teachings. Here, uniformity is required. Trouble ensues when particular parties or politicians claim to represent "Catholic politics" and demand allegiance from Catholic individuals. H. Daniel-Rops, *A Fight for God: 1870-1939*, trans. John Warrington (London: J. M. Dent & Sons, 1965), p. 122.

6.   See Pius X, *Pascendi dominici gregis* and Pius XII, *Humani generis*, 23-25. For a discussion of modernism, see Roger Aubert, "The Modernist Crisis," in Aubert et al., *Industrial Age*, pp. 420-80 and Mark Schoof, *A Survey of Catholic Theology: 1800-1970*, trans. N. D. Smith, with an introduction by E. Schillebeeckx (Paramus, N.J.: Paulist Newman Press, 1970), pp. 14-151, 157-224.

7.   A decree from the Holy Office in 1927 forbade Roman Catholics from participating in the Lausanne conference. See Oliver Stratford Tomkins, "The Roman Catholic Church and the Ecumenical Movement: 1910-1948," in Ruth Rouse and Stephen Charles Neill, eds., *A History of the Ecumenical Movement: 1517-1948*, 2nd ed. (Philadelphia: Westminster Press, 1967), pp. 680-84. Unofficial interfaith groups of Catholics and Protestants were formed after World War I and called *l'union sacré*. Similar *Una Sancta* groups were formed after the Second World War. See Eduardo Soderini, *Leo XIII: Italy and France*, trans. Barbara Barclay Carter (London: Burns Oates and Washbourne, 1935), p. 230, n. 1; and Erwin Iserloh, "History of the Ecumenical Movement," in Gabriel Adriányi et al., *The Church in the Modern Age*, trans. Anselm Biggs (New York: Crossroad, 1981), pp. 468-69.

8.   According to Adriányi, between 1918 and 1923, all Roman Catholic bishops in Russia are "imprisoned, expelled, or shot." "The Church in Northern, Eastern, and Southern Europe," in Adriányi et al., *Modern Age*, p. 510. This includes, says Rhodes, the murder of "thousands of priests, monks, nuns." *Age of Dictators*, p. 136. Violence recurs in Béla Kun's Hungary (1919) and—after World War II—in the Soviet Union (especially, Estonia, Latvia, Lithuania, Byelorussia, Moldavia, and the Ukraine), Yugoslavia (Cardinal Stepinac arrested in 1946), Poland (Cardinal Wyszynski arrested in 1953), Hungary (Cardinal Mindszenty arrested in 1948, Archbishop Grosz in 1951), Czechoslovakia (Archbishop Beran arrested in 1949), Albania, Bulgaria, China (thirty-eight bishops arrested in 1958), and North Korea. Leftist regimes in Mexico loosely observe the 1917 separation laws until the 1926 Calles regime. Then, seventy-three convents, 129 religious colleges, and ninety-two churches are closed, 185 priests are expelled, and seventy-eight priests, religious, and lay persons are killed. In Spain, leftist persecution during the Second Republic (1931-33) and Popular Front (1936) "drove the Spanish Church into a frightful catastrophe without comparison in the history of the Church." See Quintín Aldea Vaquero, "Spain," in Adriányi et al., *Modern Age*, p. 604. The situation in Spain, notes Rhodes, was a "daily tale of murder and arson." *Age of Dictators*, p. 123.

9.   "Open battle" between Italian Catholic and fascist youth groups begins in 1931; legislative struggles are reopened in 1938. After this time, says Mezzardi, "Italian

Catholicism experienced no further shocks." Luigi Mezzardi, "Catholicism in Italy," in Adriányi et al., *Modern Age*, p. 578. The German and Austrian situation is different. Overt suppression of Catholic organizations begins in 1933, including 'show trials' of priests by the late 1930s. Hitler, however, does not want to "create martyrs" in "the manner of the Russian Communists"; rather, he seeks "the mind of youth" by systematically impugning the priesthood, eliminating Catholic youth organizations, and destroying the Catholic schools. Rhodes, *Age of Dictators*, pp. 168-69. In Austria, fascists close 120 churches, thirty-six monasteries, and 188 convents; in addition, thirty-five priests are killed, 742 are arrested, 208 are exiled, and 110 are sent to concentration camps. See Radomir Luža, "Nazi Control of the Austrian Catholic Church, 1939-1941," *The Catholic Historical Review* 63 (October 1977): 561, n. 65 and 562.

10. On rule of the few over the many, see Leo XIII, *Quod apostolici muneris*, 7, *Diuturnum*, 24, *Immortale Dei*, 5, *Sapientiae christianae*, 20; Pius X, *E suprimi*, 19; Pius XI, *Ubi arcano Dei consilio*, 24, *Rerum omnium perturbationem*, 27, *Non abbiamo bisogno*, 52, *Quadragesimo anno*, 105, *Divini Redemptoris*, 23, 33; Pius XII, *Summi Pontificatus*, 52-53, 71, 73, *Datis nuperrime*, 2. On parental rights over education, see Leo XIII, *Rerum novarum*, 14, *Affari vos*, 4, 6; Pius XI, *Divini Redemptoris*, 10-11, 33; Pius XII, *Orientales Ecclesias*, 13, 17, *Luctuosissimi eventus*, 1, 3, *Fidei donum*, 15, *Ad Apostolorum Principis*, 19.

11. On worker associations, see Leo XIII, *Rerum novarum*, 51, 53; Pius XI, *Quadragesimo anno*, 38, 78, *Divini Redemptoris*, 37. On forced labor, see Pius XI, *Mit brennender Sorge*, 36, *Divini Redemptoris*, 12. On imprisonment, see Pius XII, *Ingruentium malorum*, 18. On propaganda, see Pius XI, *Mit brennender Sorge*, 33, *Divini Redemptoris*, 17; Pius XII, *Anni sacri*, 3, *Miranda prorsus*, 51, 133. In *Miranda prorsus*, 133, Pius XII decries "deliberate 'jamming'" of Western radio signals in the Eastern bloc, creating "a kind of aerial 'iron curtain' . . . with the express purpose of preventing the entry of truth." On euthanasia, eugenics, and abortion, see Pius XI, *Casti connubii*, 63-70; Pius XII, *Mystici Corporis Christi*, 94.

12. On civil violence, see Leo XIII, *Inscrutabili Dei consilio*, 2, 6, *Quod apostolici muneris*, 1, *Diuturnum*, 2, *Etsi nos*, 8, *Humanum genus*, 22-23, 25, *Immortale Dei*, 1, 5, 31, *Saepe nos*, 8, *Exeunte iam anno*, 8, *Custodi di quella fede*, 7; Pius XI, *Ubi arcano Dei consilio*, 4, 14-15, 24, 39, *Caritate Christi compulsi*, 1, 7. On anarchism and assassination, see Leo XIII, *Quod apostolici muneris*, 1-2, *Diuturnum*, 2, *Sapientiae christianae*, 20; Pius X, *Ad diem illum laetissimum*, 22. Between 1881 and 1914, assassins murder Czar Alexander II, Spanish Prime Minister Canovas, French President Carnot, Empress Elizabeth of Austria, King Humbert I of Italy, United States President William McKinley, and Austrian Archduke Franz Ferdinand. Two attempts are made on the life of German Kaiser Wilhelm I.

13. Köhler says the level of violence in Ireland (nearly one hundred attempted assassinations and twenty-six murders in 1882 alone) "has to be taken into consideration" when assessing Leo XIII's view of the Irish boycott. Oscar Köhler, "Catholic Self-Awareness in the British Empire," in Aubert et al., *Industrial Age*, pp. 144-46. For a discussion of *Saepe nos* and its author, Monsignor Persico, see Rhodes, *Power of Rome*, pp. 146-58. On Pius IX and boycotting, see his *Quod nunquam*, 7.

14. On freemasonry and fascism, see Leo XIII, *Custodi di quella fede*, 8; Pius XI, *Ubi arcano Dei consilio*, 11, 25, *Rappresentanti in terra*, 49, *Quadragesimo anno*, 108-9, *Non abbiamo bisogno*, 44, *Mit brennender Sorge*, 8. On the condemnation of war, see also Benedict XV, *Annus iam plenus*, 1; Pius XI, *Ubi arcano Dei consilio*, 10, *Quadragesimo anno*, 108; Pius XII, *Summi Pontificatus*, 23, *Communium interpretes dolorum*, 1-2, *Auspicia quaedam*, 1, *In multiplicibus curis*, 1. Rhodes admires Benedict XV's position of neutrality during World War I, especially considering that the entente powers "were all at variance with the Vatican" and the central powers implied that they would "reestablish the Pope's

temporal power, and expel the Savoyards from Rome." Anthony Rhodes, "The Pope of the First World War: Benedict XV (1914-22)," *The Month* 250 (June 1989): 249. Wars specifically noted in the Leonine period encyclicals include: World War I, the Arab Wars of Independence (1916-22), the Russian Civil War (1918-20), the Mexican 'Cristeros' War (1926-29), the Spanish Civil War (1936-39), World War II, and the Israeli-Egyptian War. On conventional weapons, see Benedict XV, *Ad beatissimi apostolorum*, 3; Pius XI, *Nova impendit*, 8; Pius XII, *Optatissima pax*, 3, *Mirabile illud*, 2, 3, *Meminisse iuvat*, 3. On nuclear weapons, see Pius XII, *Anni Sacri*, 2 and *Summi maeroris*, 5-6. On violations of state's rights, see Pius XII, *Summi Pontificatus*, 74, *In multiplicibus curis*, 3, *Redemptoris nostri cruciatus*, 16.

15.   On mixed marriage, see Leo XIII, *Arcanum*, 43, *Quod multum*, 7, *Constanti Hungarorum*, 7, *Longinqua*, 14; Pius XII, *Sertum laetitiae*, 26. In *Quod multum*, Leo XIII decries Catholic and Jewish intermarriage. However, Konrad Repgen says Pius XI defends these unions against 1938 Italian laws proscribing "interracial" marriage. Konrad Repgen, "Foreign Policy of the Popes in the Epoch of the World Wars," in Adriányi, *Modern Age*, p. 58. On civil marriage, see Leo XIII, *Inscrutabili Dei consilio*, 14, *Quod apostolici muneris*, 1, 8, *Humanum genus*, 21; Pius XII, *Sertum laetitiae*, 9. On experimental marriages, see Pius XI, *Casti connubii*, 51. On divorce, see Leo XIII, *Arcanum*, 28-32, *Humanum genus*, 21; Pius X, *Iamdudum*, 1; Pius XI, *Casti connubii*, 85-92; Pius XII, *Sertum laetitiae*, 19.

16.   On contraception, see Pius XI, *Casti connubii*, 53-57. On abortion, see sections 63-67. Here, three specific practices are admonished: therapeutic abortion, abortion as birth control, and abortion as a form of eugenics. For a discussion of this section of *Casti connubii*, see John T. Noonan, Jr., "An Almost Absolute Value in History," in John T. Noonan, Jr., ed., *The Morality of Abortion: Legal and Historical Perspectives* (Cambridge, Mass.: Harvard University Press, 1970), p. 43 and John Connery, *Abortion: The Development of the Roman Catholic Perspective* (Chicago: Loyola University Press, 1977), pp. 293-94. On sterilization, see section 65 and 68. In the latter section, Pius XI admonishes governments which stop certain couples from marrying or forcibly "deprive these of that natural faculty [of reproduction] by medical action" in order to prevent "defective off-spring." In the 1920s and 1930s, laws prescribing sterilization of "defective" persons are passed throughout Europe and the United States. See *Encyclopaedia Britannica*, 1968, s.v. "Eugenics," by Frederick Osborn.

17.   John T. Noonan, Jr., *Contraception: A History of Its Treatment by the Catholic Theologians and Canonists*, enl. ed. (Cambridge, Mass.: Harvard University Press, Belknap Press, 1986), p. 424.

18.   On working conditions, see Leo XIII, *Rerum novarum*, 36, 39; Pius XI, *Quadragesimo anno*, 135; Pius XII, *Miranda prorsus*, 18. On hours, see Leo XIII, *Rerum novarum*, 39. On wages, see Leo XIII, *Rerum novarum*, 20, 36, 43-45; Pius X, *Acerbo nimis*, 15; Pius XI, *Quadragesimo anno*, 71-74, *Divini Redemptoris*, 52. On women and children, see Leo XIII, *Rerum novarum*, 36; Pius XI, *Quadragesimo anno*, 71. On compensation, see Pius XI, *Divini Redemptoris*, 52. On spiritual needs, see Leo XIII, *Rerum novarum*, 36, 41; Pius XI, *Quadragesimo anno*, 16. On the right to organize, see Leo XIII, *Rerum novarum*, 3; Pius XI, *Quadragesimo anno*, 30, *Divini Redemptoris*, 37, 50, 53.

19.   According to Leo XIII, labor violence and strikes primarily occur due to employer callousness (*Rerum novarum*, 38). Köhler's view that "Leo XIII considered a strike categorically evil" is overstated. "Catholicism in Modern Society," p. 224. Unlike Leo, Benedict XV thinks strikes are primarily caused by "class hatred" (*Ad beatissimi apostolorum*, 12).

20.   Pius XI, *Quadragesimo anno*, 105 and 133. Heilbroner notes the decline of owner-managers in the biggest United States corporations from fifty percent in 1900, and

roughly thirty-five percent in 1925, to three percent in 1960. Robert L. Heilbroner, *The Making of Economic Society*, 3d ed. (Englewood Cliffs, N.J.: Prentice-Hall, 1970), p. 116.

21.   On distribution, see Leo XIII, *Rerum novarum*, 2; and, Pius XI, *Quadragesimo anno*, 5, 54, 58, 60, 105. Heilbroner notes that in the U.S., for example, "an extraordinary, and steadily worsening, concentration of incomes" occurs from 1919 to 1929. *Economic Society*, p. 135. On agriculture, see Pius XII, *Sertum laetitiae*, 19. On imperialism, see Pius XI, *Quadragesimo anno*, 108-9; Pius X, *Lacrimabili statu*, 1. Though these popes criticize imperialism, Habiger says Leo XIII "regarded imperialism as a noble undertaking." Matthew H. Habiger, "Papal Teaching on Private Property: 1891-1981" (Ph.D. dissertation, The Catholic University of America, 1986), p. 3. This conclusion may be based on Leo XIII's comment in *Iampridem*, 14, where he approves German colonization, whereby the state seeks to "increase its possessions, and open new avenues to commerce and trade." Christine Gudorf is correct in saying that "the papal attitude toward colonialism is not systematically developed in any of the papal documents." However, her contention that the Leonine period letters uniformly approve colonialism is incorrect. Christine E. Gudorf, *Catholic Social Teaching on Liberation Themes* (Washington, D.C.: University Press of America, 1981), pp. 145-54. On trade barriers, taxes, workers' associations, unemployment, and arms production, see Leo XIII, *Rerum novarum*, 3, 51, 53; Pius XI, *Ubi arcano Deo consilio*, 11, 15, *Quadragesimo anno*, 38-39, 78, *Nova impendit*, 8, *Divini Redemptoris*, 37, 76; Pius XII, *Summi Pontificatus*, 83.

22.   See Pius XI, *Divini Redemptoris*, 10, 12, 15, 19-20, 107. Rhodes explains that Pius XI, while Apostolic Visitor to Poland from 1918 to 1920, personally witnesses the Russian siege of Poland and deportation of 125,000 Poles and Lithuanians to Siberia. "This Polish experience," he writes, "was to determine his attitude to Communism for the rest of his life." *Age of Dictators*, p. 18.

23.   On journals and newspapers, see Leo XIII, *Humanum genus*, 14, 20, *Exeunte iam anno*, 6, *Custodi di quella fede*, 7, *Paternae*, 5, 15; Benedict XV, *Ad beatissimi apostolorum*, 15; Pius XI, *Ubi arcano Dei consilio*, 10, *Rappresentanti in terra*, 90, *Ad salutem*, 32, *Casti connubii*, 45, *Caritate Christi compulsi*, 5, 15, *Acerba animi*, 9. In Schmolke's view, the popes' attitude toward journalism, codified in the 1918 canon law rules of censorship and prohibition, "made almost impossible to Catholics a normal participation in the journalism of the time." Michael Schmolke, "Information and the Mass Media," in Adriányi, *Modern Age*, p. 412.

24.   On drunkenness and sexual licentiousness, see Pius XI, *Ad salutem*, 32, *Casti connubii*, 50; Pius XII, *Sertum laetitiae*, 19. On the theater, see Leo XIII, *Humanum genus*, 20; Pius XI, *Ad salutem*, 32, *Casti connubii*, 45. On dance and attire, see Benedict XV, *Sacra propediem*, 18-20; Pius XI, *Ubi arcano Dei consilio*, 14, *Ad salutem*, 32; Pius XII, *Sertum laetitiae*, 19. On dueling, see Leo XIII, *Pastoralis officii*. According to Charles-Louis de Beaumont, duels of honor are authorized by the German military code until World War I (and later reauthorized by German Nazis and Italian Fascists). Also, student duels (*Mensur*) are a feature of German university life during this period. "In this way," he writes, "students can obtain scars on head and cheek which are prized as marks of courage." Political duels are also common in late nineteenth century France and Italy (between 1879 and 1889, 2,759 duels are recorded in Italy alone). *Encyclopaedia Britannica*, 1968 ed., s.v. "Duel," by Charles-Louis de Beaumont. In *Pastoralis officii*, Leo XIII notes the irony that "the new age which boasts of far excelling previous ages . . . does not repudiate the base remnants of an uncouth age and foreign barbarism that we know as the custom of dueling." On suicide, see Leo XIII, *Custodi di quella fede*, 7.

25.   In 1878, virulent debate over the place of atheism in freemasonry splits the deistic English-speaking Grand Lodge from the French-speaking Grand Orient. This debate, and the political influence of the latter group in predominantly Roman Catholic

countries of Europe and Latin America, explains Leo XIII's constant attention to free-masonry. See *Catholic Encyclopaedia*, "Freemasonry" and *Encyclopaedia Britannica*, 1968 ed., s.v. "Freemasonry" by Ray Baker Harris. See Leo XIII, *Humanum genus*, 17. Other letters treating freemasonry include *Dall'Alto dell'Apostolico seggio*, *Inimica vis*, *Custodi di quella fede*, *Exeunte iam anno*, 6, and *Au milieu des sollicitudes*, 25. After Leo XIII, the next and last explicit encyclical reference to freemasonry occurs in Pius XI's 1928 *Mortalium animos*, 2.

26.   Lenin is quoted in Dennis J. Dunn, *Détente and Papal-Communist Relations, 1962-1978*, Westview Replica Editions (Boulder, Colo.: Westview Press, 1979), p. 10. The League of Godless (later, Militant Godless) is formed in the USSR in 1924. On atheistic communism, see Pius XII, *Evangelii praecones*, 17; and, *Haurietis aquas*, 13, *Fidei donum*, 17, *Miranda prorsus*, 133, *Ad Apostolorum Principis*, 11. The post-World War II communist party platform reads: "It is necessary to conduct regularly broad atheistic propaganda on a scientific basis, to explain patiently the untenability of religious beliefs . . . leaving no room for religious inventions about supernatural forces." 22nd Congress of the C.P.S.U., *Programme of the Communist Party of the Soviet Union* (Moscow: Foreign Languages Publishing House, 1961), p. 110.

27.   Sartre's quote is taken from his *Existentialism as a Humanism*, quoted in Robert C. Solomon, *Introducing Philosophy: Problems and Perspectives*, 2d ed. (New York: Harcourt Brace Jovanovich, 1981), p. 293. Pius XII's response is from *Humani generis*, 6. According to John Macquarrie, a distinction must be made between "theistic existentialism" (as represented by Kierkegaard, Marcel, and Buber) and "atheistic existentialism" (Sartre and Camus). The former philosophers "think of human existence as transcending toward God," while the latter "see human existence transcending into the nothing." John Macquarrie, *Existentialism*, Theological Resources (Philadelphia: Westminster Press, 1972), pp. 50, 199-200. In *Humani generis*, 32, Pius XII distinguishes between two types of existentialism: an "atheistic" type and "the type that [while not necessarily atheistic] denies the validity of the reason in the field of metaphysics."

28.   Pius X, *Pascendi dominici gregis*, 6. The pope's understanding of agnosticism is consistent with Gaskin's definition: "the view that there is not enough, or not good enough, evidence to decide whether God exists or not." J.C.A. Gaskin, *The Quest for Eternity: An Outline of the Philosophy of Religion* (New York: Penguin Books, 1984), p. 189.

29.   On pantheism, see Pius X, *Pascendi dominici gregis*, 39 and 19. The specific target of these accusations is theologian George Tyrrel, dismissed from the Society of Jesus in 1906 after publication of *Letter to a Professor of Anthropology* and refused the sacraments after criticizing Pius X's encyclical. See Schoof, *Survey of Catholic Theology*, pp. 64-69 and *Catholic Encyclopaedia*, 1967 ed., s.v. "Modernism," by J. J. Heaney. On fascist pantheism, see Pius XI, *Mit brennender Sorge*, 7, 9, 11. In section 7, Pius XI defines pantheism as either "lowering God to the dimensions of the world, or raising the world to the dimensions of God."

30.   Pius XI, *Pascendi dominici gregis*, 30; and 2, 6, 20. The specific target of this accusation is theologian Alfred Loisy, a former student of Ernst Renan. Loisy's works appear on the Index in 1903. See also Pius XII, *Humani genus*, 26.

31.   Pius X, *Pascendi dominici gregis*, 11; and 12. See also Pius XI, *Mortalium animos*, 9; Pius XII, *Humani generis*, 14-16. Doctrinal development is the central question among Catholic theologians during the Leonine period. In *Pascendi dominici gregis*, 27, Pius X condemns the modernist model of development which pits the so-called "conserving force" of religious authority against the "progressive force" of the laity. In this view, doctrines are created and changed when the faithful bring "pressure to bear on the depositories of authority, until the latter consent to a compromise." In 1905, Edouard Le Roy's article "Qu'est-ce qu'un dogme?" is placed on the Index over this issue. Pius XII

agrees with Pius X, but recognizes in *Humani generis*, 16 that "the terminology employed in the schools and even that used by the Teaching Authority of the Church itself is capable of being perfected and polished." According to Schoof, *nouvelle théologie* and its principal leaders (Marie-Dominique Chenu, Henri de Lubac, and Yves Congar) are indirectly admonished in *Humani generis* over the development issue. *Survey of Catholic Theology*, pp. 104-15.

32.   Pius XII, *Humani generis*, 36; and 5. Schoof suggests the pope has theologian Teilhard de Chardin in mind when warning against undue philosophical and theological extrapolations based on evolutionary theory. *Survey of Catholic Theology*, p. 118. Gudorf's claim that Pius XII wrote *Humani generis*, in part, "to condemn the acceptance of evolution" is inaccurate. *Liberation Themes*, p. 12.

33.   Maurice Cornforth, *Materialism and the Dialectical Method* (New York: International Publishers, 1971), pp. 47 and 53.

34.   From V.I. Lenin's "Materialism and Empirio-Criticism," quoted in Joseph Stalin, *Dialectical and Historical Materialism* (New York: International Publishers, 1940), p. 17.

35.   See Pius XII, *Sertum laetitiae*, 20, *Humani generis*, 5, *Haurietis aquas*, 174, *Fidei donum*, 72, *Le pèlerinage de Lourdes*, 45. Like Pius XII, Engels frequently related Marx and Darwin's thought. In his eulogy at Marx's graveside, he said: "Just as Darwin discovered the law of development of organic nature, so Marx discovered the law of development of human history." Quoted in Erich Fromm, *Marx's Concept of Man*, Milestones of Thought Series (New York: Frederick Ungar Publishing Co., 1961), p. 258.

36.   Leo XIII, *Libertas*, 15; and, *Quod multum*, 3, *Exeunte iam anno*, 6, *Providentissimus Deus*, 10, *Depuis le jour*, 15. See also Pius X, *E supremi*, 11; Pius XI, *Mens nostra*, 7; Pius XII, *Sertum laetitiae*, 20. According to Pius X, modernists hold that a natural "need for the divine" in human life "excites in the soul" a "special 'sentiment,' without any previous advertance of the mind." "It is this sentiment to which Modernists give the name faith." See Pius X, *Pascendi dominici gregis*, 7; and 14, 37. See also Pius XII, *Humani generis*, 8. Pius XI accuses fascists of identifying religious faith with the "instinct in every heart" for the "future of one's people." Pius XI, *Mit brennender Sorge*, 23.

37.   'Americanists' refers to those imbued with 'Americanism,' an error proscribed in Leo XIII's 1899 letter *Testem benevolentiae*. 'Americanists' prefer "natural virtues to supernatural ones," consider passive virtues "more suited for the past ages," and think religious vows "restrict the field of liberty." From Leo XIII's *Testem benevolentiae*, in Neuner and Dupuis, *Christian Faith*, p. 592. Though the problem of Americanism refers to purported tendencies in the United States Church, the controversy occurs in France after conservatives react to Abbé Klein's description of the 'American Way' of Roman Catholicism in his foreword to Walter Elliot's biography of Isaac Hecker. See Oscar Köhler, "The Condemnation of 'Americanism,'" in Aubert et al., *Industrial Age*, pp. 331-34. The flavor of Americanism is captured in American Archbishop Keane's remark that "in heaven, a man should feel every muscle of his body swelling with strength, every fibre eager for a day's work." Quoted in Rhodes, *Power of Rome*, p. 135. The distinction between 'passive' and 'active' virtue is synonymous with the division between the supernatural (or theological) virtues of faith, hope, and love and the natural (or cardinal) virtues of justice, prudence, temperance, and fortitude. "The natural moral virtues, if acquired," explains Davis, "give facility in action and induce one to act rightly; the supernatural give the faculty of supernatural action, each in its proper sphere, but they do not give facility of action" (Davis, *Moral and Pastoral Theology*, 1:253-54).

38.   Lenin is quoted in John Hellman, "French Left-Catholics and Communism in the Nineteen-Thirties," *Church History* 45 (December 1976): 507. An active Catholic socialist movement in Germany during the 1920s no doubt influences Pius XI's discussion, particularly in view of the fact that a German, Oswald von Nell-Breuning, drafts

the text. Notable Catholic socialists of the period are Heinrich Mertens, organizer of the Bund Katholischer Sozialisten Deutschlands (1928), and Vitus Heller, founder of the Christlich-Soziale Partei Bayern (1920). See Thomas Knapp, "The Red and the Black: Catholic Socialists in the Weimar Republic," *Catholic Historical Review* 61 (July 1975): 386-408.

39.   Leo XIII, *Immortale Dei*, 33; and 27. See also Leo XIII, *Humanum genus*, 13, *Au milieu des sollicitudes*, 9, 11, 28, *Annum sacrum*, 10; Pius X, *Vehementer nos*, 7, *Gravissimo officii munere*, 8, *Une fois encore*, 17; Pius XI, *Dilectissima nobis*, 6, 8.

40.   Leo XIII, *Humanum genus*, 22. On criticism of individual autonomy, see also Pius XI, *Caritate Christi compulsi*, 23, and *Rappresentanti in terra*, 63.

41.   Leo XIII, *Humanum genus*, 21, *Arcanum*, 8, 40.

42.   Pius XI, *Casti connubii*, 86; and 79. See also Leo XIII, *Arcanum*, 32 and *Humanum genus*, 21. Pius XI cites and condemns three arguments favoring divorce: (1) "it is for the good of either party that the one who is innocent should have the right to separate from the guilty, or that the guilty should be withdrawn from a union which is unpleasing to him and against his will"; (2) "the good of the child demands this, for either it will be deprived of a proper education or the natural fruits of it, and will too easily be affected by the discords and shortcomings of the parents, and drawn from the path of virtue"; (3) "the common good requires that these marriages should be completely dissolved, which are now incapable of producing their natural results, and that legal separations should be allowed when crimes are to be feared as a result of the common habitation and intercourse of the parties." Pius XI, *Casti connubii*, 85.

43.   Pius XI, *Divini Redemptoris*, 11. See also Leo XIII, *Quod apostolici muneris*, 1, 8, and *Arcanum*, 13. The papal discussion of socialist thought on family life is undoubtedly influenced by August Bebel's *Die Frau und der Sozialismus* (1879) which goes through many editions and translations. The most important Catholic discussion of socialism during the period is Victor Cathrein's *Socialism: Its Theoretical Basis and Practical Application* (1890), which likewise goes through several editions and translations. Cathrein's study addresses Bebel's treatment of the family. See Cathrein, *Socialism*, pp. 340-47. The Soviet communist party platform of the period reads: "The communist system of public education is based on the public upbringing of children. The educational influence which the family exerts on children must be brought into ever greater harmony with their public upbringing." 22nd Congress of the C.P.S.U., *Programme of the Communist Party*, p. 112.

44.   Pius XI, *Quadragesimo anno*, 101. Some commentators insist that the combined effect of papal charges against capitalism in the Leonine period encyclicals constitutes a *de facto* repudiation of the system as a whole. Both Donal Dorr and Renzo Bianchi make this point, the former, favorably, the latter, unfavorably. See Donal Dorr, *Option for the Poor: A Hundred Years of Vatican Social Teaching* (Maryknoll, N.Y.: Orbis Books, 1983), pp. 63 and 80; and Bianchi, *Liberalism and Its Critics*, p. 96. This debate is best approached by noting that, for the popes, capitalism and the market system of economic production and distribution are not equivalent entities. Capitalism is a theory promoting the most extensive recognition of both the right to private ownership of the means of production and an unfettered market determination of distribution. Market systems, however, can function within a broader range of property and distributional theories than the 'pure' capitalist approach. As a result, while the popes frequently criticize capitalism, they do not condemn the market system. This interpretation is supported by Franz Mueller's recollection that the theologians and philosophers of the *Königswinterer Kreis* (a study circle including Nell-Breuning, Heinrich Rommen, and Goetz Briefs) "would have distinguished laissez-faire capitalism from the market economy." Quoted in Habiger, "Papal Teaching on Private Property," p. 142.

45.   See Leo XIII, *Quod apostolici muneris*, 9, and *Rerum novarum*, 4, 10, *Graves de communi re*, 5. See also Pius XI, *Quadragesimo anno*, 112, *Divini Redemptoris*, 10. Property can be distinguished as nontangible (an idea) and tangible (an object), with the latter divided into productive (real estate, raw materials, tools, transportation, capital funds, etc.) and consumptive (food, clothing, personal effects, etc.). Though the popes do not make these distinctions, it is evident that their argument against socialism is over the latter's rejection of a personal right to tangible, productive property. Addressing Christian socialists, Leo XIII says in *Rerum novarum*, 8: "The fact that God has given the earth for the use and enjoyment of the whole human race can in no way be a bar to the owning of private property."

46.   Surplus value is the difference between the value produced by the worker and what he receives as a wage. Socialists consider the wage contract unjust because "the capitalist buys the labor-power of the worker, and in exchange for this wage, he appropriates the entire production of that worker." Ernest Mandel, *An Introduction to Marxist Economic Theory* (New York: Pathfinder Press, 1970), pp. 23-25. As Marx explains: "The value of the labour-power, and the value which the labour-power creates in the labour-process, are two entirely different magnitudes; and this difference of the two values was what the capitalist had in view, when he was purchasing the labour-power." Karl Marx, *Capital: A Critique of Political Economy*, ed. Frederick Engels, trans. Samuel Moore and Edward Aveling, 3 vols. (New York: International Publishers, 1967), 1:193.

47.   Like their predecessors, the Leonine popes recognize differences within the socialist movement itself. In *Quadragesimo anno*, 112-13, 116, 119, Pius XI distinguishes between communism and socialism. The former theory advocates violent, proletariat expropriation of power and property at an opportune moment. The latter theory endorses a nonviolent, democratic appropriation through protracted legislative process. The early and mid-nineteenth century debate among socialists over the acceptance or rejection of violence appears in the Leonine period as a conflict between 'orthodox Marxists' (destruction of the existing state) and 'state socialists' (participation in the existing state). See Cathrein, *Socialism*, pp. 66-70.

48.   Oswald von Nell-Breuning, *Reorganization of Social Economy: The Social Encyclical Developed and Explained*, trans. Bernard W. Dempsey (New York: Bruce, 1936-37), p. 303. On the problem of avarice in the capitalist and socialist systems, see Leo XIII, *Inscrutabile Dei consilio*, 2, *Quod apostolici muneris*, 1, *Auspicato concessum*, 22, 24, *Nobilissima gallorum gens*, 2, *Quod auctoritate*, 1, *Exeunte iam anno*, 6, 8, 11, *Rerum novarum*, 2-3, 42, 60, 61, *Mirae caritas*, 6; Pius X, *Lacrimabili statu*, 2; Benedict XV, *Ad beatissimi apostolorum*, 5, 12, 14, *Sacra propediem*, 13, 18; Pius XI, *Ubi arcano Dei consilio*, 22, 24, *Rerum omnium perturbationem*, 27, *Quadragesimo anno*, 53, 109, 132, 134, *Caritate Christi compulsi*, 2-3, 18, 24, *Divini Redemptoris*, 12, 44; Pius XII, *Sertum laetitiae*, 19, *Miranda prorsus*, 15.

49.   Leo XIII, *Custodi di quella fede*, 4.

50.   On artistic verism, see Leo XIII, *Humanum genus*, 20. See also Pius XI, *Ad salutem*, 12. According to Joseph Machlis, operatic composer Giacomo Puccini led "the movement known as 'verismo' which tried to bring into the lyric theater the naturalism of Zola, Ibsen, and their contemporaries." Joseph Machlis, *The Enjoyment of Music: An Introduction to Perceptive Listening*, 3d ed. (New York: W. W. Norton & Co., 1970), p. 207. C. Hugh Holman explains that Emile Zola's naturalism was a "response to the revolution in thought that modern science has produced." This response involved "the application of the principles of scientific determinism to fiction." Holman continues: "The fundamental view of man which the naturalist takes is of an animal in the natural world, responding to environmental forces and internal stresses and drives . . . none of which he fully understands." The "most influential statement ever made on the theory of 'naturalism'" is Zola's *Le roman expérimental* (1880). Zola's complete works appear on

the Index in 1894, 1895, 1896, and 1898. C. Hugh Holman, *A Handbook to Literature*, 3d ed. (Indianapolis: Bobbs-Merrill Co., Odyssey Press, 1972), pp. 337-38. On the notion of 'art for art's sake,' see Pius XII, *Musicae sacrae*, 25. The "doctrine of Art for Art's Sake" begins with the Impressionists, who assert "the painter's privilege to combine whatever elements he pleases for aesthetic effect alone." According to this view, writes H. W. Janson, "the painter's first loyalty is to his canvas, not to the outside world." The American painter James Whistler makes the earliest formal presentation of this theory in his London "Ten O'Clock" lecture in 1885. H. W. Janson, with Dora Jane Janson, *History of Art: A Survey of the Major Visual Arts from the Dawn of History to the Present Day*, 2d ed. (Englewood Cliffs, N.J.: Prentice-Hall, 1977), pp. 607-8. See also John Golding, "Whistler," in Louis Kronenberger, ed. and Emily Morison Beck, assoc. ed., *'Atlantic' Brief Lives: A Biographical Companion to the Arts* (Boston: Little, Brown and Co., Atlantic Monthly Press Books, 1965), pp. 866-68.

51.   Pius XI, *Rappresentanti in terra*, 60. The naturalist movement in European pedagogy begins in the nineteenth century under the influence of Pestalozzi, Herbart, and Fröbel. Rooted in Rousseau's notion of humanity's natural goodness and Kant's emphasis on intellectual self-sufficiency, the naturalist movement takes a psychological approach to education, stressing "development of the learner from within." Pestalozzi and Fröbel are forerunners of the "child-centered system of education." The latter establishes the first kindergarten in 1837. *Catholic Encyclopaedia*, 1967 ed., s.v. "Education, I: Modern European Education," by J. J. O'Brien.

52.   For the papal recovery of Thomas Aquinas, see Leo XIII, *Aeterni Patris*, 17-34, *Licet multa*, 5, *Officio sanctissimo*, 8, *Depuis le jour*, 22; Pius X, *Pieni l'animo*, 6; Pius XI, *Studiorum ducem*; Pius XII, *Humani generis*, 31. See McCool, *Theology in the Nineteenth Century*, pp. 81-87, 226-40; Joseph Watzlawik, *Leo XIII and the New Scholasticism* (Cebu City, Philippines: University of San Carlos, 1966); and, James Hennesey, "Leo XIII's Thomistic Revival: A Political and Philosophical Event," *The Journal of Religion* 58, supplement, 1978.

53.   On God as designer of the universe, see Leo XIII, *Inscrutabili Dei consilio* 1, *Arcanum*, 1, 25, *Vi e ben noto*, 2, *Providentissimus Deus*, 1, *Longinqua*, 4; Pius XI, *Mit brennender Sorge*, 18. On God as rational creator, see Leo XIII, *Inscrutabili Dei consilio*, 5, *Quod apostolici muneris*, 5, *Arcanum*, 25, *Diuturnum*, 11, *Nobilissima gallorum gens*, 1, *In plurimus*, 3, *Exeunte iam anno*, 9; Pius XI, *Mortalium animos*, 6, *Mit brennender Sorge*, 9. "It must be said," writes Aquinas, "that everything, that in any way is, is from God." Thomas Aquinas, *Summa Theologica*, I, q. 44, a. 1, quoted in Anton Pégis, ed., *Introduction to Saint Thomas Aquinas* (New York: Modern Library, 1948), p. 234. On God as sustainer, see Leo XIII, *Humanum genus*, 18, 29, *Etsi nos*, 21, *Vi e ben noto*, 2, *Quod anniversarius*, 1, *Exeunte iam anno*, 4, 9, *Rerum novarum*, 7, 59, *Providentissimus Deus*, 1; Pius X, *E supremi*, 7; Benedict XV, *Quod iam diu*, 1. "We must certainly admit," says Aquinas, "that things are kept in existence by God." Quoted in Mary T. Clark, ed., *An Aquinas Reader* (Garden City, N.Y.: Image Books, 1972), p. 129. On God as fulfiller, see Pius XI, *Mit brennender Sorge*, 9. For Aquinas, "divine goodness is the end of all things." Aquinas, *Summa Theologica*, I, q. 44, a. 4, quoted in Pégis, *Introduction*, p. 240.

54.   On created entities, see Leo XIII, *Libertas*, 15, *Rerum novarum*, 6. "It belongs to the perfection of every nature," writes Leo XIII in *Libertas*, 15, "to contain itself within that sphere and grade which the order of nature has assigned to it, namely that the lower should be subject and obedient to the higher." Here, the popes accept Aquinas' five-level, ascending hierarchy of physical entities (elements, minerals, plants, animals, and human beings) differentiated by "1) the intensity of its force; 2) the extension of its freedom; and 3) the width of its sphere of influence." On the levels of sentient life, animals must exercise sensory powers over the vegetative powers and humans must

exercise the deliberative powers over the sensory and vegetative powers. See Peter A. Redpath, *A Simplified Introduction to the Wisdom of St. Thomas* (Lanham, Md.: University Press of America, 1980), p. 68; and pp. 37-39. On causality, see Leo XIII, *Officio sanctissimo*, 8, *Rerum novarum*, 22, *Divinum illud munus*, 3. According to Aquinas, the movement of entities at each level of physical existence follows the "first principles of mobile being, namely its universal four causes." These are: the material cause, or "that from which a thing is made"; the formal cause, or "that in which a thing is constituted"; the efficient cause, or "that by which a thing is produced"; and the final cause, or "that on account of which a thing is made." Kenneth Dougherty, *Cosmology: An Introduction to the Thomistic Philosophy of Nature* (Peekskill, N.Y.: Graymoor Press, 1952), p. 13. For Aquinas, God is the ultimate force behind all causality, "since God is the efficient, the exemplar [formal] and the final cause of all things, and since primary matter is from Him." Aquinas, *Summa Theologica*, I, q. 44, a. 4, quoted in Pégis, *Introduction*, p. 241.

55. See Leo XIII, *Arcanum*, 25; and *Immortale Dei*, 4, *Au milieu des sollicitudes*, 6. In Aquinas' view, natural things possess matter and form. Matter is a thing's inert, potential state. Form activates a thing to realize its purpose, or end. As a result, Aquinas believes "there is an unconscious drive in all the things we find around us to exist as completely as they can by exercising all the powers at their disposal." Redpath, *Wisdom of St. Thomas*, p. 90. Because God is ultimately responsible for all matter and form, "all things are ordered to one good, as their end, and this is God." Thomas Aquinas, *Summa Contra Gentiles, Book Three: Providence, Part I*, trans. and intro. Vernon J. Bourke (Notre Dame, Ind.: University of Notre Dame Press, 1975), p. 71.

56. Marie-Dominique Chenu, *The Scope of the Summa*, trans. and ed. Robert Edward Brennan (Washington, D.C.: Thomist Press, 1958), p. 15.

57. Leo XIII, *Libertas*, 3. In Aquinas' theory of knowledge, when humans understand something a bridge is built between immediate apprehension and complex understanding by a mental "conversion to the phantasm," or to the universal essence of the object or event. Frederick Copleston explains that to cross this bridge "there is a need . . . of an activity on the part of the soul." Frederick Copleston, *A History of Philosophy*, vol. 2, *Mediaeval Philosophy, Part 2: Albert the Great to Duns Scotus* (Garden City, N.Y.: Image Books, 1962), p. 109.

58. Pius XII, *Mystici Corporis Christi*, 12. See also Leo XIII, *Libertas*, 6, *In plurimis*, 4, *Divinum illud munus*, 8, *Tametsi futura prospicientibus*, 3. The popes adopt the Thomistic understanding of original sin. In this view, Adam and Eve lost the Edenic *justitia originalis* wherein they possessed supernatural and preternatural gifts. The former gift was sanctifying grace; the latter included gifts of the soul (immunity from concupiscence and ignorance) and the body (immunity from pain and death). See Thomas Aquinas, *Summa Contra Gentiles, Book Four: Salvation*, trans. and intro., Charles J. O'Neil (Notre Dame, Ind.: University of Notre Dame Press, 1975), pp. 217-23. See also A. Tanquerey, *A Manual of Dogmatic Theology*, trans. John J. Byrnes, 2 vols. (New York: Desclee Co., 1959), 1:409-36.

59. Leo XIII, *Libertas*, 6; and *Exeunte iam anno*, 10, *Tametsi futura prospicientibus*, 6. Like Aquinas, the popes understand sin as a "disorder in the soul" in which the appetites weaken reason's already limited deliberative power, unleashing the will in a disordered pursuit of the soul's lower sensual (hearing, taste, touch, sight, and smell) and vegetative (growth, consumption, and reproduction) desires. See Thomas Aquinas, *Summa Contra Gentiles, Book Three: Providence, Part II*, trans. and intro. Vernon J. Bourke (Notre Dame, Ind.: University of Notre Dame Press, 1975), pp. 111-12, and *Summa Contra Gentiles, Book Four*, pp. 231-32.

60. Leo XIII, *Tametsi futura prospicientibus*, 6; and *Exeunte iam anno*, 10, *Rerum novarum*, 18. See also Pius XI, *Rappresentanti in terra*, 58. With Aquinas, the popes believe

Christ's death and resurrection recovered the supernatural gift of sanctifying grace, but did not restore the preternatural gifts. As a result, concupiscence, ignorance, pain, and death perdure. See A. Tanquerey, *Manual of Dogmatic Theology*, 2:80-81.

61.   Tanquerey, *Manual of Dogmatic Theology*, 2:81. See also Aquinas, *Summa Contra Gentiles, Book Four*, p. 245.

62.   Pius X took Eph 1:10 as the motto of his pontificate. See Pius X, *E supremi*, 4, *Il fermo propositio*, 1, 6, *Editae saepe*, 2, 16. See also Leo XIII, *Arcanum*, 1, 18, *In plurimis*, 2, *Mirae caritatis*, 7, *Tametsi futura prospicientibus*, 3. Another frequent Leonine period reference to Christ is Jn 14:6, where the popes emphasize Christ's 'truth' as humanity's 'way' to God. See Leo XIII, *Aeterni Patris*, 10, *Tametsi futura prospicientibus*, 5, 9, *Auspicato concessum*, 6, *Supremi Apostolatus officio*, 8, *Officio sanctissimo*, 9, *Libertas*, 26, *Divinum illud munus*, 3. The popes' use of Eph 1:9-10 and Jn 14:6 accords with the Thomistic *ordo disciplinae* of the "emanation and return of creatures." Chenu, *Scope of the Summa*, p. 15. Aquinas describes this order in the organization of his *Summa Theologica*: "we shall treat: (1) of God; (2) of the rational creature's movement towards God; (3) of Christ Who as man is our way to God." Quoted in Pégis, *Introduction*, p. 20.

63.   See Leo XIII, *Tametsi futura prospicientibus*, 6 and Pius XI, *Mortalium animos*, 6. The popes accept Aquinas' teaching that positive, revealed law is necessary for morality because, (1) "since man is ordained to an end of eternal happiness which exceeds man's natural ability . . . it was necessary that, in addition to the natural and human law, man should be directed to his end by a law given by God," (2) "by reason of the uncertainty of human judgment . . . it was necessary for man to be directed in his proper acts by a law given by God," (3) "man is not competent to judge of interior movement . . . and it was necessary for this purpose that a divine law should intervene," and (4) "human law cannot punish or forbid all human deeds . . . therefore, that no evil might remain unforbidden and unpunished, it was necessary for the divine law to supervene, whereby all sins are forbidden." Aquinas, *Summa Theologica*, I-II, q. 91, a. 4, quoted in Pegis, *Introduction*, pp. 621-22.

64.   Leo XIII, *Satis cognitum*, 13. The popes maintain their predecessors' view that there is no salvation outside the Church, with provision made for cases of invincible ignorance. See Leo XIII, *Satis cognitum*, 5; Pius XI, *Mortalium animos*, 6, 11.

65.   Leo XIII, *Satis cognitum*, 5. See also Pius X, *Ad diem illum laetissimum*, 10. Pius XII's aptly titled *Mystici Corporis Christi* is the most important encyclical statement on ecclesiology during the Leonine period. With his analysis of the Church as the Mystical Body of Christ, Pius XII employs the "admirable and luminous language used by the masters of Scholastic Theology, and chiefly by the Angelic and Common Doctor [Aquinas]." Pius XII, *Mystici Corporis Christi*, 35.

66.   Leo XIII, *Satis cognitum*, 3 and 8. See also Benedict XV, *Ad beatissimi apostolorum*, 3, and Pius XII, *Summi Pontificatus*, 15. In his encyclical on the Holy Spirit, Leo XIII emphasizes the Jn 16:12-13 image of the third person of the Trinity as the "Spirit of Truth." Leo XIII, *Divinum illud munus*, 5.

67.   Pius XI, *Nos es muy conocida*, 19; and *Ad catholici sacredotii*, 67. See also Leo XIII, *Inscrutabili Dei consilio*, 13. 'Philosophia perennis' is a term representing the view that philosophy is not a collection of unrelated systems and ideas, but "a continuous and gradual development by many philosophies and philosophers of an increasingly more adequate explanation of reality." William A. Wallace, *The Elements of Philosophy: A Compendium for Philosophers and Theologians* (New York: Alba House, 1977), p. 8. For the popes, the fundamental principles of Aquinas' philosophy represent the best articulation of *philosophia perennis*.

68.   Like their predecessors, the Leonine period popes have great concern for the religious education of the laity. Pius X wrote the encyclical *Acerbo nimis* on the topic,

composed his own catechism (hoping to have it universally adopted), and "personally explained the catechism every Sunday" to thousands of listeners. Aubert, "Concern for Pastoral Improvements: Seminaries, Cathechetical Instruction, Catholic Action," in Aubert et al., *Industrial Age*, p. 417. See also Leo XIII, *In ipso*, 8, *Depuis le jour*, 23; Pius XI, *Rerum ecclesiae*, 27. Mirroring the neo-Thomistic retrieval of Aquinas, however, catechisms of the Leonine period eliminate direct biblical references common in earlier texts. A popular catechism by Deharbe, for example, "offered a short survey of scholastic theology with clear and precise formulations" and "was free from all biblical and kerygmatic perspectives." Aubert, "Pastoral Care," pp. 18-19.

69.   In his missionary encyclical, Leo XIII insists that "faith comes by hearing the word." Leo XIII, *Sancta Dei civitas*, 1; and, *Catholicae ecclesiae*, 31. Contrariwise, Pius XII advises that missionaries "follow the same methods which the Divine Teacher used while He was on earth. Before He began to preach to the crowds, He first healed the sick." Pius XII, *Rerum ecclesiae*, 30; and *Evangelii praecones*, 22. The proximate inspiration for this shift in methodology is Cardinal Lavigerie, leader of the White Fathers of Africa. Lavigerie "forbade preaching a specifically Christian message"; rather, he pursued the "indirect apostolate (charity, schools, orphanages, visits with natives), hoping to prepare the ground gradually." Jakob Baumgartner, "The Expansion of Catholic Missions from the Time of Leo XIII until World War II," in Aubert et al., *Industrial Age*, p. 546. In general, the Leonine period encyclicals place less emphasis on preaching than the pre-Leonine period texts. An exception is Benedict XV's *Humani generis redemptionem*.

70.   Pius XII, *Evangelii praecones*, 63; and 58. In an apostolic letter, *Maximum illud*, Benedict XV warns against the 'Europeanism' of the missions by criticizing the "nationalistic attitude of individual representatives and the colonialist missionary methods." Baumgartner, "Expansion of Catholic Missions," p. 559. An example of this attitude occurs in Leo XIII's *Au milieu des solliciitudes*, where the pope admires French "enterprises in foreign lands where, by means of her gold and the labors of her missionaries who work even at the price of their blood, she simultaneously propagates her own renown and the benefits of the Catholic religion." The Leonine period popes also continue their forerunners' emphasis on native clergy and condemn racial discrimination within clerical ranks. "There should exist no discrimination of any kind between priests," warns Pius XI, "be they European missionaries or natives." Pius XI, *Rerum ecclesiae*, 26; and 16-25. See also Pius XII, *Summi Pontificatus*, 47-48, *Saeculo exeunte octavo*, 29, *Evangelii praecones*, 25.

71.   According to D. J. Geany, Pius X is "the first pope to use this term." *Catholic Encyclopeadia*, 1967 ed., s.v. "Catholic Action," by D. J. Geany. See Pius X, *In fermo proposito*, 3, 7- 8, 12, 17, *Editate saepe*, 39; Benedict XV, *Ad beatissimi apostolorum*, 26; Pius XI, *Ubi arcano Dei consilio*, 54, *Rappresentanti in terra*, 84, *Dilectissima nobis*, 25, *Divini Redemptoris*, 64, *Nos es muy conocida*, 9; Pius XII, *Evangelii praecones*, 30-40. On Leo XIII's encouragement of lay associations, see *Auspicato concessum*, 25, *Rerum novarum*, 54, *Custodi di quella fede*, 19, *Permoti nos*, 6.

72.   Aubert, "Pastoral Improvements," p. 419. The emphasis on episcopal control should not overshadow the popes' new encouragement of lay activity. Promotion of lay catechists was, says Aubert, "a novelty at this time," as was the furtherance of lay missionary activity. Ibid., p. 417. See Pius XII, *Evangelii praecones*, 37-38.

73.   These saints include: Cyril and Methodius, Francis of Assisi, Joseph, Peter Canisius, Gregory the Great, Anselm, Charles Borromeo, Boniface, Jerome, Ephrem, Dominic, Francis de Sales, Aquinas, Josaphat, Augustine, Cyril of Alexandria, Benedict, Bernard, Boniface, and Andrew Bobola.

74.   See Leo XIII, *Supremi Apostolatus officio, Superiore anno, Vi e nen noto, Octobri mense, Magnae Dei Matris, Laetitiae sanctae, Iucunda semper expectatione, Adiutricem, Fidentem*

piumque animum, Augustissimae Virginis Mariae, Diuturni temporis. See also Pius XI, *Ingravescentibus malis* and Pius XII, *Ingruentium malorum.* In addition, Pius XII writes *Deiparae virginis Mariae* on the assumption of Mary, *Fulgens corona* announcing a Marian Year, *Ad caeli reginam* on the queenship of Mary, and *Le pèlerinage de Lourdes* commemorating the centenary of Mary's apparition at Lourdes.

75.   On the Sacred Heart, see Leo XIII, *Annum sacrum*; Pius XI, *Miserentissimus Redemptor, Caritate Christi compulsi*; Pius XII, *Haurietis aquas.* On third orders, see Leo XIII, *Auspicato concessum,* 25, *Humanum genus,* 34, *Quod auctoritate,* 4; Benedict XV, *Sacra propediem*; Pius XI, *Rite expiatis,* 35. The idea of third orders take its origin from Francis of Assisi. Besides the Franciscans, the following orders sponsor 'tertiaries' during the Leonine period: Augustinians, Dominicans, Servites, Carmelites, Minims, Trinitarians, Norbertines, Benedictines, and Mercedarians.

76.   Leo XIII, *Diuturnum,* 11. On the question of a ruler's source of power, theological debate occurs during this period between 'translation' and 'designation' theorists. The former group (Joseph Mausbach, P. Tischleder, Costa-Rosetti, Cardinals Billot and Manning) believes popular selection represents a transfer of citizen power (granted by God) to the ruler. Supporters cite Cajetan, Vittoria, Soto, Bellarmine, and Suarez as fifteenth through seventeenth century translation theorists. The latter group (Luigi Taparelli, Victor Cathrein, T. Meyer, Mathias Libertore, and Cardinal Zigliara) thinks selection represents a popular choice of rulers, but not a transfer of citizen power. Advocates cite Thomas Aquinas and Leo XIII's remark in *Diuturnum* as support for the designation theory. In fact, Leo XIII "had been one of Taparelli's most promising disciples" during his student days at the Roman College. McCool, *Theology in the Nineteenth Century,* p. 226. While Leo XIII's remarks reflect the designation theory, he nowhere denounces the alternative; rather, his enmity is directed against Enlightenment social contract theories which locate political power exclusively in the citizenry, independent of God (a claim the translation theory, no less than the designation theory, rejects). Rommen notes that when Leo XIII was "asked through a cardinal if he had intended to reject the translation theory, he answered that he did not mean to reject the opinions of Catholics, but only those doctrines which denied any dependence of political authority upon God and which taught that authority in no way originates in God but exclusively in the arbitrary will of men." See Heinrich A. Rommen, *The State in Catholic Thought: A Treatise in Political Philosophy* (St. Louis: B. Herder Book Co., 1945), p. 469; and pp. 440-73. See also Gabriel Bowe, *The Origin of Political Authority: An Essay in Catholic Political Philosophy* (Dublin: Clonmore & Reynolds, 1955), pp. 16-24, 94-98; Charles, *Social Teaching of Vatican II,* pp. 205-6; Edgar Alexander, "Church and Society in Germany," in Moody, *Church and Society,* pp. 506-8.

77.   Leo XIII, *Immortale Dei,* 36; and *Diuturnum,* 7, *Au milieu des sollicitudes,* 14. Leo XIII's morally neutral approach regarding the classic governmental forms (monarchy, aristocracy, democracy) departs from Aquinas, who favored "monarchy as the best form of government." Alexander Passerin D'Entrèves, *The Medieval Contribution to Political Thought: Thomas Aquinas, Marsilius of Padua, Richard Hooker* (New York: Humanities Press, 1959), p. 37. "With this contrivance," says Köhler, "democracy is introduced as an ecclesiastically tolerable form of government." "Catholicism in Modern Society," p. 235.

78.   The popes adopt Aquinas' definition of law as "an ordinance of reason for the common good, promulgated by him who has the care of the community." Aquinas, *Summa Theologica,* I-II, q. 90, a. 4, quoted in Pégis, *Introduction,* p. 615. See Leo XIII, *Sapientiae christianae,* 8 and *Au milieu des sollicitudes,* 24. On defense of the innocent, see Leo XIII, *Tametsi futura prospicientibus,* 12, *Pastoralis officii,* 2; Pius XI, *Casti connubii,* 67, *Divini Redemptoris,* 30. Criminal justice includes the possibility of capital punishment. See Pius XI, *Casti connubii,* 64. On social coordination, see Pius XI, *Divini Redemptoris,* 32; Pius

XII, *Summi Pontificatus*, 59, *Miranda prorsus*, 35. On temporal improvement, see Leo XIII, *Rerum novarum*, 32, *Tametsi futura prospicientibus*, 12; Pius XI, *Casti connubii*, 121.

79.   Leo XIII, *Libertas*, 21; and *Immortale Dei*, 4, 6. See also Pius X, *Vehementer nos*, 3; Pius XII, *Fulgens radiatur*, 26, *Mediator Dei*, 4, *Mirabile illud*, 6. In *Immortale Dei*, 6, Leo XIII says "it is a sin for the state not to have care for religion." In his study of Leo XIII's encyclicals, John Courtney Murray claims "Leo XIII emphasized—that the purpose of the state is not the salvation of souls." John Courtney Murray, "Leo XIII: Separation of Church and State," *Theological Studies* 14 (June 1953) 203-4; and 202. See also John Courtney Murray, "Leo XIII: Two Concepts of Government," *Theological Studies* 14 (December 1953): 564. Here, Murray argues that when Leo XIII speaks of the state's direct religious responsibility this is "consequent upon social fact and social necessities of the historical, not theoretical, order." Ibid., p. 566. See also John Courtney Murray, "The Church and Totalitarian Democracy," *Theological Studies* 13 (December 1952): 551, "Leo XIII on Church and State: The General Structure of the Controversy," *Theological Studies* 14 (March 1953): 13, and "Leo XIII: Two Concepts of Government, II. Government and the Order of Culture," *Theological Studies* 15 (March 1954): 16. Close reading of the texts does not support these claims. Murray's argument misses the pope's distinction between the proximate and remote ends of government, suggesting not only the historical, but also the theoretical level of Leo XIII's concern for state care of religion.

80.   Gudorf's observation concerning the Leonine period is apt: "The dependence of human spiritual welfare upon moral activity did, however, necessitate the interference of the spiritual authority in those secular matters which concerned the moral . . . Depending upon the breadth of one's understanding of the moral, therefore, there might not really be two distinct realms—the Church could claim to be supreme in all secular matters by recognizing in them a moral component." *Liberation Themes*, p. 73. On marriage, the popes follow the pre-Leonine period view that states recognize Church law on validity, celebration, and divorce. See Leo XIII, *Arcanum*, 13, 15, 19-20, 22, 34-37, *Quam religiosa*, 4; Pius XI, *Casti connubii*, 125. Concerning education, the popes' ideal is a single state-supported Catholic school system. But "in a nation where there are different religious beliefs," writes Pius XI, Catholics should be "free to follow their own system of teaching in schools that are entirely Catholic." The principle of "distributive justice" requires that this separate system receive "financial aid granted by the state." Pius XI, *Rappresentanti in terra*, 81; and 18, 22, 44, 46, 52, 77, 82. See also Leo XIII, *Spectata fides*, 4 and *Officio sanctissimo*, 11. The idea of state censorship under Church guidance continues during the Leonine period, though the discussion is substantially reduced and new ideas—such as state selection of "committees of mothers and fathers of families, to inspect, censor and direct the published films"—are introduced. Pius XI, *Vigilanti cura*, 27; and Pius XII, *Miranda prorsus*, 35, 37-38, 112.

81.   Leo XIII, *Arcanum*, 36, *Immortale Dei*, 32, *Sapientiae christianae*, 5-6, 11. For the Leonine period popes, not only the Church, but also the state is "a perfect society, having in itself all the means for its peculiar end." Pius XI, *Rappresentanti in terra*, 12. See also Leo XIII, *Immortale Dei*, 10, *Nobilissima gallorum gens*, 2, *Libertas*, 6, 40; Benedict XV, *Pacem Dei munus pulcherrimum*, 18; Pius XI, *Mortalium animos*, 6. The concept of the Church as a *societas perfecta* was introduced in the pre-Leonine period letters to emphasize the freedom of the Church against state encroachment. The Leonine period letters are the first to give the state this designation. It would be incorrect, however, to conclude that the popes thereby endorsed the freedom of the state from observing Church teaching. On the concept of *societas perfecta*, see Patrick Granfield, "The Rise and Fall of *Societas Perfecta*," in Peter Huizing and Knut Wallf, eds., *May Church Ministers Be Politicians?*, *Concilium*, vol. 157 (Edinburgh: T. & T. Clark, 1982), pp. 3-8.

82.   Leo XIII, *Sapientiae christianae*, 25, 29 and *Libertas*, 21. John Courtney Murray

argues that Leo XIII broke from the medieval notion of two powers in one society to the notion of two powers in two societies. With this move, the pope "put an end in principle to . . . the notion of the instrumentality of political power to the proper ends of the supernatural society." Murray, "Church and Totalitarian Democracy," p. 558 and "Separation of Church and State," pp. 200-1. Close reading of the encyclicals does not support Murray's claim. Rather, Leo XIII hopes for close relations between Church and state so that an overall Christian society—a *Christianitas*—might be restored. Leslie Griffin is correct when she observes that Leo XIII "not only opposes the separation of church and state, but advocates that Catholicism should be the one religion supported by the state." Leslie Griffin, "The Integration of Spiritual and Temporal: Roman Catholic Church-State Theory from Leo XIII to John Paul II" (Ph.D. dissertation, Yale University, 1984), p. 139.

83.   Leo XIII, *Libertas*, 33; and 34. See also Leo XIII, *Arcanum*, 13 and Pius X, *Il fermo proposito*, 5. Commenting on the favorable condition of the Church in the United States, Leo XIII adds: "Yet, though all this is true, it would be erroneous to draw the conclusion that in America is to be sought the type of the most desirable status of the Church, or that it would be universally expedient for State and Church, to be, as in America, dissevered and divorced." Leo XIII, *Longinqua*, 6. In his study of this text, John Courtney Murray claims Leo XIII's remark is "a statement of fact, not of doctrine." Murray, "Church and Totalitarian Democracy," p. 552, n. 58. He adds that "one does not find in Leo XIII the notion of a double situation, one *per se* (the Ideal), the other *per accidens* (the lamentable Real). Murray, "General Structure of the Controversy," p. 26. Murray's claim that Leo XIII did not view the American situation as doctrinally unsound and that he did not contrast an ideal Church-state relationship against less than ideal arrangements cannot be supported by the texts.

84.   Leo XIII, *Immortale Dei*, 44-45. See also Leo XIII, *Libertas*, 45, *Sapientiae christianae*, 31, *Au milieu des sollicitudes*, 6, *Constanti Hungarorum*, 11; Pius X, *Il fermo proposito*, 7, 17; Pius XI, *Divini Redemptoris*, 30. Leo XIII indirectly notes the Italian exception to this general teaching on Catholic participation. See Leo XIII, *Immortale Dei*, 44 and *Libertas*, 45. Since the expropriation of the papal states by the Italian government during Pius IX's reign, a papal *non expedit* forbade Catholic participation in the new state. Pius X softens the *non expedit* before it was formally abrogated by Benedict XV. See Pius X, *Il fermo proposito*, 18-19.

85.   Dorr, *Option for the Poor*, p. 40.

86.   Pius XI, *Nos es muy conocida*, 26. During the prewar years in fascist Italy, the pope realizes "the many difficulties of the present hour" and notes "that membership in the party and the oath are for countless persons a necessary condition of their career, of their daily bread, and even of life itself." In order to reduce "the external difficulties of the situation," the pope advises Italian Catholics receiving membership cards and taking the oath to make a mental reservation such as "Saving the laws of God and the Church" and "declare also externally such reservation" if necessary. Pius XI, *Non abbiamo bisogno*, 59.

87.   Pius XI, *Nos es muy concida*, 27. Dorr's translation is used here. *Option for the Poor*, pp. 70-71. In an earlier encyclical to missionaries (*Rerum ecclesiae*, 22), Pius XI describes without acrimony how native clergy are in a better position to survive when ". . . the inhabitants of a particular territory, having reached a fairly high degree of civilization and at the same time a corresponding development in civic and social life, and desiring to become free and independent, should drive away from their country the governor, the soldiers, the missionaries of the foreign nation to whose rule they are subject. All this, of course, cannot be done without violence."

88.   On Mexico, see Pius XI, *Nos es muy conocida*, 28. Gudorf mutes the shift in papal teaching here by suggesting, without support, that Pius XI felt "there had been no

legitimate government in Mexico since the 1911 revolution." *Liberation Themes*, pp. 188-89. Gudorf adds that Pius XI probably perceived the Mexican situation as applicable to the approved criteria of the just war theory. However, no encyclical letter of the Leonine (or pre-Leonine) period explicitly refers to the just war theory. In addition, any direct reference to the just war theory would include considerations of legitimate authority and just cause, conditions not included in Pius XI's list of general principles. See also Dorr, *Option for the Poor*, pp. 71-75. On Hungary, see Pius XII, *Datis nuperrime*, 2; and *Luctuosissimi eventus*. As in the case of Pius XI, Gudorf argues that Pius XII's thought "must be understood in the light of the traditional just war theory." *Liberation Themes*, p. 214. However, she admits that "Pius XII did not connect his position on the Hungarian revolt with the just war theory explicitly." Ibid., p. 216.

89. Habiger, "Papal Teaching on Private Property," p. 50.

90. On the rights of God, see Leo XIII, *Tametsi futura prospicientibus*, 13; Pius XI, *Mortalium animos*, 6; Pius XII, *Laetamur admodum*, 3, *Le pèlerinage de Lourdes*, 49. On the rights of the Church, see Leo XIII, *Officio sanctissimo*, 13, *Libertas*, 40, 44; Benedict XV, *In hac tanta*, 25; Pius XII, *Fulgens corona*, 42, *Laetamur admodum*, 3. On the rights of the state, see Leo XIII, *Immortale Dei*, 4; Pius XI, *Ubi arcano Dei consilio*, 25, *Quas primas*, 18. Individual rights carried over from the pre-Leonine period include the family's right to educate and care for children (see Leo XIII, *Rerum novarum*, 12; Pius XI, *Rappresentanti in terra*, 44, *Mit brennender Sorge*, 31; Pius XII, *Summi Pontificatus*, 63; the right to possess and use property (see Leo XIII, *Rerum novarum*, 5-6; Pius XI, *Ubi arcano Dei consilio*, 60, *Quadragesimo anno*, 44, 46-49, *Dilectissima nobis*, 10, 21, *Divini Redemptoris*, 10, 27, *Nos es muy conocida*, 15, *Ingravescentibus malis*, 5); the right to goods necessary to physical survival (see Pius XI, *Divini Redemptoris*, 27); and the right of Catholics to publicly practice their religion (see Pius XI, *Non abbiamo bisogno*, 40, *Mit brennender Sorge*, 31, *Nos es muy conocida*, 26; Pius X, *Vehementer nos*, 9; Pius XII, *Orientales ecclesias*, 13). On this last right, the Leonine period encyclicals give no clear statement supporting the individual right of non-Catholics to profess their religion in public. The closest statement of this kind occurs in Pius XII's *In multiplicibus curis*, 3. Here, the pope decries the Palestinian wars and calls for mutual respect for the "rights of acquired traditions, especially in the religious field."

91. On the right to life, see Pius XI, *Divini Redemptoris*, 27. On bodily integrity, see ibid., 27. On language, see Leo XIII, *Reputantibus*, 2-3. On association, see Leo XIII, *Rerum novarum*, 49, 51-52, *Custodi di quella fede*, 5, *Longinqua*, 16; Pius XI, *Quadragesimo anno*, 30, 37, *Divini Redemptoris*, 27, 37; Pius XII, *Evangelii praecones*, 40. On marriage, see Leo XIII, *Rerum novarum*, 12; Pius XI, *Casti connubii*, 18, 68, *Divini Redemptoris*, 28. In *Arcanum*, 15, Leo XIII says "sons and daughters wishing to marry" cannot be "deprived of their rightful freedom by dissenting parents." On political resistance, see Leo XIII, *Libertas*, 30. On voting, see Pius X, *Il fermo proposito*, 18; Pius XI, *Nos es muy conocida*, 31. On providing for sustenance, see Leo XIII, *Rerum novarum*, 7, 45; Pius XI, *Ubi arcano Dei consilio*, 25, *Divini Redemptoris*, 27. On freedom, see Leo XIII, *Libertas*, 13; Pius XI, *Divini Redemptoris*, 27. On communication, see Leo XIII, *Libertas*, 23. On the rights of children, see Pius XI, *Rappresentanti in terra*, 45. On the rights of wives, see Pius XI, *Casti connubii*, 77.

92. Mackin, *What Is Marriage?*, pp. 201-22.

93. Pius XI, *Casti connubii*, 24; and 10, 23. See also Leo XIII, *Arcanum*, 11; Pius XII, *Sacra virginitas*, 20, 37. The popes repeat the analogy suggested in Eph 5:23-34 that as Christ is the head of His body, the Church, so "man is the head" and "woman is the heart" of the family. This "'order of love,'" says Pius XI, ". . . includes both the primacy of the husband with regard to the wife and children" and "the ready subjection of the wife and her willing obedience." Pius XI, *Casti connubii*, 27; and 26, 29, 75. See also Leo

XIII, *Arcanum*, 11; Pius XI, *Quas primas*, 19, *Rappresentanti in terra*, 19. The "subjection of wife to husband," says Pius XI in *Casti connubii*, 28, "in its degree and manner may vary according to the different conditions of persons, place and time."

94.   On artificial birth control, see Pius XI, *Casti connubii*, 54. The principal papal argument against artificial birth control is that the practice is "intrinsically against nature." Pius XI also cites Augustine's discussion of the 'sin of Onan' in Gen 38:8-10. On the rhythm method, see section 59. On abortion, see section 58. It is also noteworthy that Pius XI's letter offers no teaching on when the human conceptus receives a soul. On sterilization, see section 71.

95.   Pius XI, *Casti connubii*, 120. Though the family is naturally prior to the state, the household needs government assistance because, says Pius XI, it is "not a perfect society, that is, it has not in itself all the means necessary for its full development." Pius XI, *Rappresentanti in terra*, 45; and 12. See also Pius X, *Iucunda sane*, 19.

96.   Habiger, "Papal Teaching on Private Property," pp. 16-19.

97.   Leo XIII, *Rerum novarum*, 22. According to the Thomistic discussion at the time, situations of extreme need involve immediate threats to life. The manuals of moral theology typically distinguish three levels of need: (1)'common'—where an individual can expect aid from the immediate family, (2)'grave'—where the immediate family is incapable of providing aid to the individual, (3)'extreme'—where the individual's life (materially or spiritually) is in immediate danger unless relief is found beyond the immediate family. See Dominic M. Prümmer, *Handbook of Moral Theology* (New York: P.J. Kenedy and Sons, 1957), p. 99. Contemporary commentators correctly observe that Leo XIII's teaching on individual property ownership differs from Aquinas in three significant ways: (1) Aquinas begins his discussion not with the "power to procure and dispense" property (Leo XIII's 'right of possession'), but with a natural law claim that external things be held "as common" so that people "communicate them to others in their need" (Leo XIII's secondary 'right of use'), (2) Aquinas does not consider the "power to care and procure" property a precept of natural law, but "an addition thereto devised by human reason," (3) Aquinas' principle of 'common use' requires care of the needy not out of charity, but "by natural law." See Aquinas, *Summa Theologica*, II-II, q. 66, a. 1, 2, 7, quoted in Dino Bigongiari, ed., *The Political Ideas of St. Thomas Aquinas: Representative Selections* (New York: Hafner Press, 1953), pp. 127-31. A useful analysis of Leo XIII's divergence from Aquinas and the long-standing commentary debate over this issue appears in Elsbernd, *Papal Statements on Rights*, pp. 312-25. Habiger raises a dissenting voice in "Papal Teaching on Private Property," pp. 27-36.

98.   Pius XI, *Quadragesimo anno*, 45; and 47. See also Pius XI, *Ubi arcano Dei consilio*, 37 and *Quas primas*, 17. On property ownership as worker protection, see *Quadragesimo anno*, 61, 63; on the inviolable, natural right of ownership, sections 44, 49; on the relativity of historical forms of property, section 49; on an individual's charitable obligations in view of the community's 'right of use' over property, section 47; on the state's role in regulating communal use, sections 49 and 57.

99.   Pius XI, *Quadragesimo anno*, 52. In *Quod apostolici muneris*, 1, Leo XIII lists three 'titles' to property: "lawful inheritance," "labor of brain and hands," "thrift in one's mode of life."

100.   On profit sharing, see Pius XI, *Quadragesimo anno*, 53; and 136. On employer responsibility, see Leo XIII, *Rerum novarum*, 20.

101.   On working conditions, see Leo XIII, *Rerum novarum*, 20, 40-42; Pius XI, *Quadragesimo anno*, 135. On negotiation, see Leo XIII, *Rerum novarum*, 48, 55, 58; Pius XI, *Quadragesimo anno*, 35, 84-87, 137. On just wage, see Leo XIII, *Rerum novarum*, 43-47, *Graves de communi re*, 13, 16; Pius XI, *Quadragesimo anno*, 63-75; Pius XII, *Sertum laetitiae*, 36. On worker responsibility, see Leo XIII, *Rerum novarum*, 20. Gudorf claims Leo XIII

recognizes the "right to strike." *Liberation Themes*, p. 179. Though the pope does not explicitly condemn strikes, nowhere does he clearly acknowledge a right to strike. See Leo XIII, *Rerum novarum*, 36, 39.

102.   See Leo XIII, *Rerum novarum*, 19; Pius XI, *Quadragesimo anno*, 100. In *Quadragesimo anno*, 51, Pius XI says the virtue of liberality requires investment of excess income "in developing favorable opportunities for employment, provided the labor employed produces results which are really useful." In his commentary on *Quadragesimo Anno*, Nell-Breuning says Pius XI's emphasis on liberality constitutes a retrieval of Aquinas' *magnificentia* from the *Summa Theologica*, II-II, q. 134. Though originating in the Middle Ages, *magnificentia* "is a genuinely capitalistic virtue" in that it encourages capital formation and investment of excess income. *Reorganization of Social Economy*, p. 115.

103.   On the double character of capital, see Pius XI, *Quadragesimo anno*, 110. On equity, see section 136; investment trustees, section 105; corporations, section 132; credit, section 106.

104.   On the natural dignity of work, see Pius X, *Iucunda sane*, 21; Pius XI, *Quadragesimo anno*, 61; Pius XII, *Haurietis aquas*, 74. The spiritual dignity of labor is enhanced by the fact that Jesus Christ was "not only the 'Son of a Carpenter' but Himself a 'Carpenter.'" Pius XI, *Divini Redemptoris*, 36; and, *Quadragesimo anno*, 23, 101. See also Leo XIII, *Rerum novarum*, 23. On worker advancement, see Leo XIII, *Rerum novarum*, 28; and, *Quamquam pluries*, 5. See also Pius XII, *Summi maeroris*, 3. The popes hold what Gudorf calls a "static view of classes," but it does not follow that they discourage the poor to become rich, the employee to become an employer, and the laborer to become a capitalist. *Liberation Themes*, p. 44. On worker association, see Leo XIII, *Rerum novarum*, 13, 49, 51-52, 54, 59-61. See also Leo XIII, *Quod apostolici muneris*, 11, *Humanum genus*, 35, *Etsi nos*, 16, *Libertas*, 16, *Custodi di quella fede*, 13, *Graves de communi re*, 3; Pius X, *Singulari quadem*, 4, 6-7; Pius XI, *Quadragesimo anno*, 30, 35, 37, 87, *Divini Redemptoris*, 27, 37; Pius XII, *Evangelii praecones*, 40. On equal opportunity, see Pius XII, *Sertum laetitiae*, 37.

105.   On avoiding evil associations, see Leo XIII, *Rerum novarum*, 20. In *Quadragesimo anno*, 123, Pius XI proscribes Catholic collaboration with socialists and communists. On inappropriate wage scales, see Pius XI, *Quadragesimo anno*, 74. On strikes, see Leo XIII, *Rerum novarum*, 36; and 38-39.

106.   On training in Roman Catholic social ethics, see Leo XIII, *Rerum novarum*, 26, *Fin dal principio*, 15; Pius XI, *Quadragesimo anno*, 19-20, 142, *Divini Redemptoris*, 55. Pius XI is the first pope claiming that papal documents offer a distinct "Catholic doctrine" on economic life. See Pius XI, *Quadragesimo anno*, 44; and, 18, 39, 96. See also Pius X, *Singulari quadem*, 3; Pius XI, *Divini Redemptoris*, 34, 69. For a linguistic and interpretive analysis of the shift from the broad term *doctrinae* in Leo XIII's *Rerum novarum*, 16 to the more technical term *doctrina* in Pius XI's *Quadragesimo anno*, 18, see Elsbernd, *Papal Statements on Rights*, 586-91. See also Chenu, *La 'doctrine sociale' de l'église comme idéologie* (Paris: Les éditions du Cerf, 1979), pp. 7-13, 87-96. On practical aid, see Leo XIII, *Quod apostolici muneris*, 9, *Rerum novarum*, 29-30, *Spesse volte*, 9, *Graves de communi re*, 3; Pius XI, *Nos es muy conocida*, 18; Pius XII, *Fulgens corona*, 39.

107.   On working conditions, see Leo XIII, *Rerum novarum*, 42; Pius XI, *Caritate Christi compulsi*, 18. On wages, see Leo XIII, *Rerum novarum*, 44; Pius XI, *Quadragesimo anno*, 71-74, *Divini Redemptoris*, 52. On Sunday rest, see Leo XIII, *Rerum novarum*, 41; and 30, 40. See also Pius XI, *Caritate Christi compulsi*, 18. On business competition, see Pius XI, *Quadragesimo anno*, 110. On distribution, see Leo XIII, *Rerum novarum*, 33. On strikes, see ibid., 36, 39.

108.   See Pius XI, *Studiorum ducem*, 27, *Quadragesimo anno*, 57-58, 71, 74, 88, 101, 110, 126, *Divini Redemptoris*, 32, 51-52, 54, *Nos es muy conocida*, 15-16. Pius X is the first pope

to use the term 'social justice' in an encyclical, but without elaboration. See Pius X, *Iucunda sane*, 3. Hollenbach's association of the term 'social justice' with Leo XIII is an anachronism. See David Hollenbach, "Modern Catholic Teaching Concerning Justice," in John Haughey, ed., *The Faith That Does Justice: Examining the Christian Sources for Social Change* (New York: Paulist Press, 1977), pp. 222, 224. Elsbernd locates each use of the term 'social justice' in Pius XI's letters and concludes: "Social justice in the encyclicals of Pius XI could be termed justice as considered under the aspect of the common good of the whole social order including its individual members and structures. The primary field of application, however, was the socio-economic order." *Papal Statements on Rights*, p. 600. For a further discussion of this term in encyclical and commentary literature, see Habiger, "Papal Teaching on Private Property," pp. 110-32.

109.   See Normand J. Paulus, "Uses and Misuses of the Term 'Social Justice' in the Roman Catholic Tradition," *The Journal of Religious Ethics* 15 (Fall 1987): 274. Leonine period manuals of moral theology utilize Aquinas' distinction between general and particular justice, with the latter category further divided into commutative and distributive forms. General justice oversees the political and economic structure of society, ensuring that both serve the common good. Commutative justice concerns fairness, freedom, and fidelity in agreements between individuals and groups in society. Distributive justice requires that a rightful proportion of society's benefits and burdens be shared by all citizens. See Aquinas, *Summa Theologica*, II-II, q. 57, a. 2; q. 58, aa. 5-7, quoted in Bigongiari, *Political Ideas*, pp. 98-126. See also Eberhard Welty, *A Handbook of Christian Social Ethics*, 2 vols. (New York: Herder & Herder, 1963), 1:289-319. The popes use the terms 'commutative' and 'distributive' (see Leo XIII, *Rerum novarum*, 33), but no encyclical letter explicitly discusses Aquinas' theory of justice. As a result, Hollenbach's claim that the Leonine period popes offer "refined and critical thought on the nature of justice" is overstated. "Teachings Concerning Justice," p. 209.

110.   Pius XI, *Quadragesimo anno*, 79. Nell-Breuning suggests the origin of Pius XI's subsidiary principle is Aquinas' *Summa Contra Gentiles*, book 3, chap. 71. *Reorganization of Social Economy*, p. 206, n. 3. In *Rerum novarum*, 35-36, Leo XIII discusses the idea behind subsidiarity without explicitly naming the principle or its source.

111.   The origin and intent of this insertion is clouded by Leonine period debates between the German 'Solidarist,' or *Sozialpolitik* school of social thought (Ketteler, Pesch, Biederlack, Cathrein, Schilling, Gundlach, Nell-Breuning) and the Austrian 'Romantic,' or *Sozialreform* school (Müller, Schlegel, Vogelsang, Orel, Spann). Both schools support a vocational group concept, but their understanding of it differs. The German Solidarists stress the human person as "the foundation of society" and hope for gradual movement toward vocational groups within the trade union movement as a method of protecting human personhood. Alfred Diamant, *Austrian Catholics and the First Republic: Democracy, Capitalism, and the Social Order, 1918-1934* (Princeton, N.J.: Princeton University Press, 1960), p. 161. The Austrian Romantics stress the personality of the *Genossenschaft* and hope, through a compulsory, state-controlled corporative system, to "revive medieval German folk culture." Ibid., p. 19. Diamant suggests Pius XI's discussion of corporatism represents a turn toward *Sozialreform* and adds that under the "guise of a commentary," Nell-Breuning tries to make "the encyclical into a *Sozialpolitik* document." Ibid., p. 183. But Pius XI's concern that the vocational groups remain noncompulsory and autonomous—plus Nell-Breuning's 1971 article discussing his role in drafting *Quadragesimo Anno*—challenges Diamant's thesis. See Oswald von Nell-Breuning, "The Drafting of *Quadragesimo Anno*," in Curran and McCormick, *Readings in Moral Theology No. 5*, pp. 60-68. Philippe C. Schmitter mistakenly credits Leo XIII with the "modern ideological revival" of corporatism. "Corporatism Is Dead! Long Live Corporatism!," *Government & Opposition* 24 (Winter 1989): 67.

112.   On the noncompulsory character of the vocational groups, see Pius XI, *Quadragesimo anno*, 87. On the autonomy of vocational groups from inappropriate state interference, see ibid., 83 and *Divini Redemptoris*, 32. In *Quadragesimo anno*, 91-95, Pius XI indirectly criticizes Mussolini's corporative system for giving too much power to the state. For useful descriptions of corporatism, see Joseph David Munier, "Some American Approximations to Pius XI's 'Industries and Professions'" (Ph.D. dissertation, The Catholic University of America, 1943) and Philippe C. Schmitter, "Still the Century of Corporatism?," in Philippe C. Schmitter and Gerhard Lehmbruch, eds., *Trends toward Corporatist Intermediation, Contemporary Political Sociology*, vol. 1 (London: Sage Publications, 1979), pp. 7-52. On the common good, see Pius XI, *Quadragesimo anno* 90; and *Divini Redemptoris*, 32. Given Pius XI's economic vision, Gudorf's claim that "the basic structures of society were not called into question by the popes" is incorrect. *Liberation Themes*, p. 23. Dorr is accurate when he suggests that Pius XI's corporative vision "amounts to a radical change in the structures that had shaped the Western world." Dorr, *Option for the Poor*, p. 61. Calvez shares Dorr's interpretation in "Economic Policy Issues in Roman Catholic Social Teaching: An International Perspective," in Thomas M. Gannon, ed., *The Catholic Challenge to the American Economy: Reflections on the U.S. Bishops Pastoral Letter on Catholic Social Teaching and the U.S. Economy* (New York: Macmillan, 1987), p. 18.

113.   Habiger, "Papal Teaching on Private Property," p. 106. See also Pius XI, *Quadragesimo anno*, 45, 57-58, 74, 84-85, 101, 110.

114.   Nowhere in the encyclical letters do the popes define obscenity. A widely held view among moral theologians during the period is proposed by Arthur Vermeersch. He defines visual obscenity as a "'degrading manifestation of the mind . . . or a degrading solicitation of the mind . . . in and through the [sic] nudity.'" Quoted in Harold C. Gardiner, *Catholic Viewpoint on Censorship*, rev. ed. (Garden City, N.Y.: Image Books, 1961), p. 64. Gardiner suggests Vermeersch's 'degrading element' can be further specified as "the intrinsic tendency or bent of the work to arouse sexual passion, or, to put it more concretely, the motions of the genital apparatus which are preparatory to the complete act of sexual union."

115.   Leo XIII, *Libertas*, 23. See also Pius XII, *Miranda prorsus*, 35, 38, 112. Through Leo XIII's apostolic constitution on book censorship (*Officiorum ac munerum*), the "severity of the previous rules was lessened and a more positive tone was introduced." National Literary Commission, *Study Guide*, p. 12. Leo XIII publishes a shortened list of condemned books in 1900. Seven years later, Benedict XV abolishes the separate office of the Sacred Congregation of the Index, merging its duties with those of the Congregation of the Holy Office. A new list of prohibited books and periodicals appears in 1922 and, in 1948, Pius XII conducts a second major revision of Index regulations.

116.   Pius XI, *Vigilanti cura*, 38; and 39, 46. See also Pius XII, *Miranda prorsus*, 69-73, 78-79, 82, 132. The Legion of Decency is first organized in the United States in 1933. Pius XI adopts the Legion as a world model, recommending episcopal offices be established in each diocese to initiate and support its work. Pius XII further creates the Pontifical Commission for Motion Pictures, Radio and Television in Rome. The popes desire that not only viewers honor the Legion lists, but also directors, managers, producers, writers, and actors confer with diocesan offices over artistic projects. See Pius XI, *Vigilanti cura*, 31, 36, and Pius XII, *Miranda prorsus*, 90-96, 99-111. It is noteworthy that while Pius XI thinks "it would be desirable that a single list [of approved and condemned films] should be published for the whole world," he concedes that "customs and circumstances vary in different lands" making it impossible to "obtain a unanimous and universal list." Pius XI, *Vigilanti cura*, 38.

117.   Pius XII, *Musicae sacrae*, 24; and *Miranda prorsus*, 43. See also Pius XI, *Vigilanti cura*, 4, 15-16, 21.

118.   Pius XII, *Miranda prorsus*, 99-102.

119.   Pius XI, *Rappresentanti in terra*, 25-26.

120.   On family education, see Pius XI, *Rappresentanti in terra*, 12, 35, 39, 45, 67. Given the parent's natural right of education, "children of infidels" (pagans, Moslems, and Jews) must not receive Roman Catholic instruction "against the will of the parents"—except "under peculiar circumstances and with special cautions." Ibid., 39. The popes are silent, however, concerning the educational rights of heretical (Protestant) and schismatic (Orthodox) Christian parents.

121.   On the state and education , see Pius XI, *Rappresentanti in terra*, 14, 44-47. The state may not, writes Pius XI in section 45, force families to "make use of government schools, contrary to the dictates of their Christian conscience."

122.   Pius XII, *Miranda prorsus*, 1. On the pursuit of science, see sections 28 and 55. See also Leo XIII, *Aeterni Patris*, 29; Pius X, *Iucunda sane*, 35; Pius XI, *Vigilanti cura*, 6; Pius XII, *Miranda prorsus*, 23. On progress, see Pius XII, *Miranda prorsus*, 1, 3. While extolling authentic social progress, Pius XII observes in 1939 that the "illusions of limitless progress" are "gone." Pius XII, *Summi pontificatus*, 78. Gardiner notes that the "Catholic concept" of progress "implies necessarily the correlative idea of measure and restraint, internally in a man's own conscience and motives, and externally through the operation of law and of social forces which are not formally legal." *Censorship*, p. 26.

123.   Egal Feldman notes two signs of improved Jewish-Roman Catholic relations during the Leonine period: Pius XI's 1938 remark that "spiritually we [Christians] are Semites" and Pius XII's deletion of Jews as *perfidi* in the Good Friday liturgical prayer for unbelievers. *Encyclopaedia Judaica*, s.v. "Church, Catholic," by Egal Feldman. On the international status of Jerusalem, see Pius XII, *Auspicia quaedam*, 12, *In multiplicibus curis*, 8, *Redemptoris nostri cruciatus*, 9. Willehad Eckert claims Pius X rejected Zionism in a 1904 audience with Theodor Herzl. *Encyclopaedia Judaica*, s.v. "Pius X," by Willehad Paul Eckert.

124.   On "equality of rights," see Pius XI, *Casti connubii*, 76. Gudorf argues that *Casti connubii* begins a "shift from a total denial of equality between the sexes" to the view that "men and women were completely equal and therefore deserving of equal rights." The popes still hold, however, that men and women are "not the same and therefore did not deserve the same rights." An example of this type of shift occurred in United States Constitutional law when jurists moved from a denial of rights to blacks, to the concept of 'separate-but-equal.' *Liberation Themes*, pp. 271-72. On the "noble office" of women, see Pius XI, *Casti connubii*, 75. On the "nature" of women, see Pius XI, *Rappresentanti in terra*, 68. Gudorf correctly observes that papal literature does not give equal attention to the "nature of men, of fatherhood, and of masculinity." Ibid., p. 255. An exception occurs in *Rappresentanti in terra*, 31, where Pius XI quotes Aquinas' *Summa Theologica*, II-II, q. 102, a. 1: "The father is the principle of generation, of education and discipline."

125.   On the parallel histories of the Church and civilization, see Pius XI, *Rappresentanti in terra*, 99. Every Leonine period pope believes that Roman Catholic Christianity undergirds what Pius XI calls in section 7 the "true *civitas humana*." On the "peculiar gifts" of non-Western cultures, see Pius XII, *Summi Pontificatus*, 43; and 45. See also Leo XIII, *Inscrutabili Dei consilio*, 7; Pius XII, *Evangelii praecones*, 56. According to Ritter, in pre-World War II scholarship the terms 'culture' and 'civilization' were "rarely considered completely synonymous." See Harry Ritter, *Dictionary of Concepts*, p. 42. Similarly, the Leonine period popes regard true 'civilization' as a higher stage of social evolution requiring, among other things, Christian religiosity. Joseph Komonchak argues that during this period "modern Roman Catholicism was inextricably linked . . . with the project of constructing a world alternate to that of modern society and culture." Joseph A. Komonchak, "The Enlightenment and the Construction of Roman

Catholicism," *Catholic Commission on Intellectual and Cultural Affairs* (1985): 50. It would be more accurate to say the popes thought in terms of recalling the world of Western civilization to its Christian foundations than constructing an alternate world. As Leo XIII says in *Rerum novarum*, 27: "When a society is perishing, the wholesale advice to give to those who would restore it is to call it to the principles from which it sprang; for the purpose and perfection of an association is to aim at and to attain that for which it is formed, and its efforts should be put in motion and inspired by the end and object which originally gave it being."

126.   Daniel A. O'Connor, *Catholic Social Doctrine* (Westminster, Md.: Newman Press, 1956), p. 73.

127.   Chantel Mouffe, "American Liberalism and Its Critics: Rawls, Taylor, Sandel and Walzer," *Praxis International* 8 (July 1988): 198.

128.   Ken Anderson, Paul Piccone, Fred Siegel, Michael Taves, "Roundtable on Communitarianism," *Telos* 76 (Summer 1988): 13.

129.   George L. Mosse, "Nationalism, Fascism, and the Radical Right," in Eugene Kamenka, ed., *Community as a Social Ideal* (New York: St. Martin's Press, 1982), p. 27.

3

THE POST-LEONINE PERIOD 1959–89

Many contemporary encyclical commentators note significant changes in papal letters beginning with the pontificate of John XXIII. Variously located in the encyclicals' sources, methods, and conclusions, these alterations suggest "cracks in what had been a rather monolithic body of social teaching."[1] But if this is true, are these changes of any greater significance than those which already occurred between the pre-Leonine and Leonine period letters? And if the post-Leonine period represents a second major shift in papal letters, do the common teachings which endured across the pre-Leonine and Leonine periods survive?

This chapter argues that significant changes occur in the post-Leonine period encyclicals, paralleling the shift from pre-Leonine to Leonine period letters. Yet, as in the former transition, commonalities also remain.

The pattern of encyclical study established in previous chapters is repeated here. A brief overview introduces the period, followed by sections indicating the problems and solutions discussed by the popes. The chapter concludes with a summary interpretation of post-Leonine period social teaching.

Overview

At the present time, the post-Leonine period corpus includes twenty-two letters from John XXIII's 1959 *Ad Petri Cathedram* to John Paul II's 1987 *Sollicitudo rei socialis*. Compared to the previous period, a dramatic decline in encyclical output occurs. Bishops remain the first addressees of every encyclical, but only three letters cite them exclusively. Instead, a more inclusive salutation evolves. In *Pacem in Terris*, John XXIII greets not only bishops, but also "all men of good will." This continues throughout the period until John Paul II's *Redemptor hominis* amends it to read "all men and women of good will." The long-standing use of *epistolae encyclicae* (letters addressed to specific national bishops or nonclerical groups) discontinues; all post-Leonine period encyclicals are *litterae encyclicae* (letters written to all bishops and people).

Like earlier papal letters, the principal encyclical topics are faith, morality, and worship. Noteworthy is the increase in proportionate attention given specific questions of faith and worship during the period. Four letters treat matters of faith, five letters discuss worship, and thirteen letters focus on moral issues.

The post-Leonine period spans the pontificates of John XXIII (1958-63), Paul VI (1963-78), John Paul I (1978), and John Paul II (1978-). This period witnesses the momentous Second Vatican Council and the development of liberation theology. In politics, United States and Soviet tensions persist while new independent nations emerge, joining what comes to be called the 'Third World.' As Eastern-bloc communist nations vacillate between economic centralization and experiments in decentralization, Western nations of the northern hemisphere undergo unprecedented economic growth. At the same time, most nations on the continents of South America, Africa, the Indian Peninsula, and East Indies experience prolonged periods of poverty. The development of Western science and technology mushrooms during the period, led by nuclear physics, laser technology, cybernetics, computers, and robotics. The analytical school continues its domination of Western philosophical inquiry, though challenged by Marcuse, Habermas, and Lukacs of the Frankfort School and Derrida's deconstructionism. The plastic arts move through 'pop,' 'op,' and 'conceptual' stages, associated with such names as Lichtenstein, Vasarely, Javacheff, and Warhol. New directions in music are introduced by Leonard Bernstein, Samuel Barber, and Philip Glass. Still influenced by earlier existentialist literature, the dominant literary figures of the period include Edward Albee, Harold Pinter, Günther Grass, and Samuel Beckett. Fellini, Bergman, and Godard break new ground in artistic film making, though American-produced motion pictures receive the greater share of popular attention. Similarly, television continues an unchallenged reign as the major shaper of contemporary Western culture.

Problems

As in previous chapters, problems discussed in the post-Leonine period texts can be divided into troublesome practices and ideas. The former occur in religious, political, family, economic, and cultural life.

The latter involve not only general theological and philosophical concepts, but also ideas specific to each sphere of social interaction.

Problematic Practices

Religious Practices. Though earlier problems regarding episcopal leadership, Roman Catholic journalism, and intercreedal relations disappear in the post-Leonine period texts, the popes retain their predecessors' concerns over clerical discipline, lay religiosity, and theological study. Regarding clerical discipline, the popes identify poor catechesis, insubordination toward bishops, and sacramental irregularities as ongoing problems.[2] In *Sacerdotalis caelibatus*, 83-84, Paul VI registers a new complaint over "defections" from the priesthood.[3]

Repeated problems in lay religious practice include lack of religious vocations, rejection of Christian asceticism, and apathy.[4] In *Dives in misericordia*, 47, John Paul II laments a "hardness of heart" among Christians, "reflected in the loss of the sense of sin."

Warnings against imprudent theological investigation continue in the post-Leonine period letters. In *Redemptor hominis*, 8, John Paul II says the Church must maintain "a critical sense with regard to all that goes to make up her human character"; however, "criticism too should have its just limits." Thus, the theologian who "ceases to be constructive," seeking only to "direct the opinion of others in accordance with one's own," threatens religious life.

Political Practices. The popes sustain—though sometimes in altered form—earlier encyclical diatribes against state encroachment on Church affairs, government oppression of citizens, civil violence, excessive nationalism, neocolonialism, weapons production, and war. New criticism focuses on inadequate structures of world governance.

Denunciation of state encroachment on Church prerogatives and institutions markedly declines in post-Leonine period letters. Relations between the Church and Western democracies improve after World War II and, while the oppressed condition of the "Church of Silence" in communist countries receives occasional attention, papal denunciation of specific communist states recedes.[5] Dennis Dunn cites four reasons for this shift. First, John XXIII thought Khruschev's policy of 'peaceful coexistence' created a new opening for negotiation over repair of the Roman Catholic Church in Russia. Second, John XXIII wanted to encourage communist leaders outside the Soviet Union who permitted "qualified toleration" of the Church. Third, he wanted reduced hostility between the Roman Catholic Church and the 'revisionist' communist parties of Italy and France. Fourth, John XXIII thought improved communication with the Soviet Union would aid Church-state relations in other communist countries.[6]

The post-Leonine period encyclicals expand and shift long-standing papal protest against state oppression of citizens. Abuses include torture, unjust imprisonment, racial discrimination, and enforced contraception.[7] In *Sollicitudo rei socialis*, 24, John Paul II observes how all these problems exacerbate the "millions of refugees . . . deprived of home, employment, family, and homeland." For the first time, the popes also criticize government disregard for an individual's right to practice religion publicly, "independent of the religion professed or of the concept of the world which these individuals and communities have."[8]

The popes warn against civil violence, whether in the form of "disorders and excesses" committed in an otherwise legitimate pursuit of political freedom, or "in the name of alleged justice (for example, historical justice or class justice)." Terrorist murder and hostage-taking are also decried.[9]

The most repeated political problems cited in post-Leonine period letters are proliferation of military weaponry and war. John XXIII's *Ad Petri Cathedram*, 34 denounces increased international production and possession of "the monstrous weapons our age has devised." In *Pacem in terris*, 128, he notes that the expenditure of "fabulous sums" on nuclear weapons for the sake of deterrence is based on the "law of fear." During the Vietnam War, Paul VI exclaims in *Christi Matri*, 6: "In the name of the Lord We cry out to them to stop." Like their forerunners, the popes identify excessive nationalism as one cause of this ongoing militarism.[10]

A particular papal concern is neocolonialism through unjust international trade relations. First World commodity price fluctuations inordinately harm Third World countries dependent upon raw material exports. In *Populorum progressio*, 57, Paul VI explains that because brokers and producers influence prices to suit cost constraints of First World consumers and producers, "the poor nations remain ever poorer while the rich ones become still richer." Yet, economically undeveloped nations are drawn to the volatile raw material export market (as opposed to enhancement of domestic markets) "under the cloak of financial aid or technical assistance" from developed countries. Through this "neocolonialism," he says in section 52, powerful nations seek "complete dominance" over weaker nations "in the form of political pressures and economic suzerainty." In *Sollicitudo rei socialis*, 16, John Paul II thinks these conditions have grown "notably worse" since Paul VI's *Populorum progressio*.

New papal complaints concern the lack of adequate structures for international political governance. With burgeoning international problems, says John XXIII, "public authorities of the individual political communities . . . are no longer able to face the task of finding an adequate solution." This lack of political organization beyond the nation-state constitutes a global "structural defect." "The present system of organization and the way its principle of authority operates on a world basis," continues the pope, "no longer correspond to the objective requirements of the universal common good."[11]

Family Practices. Though the popes discontinue their forerunners' attacks on mixed and civil marriage and secular school systems, they sustain earlier papal concern over occupational and sexual practices threatening family life. In addition, new criticism appears regarding oppressive family structures.

In the popes' view, the growing necessity to emigrate in search of work destabilizes the family. In *Ad Petri Cathedram*, 134, John XXIII complains: "Since husbands are often separated from their wives and parents from their children, the bonds and ties that hold them together are stretched thin and serious injury is done to the family."

In *Humanae vitae*, Paul VI adopts and abridges Leonine period complaints regarding contraceptive birth control. In section 14, he says the divine order of marriage is violated by "conjugal acts made intentionally infecund." Unlike the earlier papal view, however, God's order is obtained not only in biological "laws and rhythms of fecundity," but also in the interpersonal character of marital sexuality, wherein husband and wife share conjugal love as a way of "expressing and consolidating their union" (section 11). As a result, writes John Noonan, artificial birth control is wrong not simply because it violates normal biological activity, but "because it is contrary to something in the special relation of two persons" having both a procreative and unitive aspect.[12] On this ground, Paul VI also rejects birth control through "directly willed and procured abortion" and "direct sterilization, whether perpetual or temporary" (section 14).

In section 13, Paul VI also says the "unitive meaning" of conjugal relations proscribes sexual intercourse "imposed upon one's partner." For the first time in encyclical literature, marital intercourse without the honest consent of both partners is condemned, regardless of the couple's fertility at the time of the act. This perspective recurs in Paul VI's warning that contraceptive use could encourage man to view woman as "a mere instrument of selfish enjoyment" (section 17).

Paul VI also introduces new criticism of oppressive family structures. *Populorum progressio*, 36 decries "long-standing social frameworks" in developing countries wherein families impair the "fundamental rights of the individual." He adds that such conditions have also existed in developed countries "at some periods of history and in some places." Whereas previous popes recognized the issue of abuse within families, Paul VI is the first to suggest that certain understandings of power and authority between husbands, wives, and children can be—and have historically been—oppressive.

Economic Practices. The popes devote significant attention to economic problems. Compared with earlier discussions, the scope of papal criticism widens. "The social question," exclaims Paul VI in *Populorum progressio*, 3, "has become world-wide."

Like their predecessors, the popes reprove employer injustices affecting workplace conditions, hours, wages, compensation, female and child labor, and the religious needs and associational rights of employees.[13] New papal concerns include exploitation of seasonal emigrant, permanent immigrant, and agricultural workers, disregard for employee input during production, and neglect of the disabled.[14]

Paul VI's *Populorum progressio*, 23-34 raises several problems regarding property ownership and financial investment. First, owners of extensive "landed estates" who use the land poorly or continually leave it fallow are admonished for harming "the interests of the country." Second, citizens who possess "abundant incomes from the resources and activity of their own country" are admonished against transferring "a considerable part of this income abroad purely for their own advantage." Finally, the pope thinks it a violation of justice—not simply charity—for one to "keep for his exclusive use what he does not need, when others lack necessities."

The popes repeat and expand previous encyclical diatribes against inappropriate business activity. The evils of unlimited competition, greed, usury, concentration of wealth, monopoly, absentee ownership, and business control of the state are attacked.[15] In *Populorum progressio*, 70, Paul VI decries industrialists who "are not lacking in social sensitivity in their own country," but "return to the inhuman principles of individualism when they operate in less developed countries."

Regarding employee activity, the popes reject worker violence, specifically if motivated by the ideology of "class struggle in the 'Marxist sense.'" On the other hand, the pontiffs consider that most workplace violence is precipitated by employer injustice.[16] New papal scrutiny focuses on union activities. Union demands, warns John Paul II in *Laborem exercens*, 97–98, "cannot be turned into a kind of group or class 'egotism.'" Nor should unions "'play politics'" by using strikes for political purposes.

Problematic state economic practices also concern the popes. Older encyclical complaints over suppression of Sunday labor laws, weapons manufacturing, unjust expropriation of property, unemployment, neglect of workers, and imperialism are sustained.[17] In *Populorum progressio*, 29, Paul VI criticizes government programs promoting hasty industrial growth without concern for the immediate community.

Also carried forward from the Leonine period are practical criticisms of both the capitalist and communist systems of economic organization. Capitalism tempts avaricious individualism, skews just distribution, and devalues agricultural work.[18] For its part, communism poses the "danger of complete collectivism" wherein "human liberty is excessively restricted and the true concept of social authority is overlooked."[19] In *Sollicitudo rei socialis*, 15, John Paul II notes how economic "totalitarianism" denies or unduly limits a person's "right of economic initiative."

Beyond the idiosyncratic liabilities of capitalism and communism, John Paul II's *Laborem exercens*, 9 reproves the "world sphere of inequality and injustice" for which both systems are accountable. Later, in *Sollicitudo rei socialis*, 20, he indicts the East-West superpowers for impairing world economic production and distribution. Here, he develops a theme introduced in John XXIII's *Mater et Magistra*.

From the standpoint of production, global economics suffers in several ways. Modern production processes deplete and pollute natural resources, raise the objective structure of work over its subjective meaning, and place humanity "under threat from what it produces."[20] Also, as global production increasingly emphasizes the industrial and service sectors, agricultural life erodes. Throughout the world, independent farmers and agricultural regions and nations "are left such primitive and obsolete methods of cultivation that they are unable to produce what is needed for the entire population." At the same time, says John XXIII in *Mater et Magistra*, 154, First World agribusinesses "produce surpluses which to some extent harm the economy of the entire nation." In section 161, the pope writes that, in some cases, independent farmers are driven to "destroy entirely or waste goods" to affect prices "while elsewhere large masses of people experience want and hunger."[21] In addition, some countries have an imbalance between the number of citizens and the availability of land, while others "experience a shortage of citizens, but have rich land resources." Because independent farmers and peasants have been reduced to inferior economic status worldwide, "nothing can be done to keep men from deserting the fields" and migrating into the already overcrowded urban *barrios*.[22]

The most repeated complaint in post-Leonine letters is inequity in global economic distribution. In *Redemptor hominis*, 51-52, John Paul II calls this problem a "gigantic development of the parable in the Bible of the rich banqueter and the poor man Lazarus." "Rich, highly developed societies" retain a "surplus of goods," says the pope, "while the remaining societies—at least broad sectors of them—are suffering from hunger, with many people dying each day of starvation and malnutrition." Eight years later, in *Sollicitudo rei socialis*, 14, the pope specifically notes a "widening of the gap between the areas of the so-called developed North and the developing South." Paul VI's *Populorum progressio*, 55 earlier warned that upon this issue "the very life of poor nations, civil peace in developing countries, and world peace are at stake."

Cultural Practices. Several problematic cultural practices undergo papal scrutiny. As in earlier encyclicals, these problems concern informational and artistic communications, life-style, education, science and technology, and group relations. The popes also add new warnings regarding environmental abuse, discrimination, and population increase.

Immoral speech and literature, as well as licentious motion picture and television presentations, earn papal opprobrium. Of these problems, dishonest speech receives the greatest post-Leonine period attention. John XXIII's *Ad Petri Cathedram*, 11, condemns the "despicable business" of anyone who "consciously and wantonly attacks known truth, who arms himself with falsehood in his speech." "Lack of responsibility for what one says," adds John Paul II in *Dives in misericordia*, 123, bears on the widespread "crisis of truth" affecting modern human relations.

The popes also repeat long-standing encyclical warnings against life-styles of sexual permissiveness, violence, and excessive material accumulation and consumption. Regarding the last issue, John Paul II's *Dives in misericordia*, 113 scorns "wealthy and surfeited people and societies, living in plenty and ruled by consumerism and pleasure." In *Sollicitudo rei socialis*, 28, he condemns the "superdevelopment" of some nations which have created a "civilization of 'consumption' or 'consumerism.'" Consequently, in *Dominum et vivificantem*, 60 he observes that such life-styles are not always self-consciously chosen, but sometimes follow upon "conditionings and pressures exerted . . . by dominating structures and mechanisms in the various spheres of society."

Though Leonine period complaints against adolescent coeducation, sex education, and excessive emphasis on military and athletic skills disappear from post-Leonine period letters, educational problems still occupy papal attention. The primary worry concerns declining religious instruction in private and public schools. This problem, however, results less from secular state influence than from the cultural impact of Western science and technology. "It happens in many quarters and too often," notes John XXIII in *Pacem in terris*, 153, "that there is no proportion between scientific training and religious instruction."

Alongside its inordinate cultural influence, the threatening products of science and technology receive critical papal attention. John XXIII's *Mater et Magistra*, 244 claims that "discoveries of science, technical advances, and economic productivity" are too often used as "means whereby the human race is led toward ruin and horrible death." Not only do people frequently "neglect themselves" while admiring "their own works as if these were gods," but they also neglect the dangerous environmental impact of their discoveries.[23]

While maintaining warnings against racism and mistreatment of women at workplace and home, the popes identify new problems regarding the treatment of ethnic minorities and generational conflict.[24] According to the popes, minorities often find their cultural traditions subtly or explicitly repressed by society's dominant majority. Such cultural abuse also occurs in the "conflict between traditional civilizations and the new elements of industrial civilization." John XXIII warns that cultural discrimination can fuel a backlash wherein "minority groups either because of a reaction to their present situation or because of historical difficulties . . . exalt beyond due measure anything proper to their own people." Linked with these cultural conflicts is a new "conflict of the generations," particularly in countries experiencing rapid political and economic change.[25]

Post-Leonine period discussion of the population issue is ambiguous. In *Mater et Magistra*, John XXIII says the "interrelationships on a global scale between the number of births and available resources" present no "grave difficulties" now or "in the immediate future." Contrariwise, John Paul II's *Sollicitudo rei socialis*, 25 says "one cannot deny the existence, especially in the southern hemisphere, of a demographic problem which creates difficulties for development." At the same time, the northern hemisphere's declining birthrate has serious "repercussions on the aging of the population."

Problematic Ideas

Like their predecessors, the post-Leonine period popes scrutinize the false premises underlying practical problems of everyday life. These ideas can be differentiated into those of a general theological or philosophical nature and those addressing specific social issues.

General Theological and Philosophical Concepts

God. Though disregard for Christ's divinity and modernist interpretations of revelation, grace, and God's Kingdom receive no explicit post-Leonine period attention, the popes retain vigorous concern over atheism. In *Ecclesiam suam*, 99, Paul VI says atheism constitutes "the most serious problem of our time." Three features distinguish the post-Leonine period treatment of atheism.

While the popes consider the underlying principles of atheism false, they introduce a new sensitivity toward its complex origins and expressions. Noting sections 19-21 of the Second Vatican Council's pastoral constitution *Gaudium et spes*, John Paul II writes: "It is not possible to speak of atheism in a univocal way . . . since there exist numerous forms of atheism and the word is perhaps often used in a wrong sense."[26] One motive for acknowledging this diversity is to forestall precipitous and simplistic interpretations of atheism. In Paul VI's view, expressed in *Ecclesiam suam*, 104, Christians should make every effort at probing the "mind of the modern atheist, in an effort to understand the reasons for his mental turmoil and his denial of God."

Second, Paul VI introduces a new suggestion that Christians are partially culpable for contemporary atheism. Anticipating the discussion in Vatican II's *Gaudium et spes*, the pope says some forms of atheism "spring from the demand for a more profound and purer presentation of religious truth, and an objection to forms of language and worship which somehow fall short of the ideal."[27] With this in mind, Paul VI's *Ecclesiam suam*, 85 says Christians should not "hold fast to forms of expression which have lost their meaning and can no longer stir men's minds."

A third new element in post-Leonine period treatment of atheism concerns the mid-1960s 'death of God' movement. Inspired by theologian Thomas J. J. Altizer and others, the new 'Christian atheists' announce the death of conventional Christianity's repressive "Wholly Other God" so that "the authentically liberated human being may live."[28] Advocates locate their Christian identity in the recognition of Jesus as the most authentic example of a liberated human life. In *Dominum et vivificantem*, 37-38, John Paul II denounces as "an absurdity, both in concept and expression," the "process of thought and historico-sociological practice in which the rejection of God has reached the point of declaring his 'death.'" "Showing God as an enemy of his own creature," says the pope, is a "complete falsification of the truth about who God is."

World. The popes repeat earlier charges against the false interpretations of the world proffered by philosophical naturalism and dialectical materialism. Alluding to the first theory, Paul VI's *Ecclesiam suam*, 104 decries any absolute "scientific explanation of the universe by human reasoning." In *Dominum et vivificantem*, 56, John Paul II calls dialectical materialism "a reading of the whole of reality as 'matter.'" Though dialectical materialism "sometimes also speaks of the 'spirit' and of 'questions of the spirit,'" it does so "only insofar as it considers certain facts as derived from matter ('epiphenomena'), since according to this system matter is the one and only form of being."

Humanity. The popes repeat several of their predecessors' complaints over problematic ideas regarding human existence. These include notions treating the spiritual dimension of human life, the power of reason, the criteria of morality, the reality of sin, and the nature of freedom.

Post-Leonine period encyclicals protest materialistic denial of the immaterial and immortal human soul. In *Mater et Magistra*, 214, John XXIII rejects the claim that humanity's soul-based "sense of religion" is simply "adventitious or imaginary." John Paul II's *Dominum et vivificantem*, 57 asserts that materialism promotes belief that death constitutes "the definitive end of human existence." "Hence one can understand," he adds, "how it can be said that human life is nothing but an 'existence in order to die.'"

Earlier papal protest against rationalism recurs in post-Leonine period letters. In typical fashion, Paul VI's *Ecclesiam suam*, 28 says elevating pure reason to the "most perfect and highest function" of life and "the measure and source of reality" leads philosophers to "abstruse, barren, absurd, and wholly fallacious conclusions."

In the area of human morality, the popes continue encyclical diatribes against ethical positivism, utilitarianism, subjectivism, and relativism. New warnings are raised against a hedonistic "philosophy of life," misinterpretations of conscience as an "exclusive capacity to decide what is good and what is evil" independent of the objective moral order manifested in "the voice of God" and the notion that one must "abandon the activities of this world in order to strive for Christian perfection."[29]

Lastly, the popes decry philosophies which deny sin and distort human freedom. In *Mater et Magistra*, 213, John XXIII bemoans "systems of thought" which "fail to take into account the weaknesses of human nature." Such philosophies exaggerate human freedom. Materialistic philosophies, on the other hand, underestimate human freedom. Though "men are not altogether free of their milieu," writes John XXIII in *Mater et Magistra*, 255, this by no means implies that human life is a "blind drive of natural forces."

Specific Social Concepts. The popes continue the encyclical pattern of highlighting specific ideas threatening social life. Again, for clarity, these ideas can be divided into the religious, political, family, economic, and cultural areas of human relations.

Religion. Though papal exhortation against religious indifference and radical alterations of Church structure perdure, the popes drop earlier encyclical attacks on freedom of conscience in worship and Roman Catholic cooperation with socialists. New warnings are directed against excessive religious adaptation to secular thought.

A novel element appears in the papal treatment of religious indifference. The popes still denounce indifference as either the attribution of equal salvific value to all churches or the agnostic idea that all religious claims are equally unverifiable. New, however, is association of religious indifference with spiritual apathy. In *Dives in misericordia*, 168, John Paul II laments how "modern man" can make God "extraneous to himself, proclaiming in various ways that God is 'superfluous.'"[30]

The popes continue encyclical protest against 'conciliarist' theories of church reorganization. In *Ecclesiam suam*, 26, Paul VI labels as "outlandish" any idea suggesting "that the Church should abdicate its proper role, and adopt an entirely new and unprecedented mode of existence." He cites two of the "various new guises" under which this error appears: the theory that the Church "should be reduced to the modest proportions which it had in its earliest days" or the notion that nonordained or nonepiscopal members who "consider themselves divinely inspired" should govern the Church (section 46).

In section 48 of the same encyclical, Paul VI also rejects "craving for uniformity" among those "who think that the reform of the Church should consist principally in adapting its way of thinking and acting to the customs and temper of the modern secular world." Such "irenism and syncretism," he says in section 88, "is ultimately nothing more than skepticism about the power and content of the Word of God which we desire to preach."

Politics. Despite ample concern over inappropriate political practices, the popes pay less attention than their predecessors to problematic political theories. Mistaken views of state authority, law, freedom, and human rights are briefly discussed, while complaints over dissolute Church-state theories cease. New concern is shown for mistaken views of international relations.

In *Pacem in terris*, 78, John XXIII reiterates papal complaint against social contract theories of government. Neither "the binding force of the constitution" nor the "government's right to command" can be exclusively located in the popular will. "No folly seems more characteristic of our time," the pope adds in *Mater et Magistra*, 217, "than the desire to establish a firm and meaningful temporal order, but without God, its necessary foundation."

Mistaken theories of legal justice and political freedom draw papal attention. The popes decry positivistic interpretations of justice which locate law entirely in the will of either rulers or popular majorities. If "there exists no law of truth and right which transcends external affairs and man himself," fears John XXIII in *Mater et Magistra*, 205-6, ". . . men can agree fully and surely about nothing, since one and the same law of justice is not accepted by all." As a logical consequence, people "conclude that there is no way of achieving their rights or advantages, unless they resort to force." Concerning freedom, John Paul II laments in *Redemptor hominis*, 35: "Nowadays it is sometimes held, though wrongfully, that freedom is an end in itself, that each human being is free when he makes use of freedom as he wishes."

Corresponding to their worries over mistaken theories of law and freedom, the popes reject rights theories based solely on human will.

In *Pacem in terris*, 78, John XXIII writes: "It is of course impossible to accept the theory which professes to find the original and single source of civic rights and duties . . . in the mere will of human beings, individually or collectively."

Finally, John Paul II decries the theoretical and practical division of the world into blocs of superpower influence. This division, he writes in *Sollicitudo rei socialis*, 22, harbors "a tendency towards imperialism," wherein superpowers envision the Third World as a sphere of influence without giving consideration to either "the priorities and problems of such countries" or their unique "cultural make-up."

Family. Like their predecessors, the post-Leonine period popes scrutinize false interpretations of marriage and illicit rationales for artificial birth control. Gone, however, are explicit criticisms of theories denying parental rights over adolescent education and negative assessments of the impact of women's emancipation on family life.

The popes shift critical attention away from inappropriate contractual and sentimental interpretations of marriage to views construing matrimony as simply a historical, sociological construct. "Marriage is not," says Paul VI's *Humanae vitae*, 8, ". . . the effect of chance or the product of evolution of unconscious natural forces."

Regarding artificial birth control, Paul VI rejects justifications based on marital freedom, the principle of totality, and the principle of lesser evil. "In the task of transmitting life," insists the pope in *Humanae vitae*, 10, couples "are not free to proceed completely at will, as if they could determine in a wholly autonomous way the honest path to follow." "Just as man does not have unlimited dominion over his body," Paul VI adds in section 13, ". . . he has no such dominion over his generative faculties as such, because of their intrinsic ordination towards raising up life, of which God is the principle." As for the principle of totality (the idea that "it is permissible for an injury to be done to one part of the body in order that the whole body may benefit"), the pope argues that "it is an error to think that a conjugal act which is deliberately made infecund . . . could be made honest and right by the ensemble of a fecund conjugal life."[31] Finally, Paul VI cites Rom 3:8 in section 14, saying "one cannot invoke" the principle of the lesser evil because "it is not licit, even for the gravest reasons, to do evil so that good may follow therefrom."

Economics. Capitalist and socialist economic theory receive ample criticism in post-Leonine period texts. "The Church's social doctrine," writes John Paul II in *Sollicitudo rei socialis*, 23, "adopts a critical attitude towards both liberal capitalism and Marxist collectivism." As in previous periods, the popes scrutinize the distinct and shared problems affecting both theories.

Like their predecessors, the popes focus on two general problems impairing capitalist economic theory. With its underlying ethic of individual self-interest, capitalism unduly elevates profit "as the key motive for economic progress." Second, capitalism holds that competition for profit, when unrestrained, automatically effects a socially optimal distribution of material goods.[32] These two problems incorporate several additional errors.

Unrestrained profit maximization assumes and promotes false notions of property ownership, economic justice, and international trade. In *Populorum progressio*, 26, Paul VI accuses capitalists of raising "private ownership of the means of production as an absolute right that has no limits and carries no corresponding social obligation." In this way, capitalists shrink the concept of economic justice to simple satisfaction of legal contracts, concealing the contractors' often inordinate economic power. Recalling Leo XIII's remarks on wage contracts, Paul VI writes in section 59: "If the positions of the contracting partners are too unequal, the consent of the parties does not suffice to guarantee the justice of their contract." The same criticism applies to capitalist notions of free trade between nations. Because vast inequalities of wealth and power differentiate nations, "prices which are 'freely' set in the market can produce unfair results." As a result, "the rule of free trade, taken by itself, is no longer able to govern international relations." "One must recognize," says the pope, "that it is the fundamental principle of liberalism, as the rule for commercial exchange, which is questioned here."[33]

The capitalist concept of automatic justice through unrestrained competition entails a false view of distribution, an inappropriate separation of economics and morality, and a minimalist interpretation of state responsibility. In *Mater et Magistra*, 11, John XXIII rejects the idea, overtly promoted at the turn of the century, that "interest on capital, prices of goods and services, profits and wages" should "be determined purely mechanically by the laws of the marketplace." "Hence, it was held," he adds, "that no connection existed between economic and moral laws" and "every precaution was taken lest the civil authority intervene in any way in economic affairs." According to John Paul II in *Laborem exercens*, 30, this "reversal of order"—wherein objective economic "forces" dominate human subjectivity—"should rightly be called 'capitalism.'"

Socialism (understood as Marxist scientific socialism) also contains a twofold problem. On one hand, it promotes a false "program of collectivism as proclaimed by Marxism," and on the other hand, it proclaims the idea of "class struggle in the 'Marxist sense.'"[34] These general problems include several more specific errors.

Socialist collectivism assumes and advances mistaken views of property ownership and state economic power. According to John Paul II's *Laborem exercens*, 65, both productive and nonproductive personal property involve human labor. By accepting Marx's theory of surplus value, socialists wrongfully denounce individual ownership of productive property by "isolating these means as a separate property in order to set it up in the form of 'capital' in opposition to 'labor.'" This encourages the similarly flawed idea of transferring administration of all productive property to the state. Because the Marxist "principle of the dictatorship of the proletariat" emphasizes a one-party "monopoly of power," John Paul II warns that "merely taking these means of production (capital) out of the hands of their private owners is not enough to ensure their proper socialization."[35]

The socialist theory of class struggle incorporates mistaken notions of dialectical materialism and inevitable conflict between capital and labor. The philosophy of dialectical materialism, says John Paul II in *Laborem exercens*, 61, incorrectly reduces human beings to "a kind of 'resultant' of the economic or production relations prevailing at a given period." Second, belief that the capitalist mode of production inevitably generates capital-labor struggle founders on a false separation. In section 59, the pope says that 'capital' is an economic concept, not a person; as such, it cannot be separated from labor because "labor and what we are accustomed to call capital are intermingled." Though the "actual people behind these concepts" are frequently opposed, class tension is not automatically created by "the structure of the production process itself," but by two human errors latent in any economic system: the personalization of 'capital' and the depersonalization of 'labor' (sections 59-62).

In *Sollicitudo rei socialis*, 20, John Paul II notes that the ideologies of "liberal capitalism" and "Marxist collectivism" present "two very different visions of man and of his freedom and social role." At the same time, the post-Leonine period popes join their earlier colleagues in identifying certain shared premises within both economic systems. According to John Paul II's *Laborem exercens*, 28, both capitalism and socialism are rooted in "materialistic and economistic thought." As 'materialistic' theories, capitalism and socialism mistakenly correlate human economic happiness with quantity of material goods possessed.

The former theory emphasizes individual acquisition, while the latter stresses collective accumulation. As 'economistic' theories, capitalism and socialism incorrectly separate capital and labor, setting them up as opposing, impersonal forces. For the former, the force of capital in economic competition, if uninhibited, automatically advances society's economic well-being. For the latter, the force of labor in class conflict, if unsuppressed, promotes society's economic welfare. Finally, each system "harbors in its own way," attests John Paul II in *Sollicitudo rei socialis*, 22, "a tendency towards imperialism."

Though modern socialism constitutes a more philosophically self-conscious—and, thus, more challenging—economic theory, capitalism remains its progenitor. According to John Paul II's *Laborem exercens*, 61-62, "the philosophy and economic theories of the 18th century" and "the whole of the economic and social practice of the time" introduced both "practical materialism" and economism. Socialism developed out of this "most elementary and common phase" of capitalistic materialism and economism into "the phase of what is called dialectical materialism."

Culture. As in earlier periods, the popes' overall cultural concern is the "desacralization" of society. "There are today those," bemoans John XXIII, "who assert that . . . men can achieve the highest civilization even apart from God and by their unaided powers."[36] Specifically, the popes continue their predecessors' criticism of faulty ideas concerning communication and science. A new concern is raised over troublesome theories of cultural development.

As in earlier encyclicals, the popes reject rationalizations of dishonest speech and pornography on grounds of utility or freedom. In *Ecclesiam suam*, 102, Paul VI attacks the view that oral communication should "serve not the investigation and formulation of objective truth, but purely subjective expediency." Similarly, in *Humanae vitae*, 22, he denounces those who support "pornography and licentious performance . . . with the pretext of artistic or scientific exigencies, or to deduce an argument from the freedom allowed in this sector by the public authorities."

The popes repeat their predecessors' warnings against viewing science as an exhaustive, self-sufficient tool for interpreting reality. In *Pacem in terris*, 152, John XXIII decries the belief of some scientists that a separation must occur "between religious belief and their action in the temporal sphere." Quoting Henri de Lubac, Paul VI says in *Populorum progressio*, 42: "True, man can organize the world apart from

God, but 'without God man can organize it in the end only to man's detriment.'"

In *Sollicitudo rei socialis*, 27, John Paul II rejects the idea that cultural development is an "automatic," "limitless," primarily economic process. This idea is "linked to the notion of 'progress' with philosophical connotations deriving from the Enlightenment." These connotations invoke a "naive mechanistic optimism." In section 28, John Paul II argues that reducing the concept of cultural development to "having" a greater store of material goods threatens the social, cultural and spiritual dimensions of "being" human.

Solutions

Encyclical solutions to humanity's social problems are a blend of theological and social insight. As in previous chapters, distinguishing and analyzing these insights helps disclose the characteristic features of positive encyclical social teaching in the post-Leonine period letters.

Theological Perspectives

The post-Leonine period encyclicals adopt a new controlling image for communicating key themes of Christian faith. Just as the transition from pre-Leonine to Leonine period letters marked a shift in the dominant theological metaphor from sheepfold intimacy to cosmological design, the post-Leonine period letters deemphasize cosmic order and introduce the metaphor of dialogical journey. This new image, bolstered by theological developments at the Second Vatican Council, modifies papal perspectives on God, the world, and humanity.

One source for this metaphor shift is the popes' new emphasis on the Holy Spirit. Whereas earlier encyclicals presented God through the pastoral image of Christ the Good Shepherd and the cosmological image of a creating and sustaining Father of the Universe, post-Leonine period letters accentuate the image of God as dialogical Spirit. "The method employed by God in revealing himself to men," explains Paul VI in *Ecclesiam suam*, 19 and 70- 71, is a "two-way relationship," a "long, varied dialogue" initiated by God "through Christ in the Holy Spirit." Enlivened by Vatican II, John Paul II believes contemporary humanity has made "a fresh discovery of God in his transcendent reality as the infinite Spirit."[37] In section 54 of *Dominum et vivificantem* (written on the topic of "the Holy Spirit in the Church and the world"), John Paul II says this discovery echoes Jesus' Jn 4:24 message to the Samaritan woman at the well: "God is spirit."

Emphasis on the Holy Spirit's dialogical journey with humanity encourages a new papal perspective on the world. Unlike earlier images of the world as a necessary, yet ominous, pasture and a cosmic structure of divinely actuated causes and entities, post-Leonine period letters regularly present the world as the cultural, physical and historical context for God's conversational pilgrimage with humanity. In *Dominum et vivificantem*, 24, John Paul II says the redemptive message of the Holy Spirit is "constantly carried out" within the physical and social "history of the world."[38]

As a result, Christians must "give careful consideration to the signs of the times," differentiating "relapses into barbarism" from the world's Spirit-informed "steps towards its Creator."[39] In *Dominum et vivificantem*, 59, John Paul II says human beings can promote God's kingdom "within the world" by correctly discerning the Spirit. Unlike earlier encyclicals, where the temporal dimension of God's kingdom is considered strictly coextensive with the Roman Catholic Church, post-Leonine period letters acknowledge the presence of the kingdom in not only the Catholic Church, but in all Christian churches and wherever social activities authentically contribute to a "greater humanity."[40]

The popes' novel emphasis on Spirit also generates fresh perspectives on humanity. These perspectives, however, are placed alongside a continued commitment to anthropological claims developed during the Leonine period. Because these earlier ideas flow from a significantly different outlook on God and the world, the treatment of humanity in post-Leonine period encyclicals is a motley.

Alongside Leonine period emphasis on human nature as ontologically linked with the Father's cosmological design, the popes add a new focus on human experience as psychologically joined in a dialogical journey with the Spirit. Use of the "pilgrimage metaphor," observes Margaret Miles, invariably creates a "heightening and intensification of experience."[41] George Grima cites the Vatican II preference "to speak of 'human experience'" rather that "'human nature'" as the immediate influence on this new approach in the post-Leonine period letters.[42]

In some encyclicals the discussion of human nature and experience appear separately, in others they are joined. In *Dominum et vivificantem*, 34, John Paul II attempts the latter, identifying "not only rationality and freedom as constitutive properties of human nature, but also, from the very beginning, the capacity of having a personal relationship with God, as 'I' and 'you.'" Here, the pope combines Leonine period emphasis on human powers of intellect and will with new attention to the heart as a symbolic locus of humanity's personal encounter with God. Thus, in both *Redemptor hominis* (sections 2, 18, 22, 40) and *Dominum et vivificantem* (sections 54, 58), the pope considers the *imago dei* in humanity "an ontological and psychological reality" encompassing the trilogy of intellect, will, and heart.

This new approach affects the entire post-Leonine period discussion of faith, morality, and fellowship. Though not rejecting the Leonine period view of faith as an intellectual ascent to divinely revealed truths, the popes append a new, conciliar-supported understanding of faith as the response of a person's whole being to God's self-revelation. In so doing, they combine earlier papal emphasis on human reason and religious dogma with fresh interest in the human heart and interrelationship with God.

According to John Paul II's *Dominum et vivificantem*, 67, the heart is "the hidden place of the salvific encounter with the Holy Spirit." This corresponds with the event of Christ's redemption, wherein divine and human hearts were reconciled. "The redemption of the world," writes John Paul II in *Redemptor hominis*, 22, ". . . is, at its deepest root, the fullness of justice in the human heart—the heart of the first-born Son—in order that it may become justice in the hearts of many human beings."

The act of faith, then, is not simply an intellectual acceptance of religious truths, but a heartfelt conversion of faith in a personal God. Because personal relationships require time to develop and deepen, conversion occurs "not only as a momentary interior act but also as a permanent attitude." "Those who come to know God in this way," says the pope, live "in a state of being continually converted to him."[43]

The capacity for this ongoing, affective relationship with God undergirds human dignity. John Paul II writes in *Dives in misericordia*, 2: "Man cannot be manifested in the full dignity of his nature without reference—not only on the level of concepts but also in an integrally existential way—to God." Here again, the popes attempt to retain both the Leonine emphasis on humanity's divinely created nature and the view that human dignity flows from "man's intimate relationship with God in the Holy Spirit."[44]

These post-Leonine period appositions (reason and affectivity, faith as an intellectual ascent to dogma and a personal relationship to God) recur in the popes' discussion of human morality. Alongside Leonine period emphasis on humanity's rational awareness of natural laws, the popes add a novel regard for affective appreciation of moral values.

Like faith, appreciation of value comes through conversion. In *Dominum et vivificantem*, 45, John Paul II speaks of an "authentic conversion of the heart," or "evangelical 'metanoia,'" which follows upon one's recognition of "the evil he has committed." Using language employed by the Latin American bishops in their Medellín and Puebla statements, John Paul II calls sin 'personal' and 'structural': 'personal' in regard to "the concrete acts of individuals," 'structural' as reflected in the ideological and institutional systems which embody "the sum total of the negative factors working against true awareness of the universal 'common good' in society."[45]

The Spirit, writes John Paul II in *Dominum et vivificantem*, 45, both encourages the "great effort" necessary to recognize sin and effects one's openness to others. Moral conversion, he says in *Sollicitudo rei socialis*, 38, entails an affective "awareness of interdependence among individuals and nations" in human conscience. "When interdependence becomes recognized in this way, the correlative response as a moral and social attitude, as a 'virtue,' is solidarity." Thus, he states in section 40: "Solidarity is undoubtedly a Christian virtue," the avowal of the neighbor as the "living image of God . . . placed under the permanent action of the Holy Spirit."[46]

Using the dialogical journey metaphor, John Paul II warns that the "path" out of sin and into solidarity is "long and complex." The "journey" requires spiritual courage and openness, because of both the "intrinsic frailty of human resolution" and the "mutability" of circumstances. Moral freedom, then, entails recognizing and obeying God's objective law (as in the Leonine period letters), as well as staying alert to the liberating "power of the Spirit."[47]

The understanding of religious fellowship in post-Leonine period teaching also combines old and new perspectives. Faithful membership in the Roman Catholic Church—portrayed in the Leonine period image of the Mystical Body of Christ—remains a critical criterion in the popes' outlook on personal salvation. However, the popes' most frequent metaphor portraying the Church is the "pilgrim People of God."[48] This image adds two new elements to encyclical discussion of religious fellowship.

First, by treating religious fellowship as "a great historical process comparable 'to a journey,'" the popes show greater openness to ecclesiological change as compared with their predecessors.[49] As it moves through the "vicissitudes of this life," says Paul VI in *Sacerdotalis caelibatus*, 33, the Church must conduct a "continual process of self-examination." In this examination, he continues in *Ecclesiam suam*, 42, the Church must be willing to "adapt itself to the forms of thought and living which the temporal environment induces," without sacrificing "the basic principles of its religious and moral teaching."

Second, by employing the title 'People of God,' the popes accentuate the Spirit's active presence within not only the Roman Catholic Church, but also Christians outside the Roman Catholic Church. The Spirit, says John Paul II's *Dominum et vivificantem*, 4, helps all people "to understand the correct meaning of the content of Christ's message." In section 53, he adds: "The Second Vatican Council reminds us of the Holy Spirit's activity also 'outside the visible body of the [Roman Catholic] church.'" With this view, the popes reverse the ecclesiological claims of the pre-Leonine and Leonine periods. As Patrick Granfield explains, the Vatican II "Church of Christ" is "broader than any one denomination, even though it is present in a special or full manner in the Catholic Church."[50]

Social Recommendations

The metaphor of dialogical journey influences papal interpretation of key Christian themes. This distinct theological perspective impacts the popes' positive teaching regarding human relations in the religious, political, family, economic, and cultural spheres of social life.

Religious Ideas and Practices. Like their predecessors, the post-Leonine period popes seek unity in religious life through the organization and operation of the Roman Catholic Church. To promote religious unity, the popes combine Leonine period insights with teachings inspired by the new 'People of God' ecclesiology. These latter recommendations include greater episcopal collegiality, more self-directed lay participation, support for ecumenism.

While reiterating previous encyclical teaching on the organizational necessity of papal authority and obedience between ranks in the Church, the popes place new emphasis on the importance of dialogue among the 'People of God.'[51] "The Church's internal relationships," writes Paul VI in *Ecclesiam suam*, 114, "should take the form of a dialogue between members of a community founded on love." Encyclical encouragement of this dialogue takes two forms.

First, the popes place new value on ideas of local bishops by encouraging national synods and episcopal conferences, as well as by establishing the international Synod of Bishops in Rome. In the spirit of Vatican II, which gave the principle of collegiality "immense new life," John Paul II's *Redemptor hominis*, 10-12 says that episcopal bodies "should pulsate in full awareness of their own identity and, at the same time, of their own originality within the universal unity of the church."

The popes also encourage a new "spirit of collaboration and responsibility" within the laity. Whereas Leonine period interest in the "lay apostolate" focused entirely on affairs of piety and social action, the post-Leonine popes support lay participation "in the spheres of diocesan synods" and "pastoral councils in the parishes and dioceses." Because the "grace of Pentecost" is transmitted through not only episcopal ordination but also the sacrament of confirmation, the gift of the Spirit is "both hierarchical and charismatic."[52]

As in earlier periods, the popes consider social action, education, evangelization, and spiritual renewal to be key operational activities of religious life. Again, post-Leonine period discussion of these activities is nuanced by the new 'People of God' ecclesiology.

Social action as a dimension of religious discipleship receives paramount encyclical attention. In this dimension, two claims made by the post-Leonine period popes reverse earlier papal teaching. First, a change occurs from earlier papal support for Catholic Action—where laity work "in union with their bishops and in constant obedience to them"—to encouragement of lay-initiated social action.[53] In *Populorum progressio,"* 81, Paul VI writes:

> It belongs to the laymen, without waiting passively for orders and directives, to take the initiative freely and to infuse a Christian spirit into the mentality, customs, laws and structures of the community in which they live.

Second, John XXIII's *Pacem in terris*, 159, permits Catholic cooperation with people holding "false philosophical teachings" if the purpose of meeting is for "the attainment of some practical end." However, the episcopal hierarchy retains the power to "intervene authoritatively" if need arise.[54]

The popes also introduce changes in religious education. Instruction of the laity, says Paul VI's *Ecclesiam suam*, 38, should incorporate experiences of "actually living the Church's life." "A Christian formation and education which would only consider teaching the faithful the formulas of the Catechism," advises John XXIII, " . . . would run the serious risk of acquiring for the Church a passive flock." An "active" curriculum in "Catholic schools at all levels" should include the "social teaching proclaimed by the Catholic Church."[55]

This new pedagogical emphasis on what Paul VI's *Ecclesiam suam*, 37 calls "intuitive experience" should also influence seminary education. According to John XXIII's *Princeps Pastorum*, 16, seminarians—especially in missionary lands—should "never be 'educated in

places too far removed from human society'" in order that they
'gradually and prudently penetrate the mentality and feelings of the
people.'"

Theologians, too, are encouraged to investigate the wide range of
human experience. It "is permissible and even desirable," writes John
Paul II in *Redemptor hominis*, 75, "that the enormous work to be done
in this direction should take into consideration a certain pluralism of
methodology." This sentiment parallels the intellectual developments
at Vatican II, which effectively ended the theological hegemony of
Thomism initiated during the Leonine period. "Close collaboration by
theology with the magisterium," however, remains "indispensable."[56]

In part, post-Leonine period teaching on missionary activity expands
insights first suggested in the Leonine period. The popes believe
missionaries should pursue social work; respect, encourage, and learn
from indigenous cultures; and encourage native clergy.[57] Influenced by
the Vatican II decree *Ad gentes*, the popes also introduce the new idea
that the Church, through missionary activity, "not only gives, but
receives."[58] In *Princeps Pastorum*, 19, John XXIII says the Church is
"willing, at all times, to recognize, welcome, and even assimilate
anything that redounds to the honor of the human mind and heart."

Vatican II shapes the popes' discussion of spiritual renewal. Distinct
from Leonine period stress on recitation of specific prayers, observance
of devotions, and membership in religious sodalities and orders, the
post-Leonine period popes seek a general intensification and commu-
nalization of spiritual energy. "Discussions concerning Christian
perfection," says Paul VI in *Ecclesiam suam*, 41, should "arouse the
faithful, not indeed to formulate new rules of spirituality, but to generate
new energies in striving after the holiness which Christ has taught us."
In section 38, the pope considers active participation in the social and
sacramental life of the 'People of God' "the best type of spirituality."

Finally, reversing Leonine period teaching, the popes endorse both
ecumenical dialogue with non-Roman Catholic Christians and openness to non-Christian religious traditions. Inspired by ecclesiological
developments at Vatican II, the popes support Christian ecumenism
"with a will."[59] "In the present historical situation of Christianity and
the world the only possibility we see of fulfilling the church's universal mission," writes John Paul II in *Redemptor hominis*, 15, ". . . is that
of seeking sincerely, perseveringly, humbly and also courageously the
ways of drawing closer and of union." This "must also be applied,"
he adds in section 16, ". . . to activity for coming together with the
representatives of the non-Christian religions." The Spirit, says John
Paul II, "'blows where it wills.'"[60]

Political Ideas and Practices. The popes adopt and, in some cases, change encyclical recommendations regarding political life. As in earlier periods, this teaching treats the origin, forms, and purpose of state authority, Church-state relations, citizenship, political freedom, and rights.

God remains the ultimate source of state authority in post-Leonine letters. For the popes, this teaching provides the only consistent ground for holding state authority morally accountable. Rulers may "oblige men in conscience," insists John XXIII in *Pacem in terris*, 49, "only if their authority is intrinsically related with the authority of God."

On the topic of governmental structure, however, the popes change earlier encyclical teaching. Whereas the Leonine period popes acknowledge democracy as one acceptable form of government, the post-Leonine period popes give it preferred status. In *Pacem in terris*, 52–79, John XXIII prescribes several basic features of participatory democracy: popular election, fixed-term political offices, popular consultation, separation of powers, and written constitutions with appended charters of human rights.[61] When John XXIII says "it is impossible to determine, once and for all, what is the most suitable form of government," he is referring not to the classical choices between monarchy, aristocracy, and democracy (as in Leonine period teaching), but to alternative forms of participatory democracy.[62] Concomitantly, John Paul II insists in *Sollicitudo rei socialis*, 44: "corrupt, dictatorial, and authoritarian forms of government" must be replaced by "democratic and participatory ones."

Consistent with earlier encyclical teaching, the popes believe state authority exists to promote the common good. In *Mater et Magistra*, 65, John XXIII defines 'common good' as "the sum total of those conditions of social living, whereby men are enabled more fully and more readily to achieve their own perfection." According to Wilhelm Weber, this definition resolved a long-standing Catholic debate over whether the common good refers to a collection of 'goods' or an organizational context for human flourishing. In Weber's view, John XXIII favors the latter approach.[63]

As in Leonine period thought, the common good entails the material and spiritual development of both the national and international community. While reasserting earlier papal emphasis on just law, mass education, poor relief, social progress, and peace, the popes add several new recommendations regarding state support of the domestic common good. These suggestions concern minority groups, overpopulation, military service, and human rights.

In *Pacem in terris*, 96, John XXIII says civil authorities must "promote the natural betterment of those citizens belonging to a minority ethnic group, particularly when that concerns their language, the development of their natural gifts, their ancestral customs, and their accomplishments and endeavors in the economic order." Regarding the difficulties accompanying "an accelerated demographic increase," Paul VI thinks "public authorities can intervene, within the limits of their competence, by favoring the availability of appropriate information and by adopting suitable measures, provided these be in conformity with the moral law and that they respect the rightful freedom of married couples."[64]

As for participation in the military, Paul VI says in *Populorum progressio*, 74, that he is "pleased to learn that in certain nations 'military service' can be partially accomplished by doing 'social service.'" This attitude is consistent with the general condemnation of war and weaponry in post-Leonine period letters. In *Pacem in terris*, 112, John XXIII urgently demands that

> . . . the arms race should cease; that the stockpiles which exist in various countries be reduced equally and simultaneously by the parties concerned; that nuclear weapons should be banned; and that a general agreement should eventually be reached about progressive disarmament and an effective method of control.

In section 127 he adds: "It is hardly possible to imagine that in the atomic era war could be used as an instrument of justice."[65] Finally, John XXIII insists in *Pacem in terris*, 65, that civil authorities "maintain a careful balance between co-ordinating and protecting the rights of the citizens, on the one hand, and promoting them on the other."

Post-Leonine period political teaching heightens concern over the universal common good of all nation states. The Church "offers men," says Paul VI's *Populorum progressio*, 13, "what she possesses as her characteristic attribute: a global vision of man and of the human race." This vision includes increased attention to relations between states and a new proposal for world government.

Concerning international relations, the popes believe states should cooperate in "truth and justice" not only to prevent war, but to foster social development. "The common good of a particular civil society," explains John XXIII in *Pacem in terris*, 98, ". . . cannot be divorced from the common good of the entire human family." As a result, the popes implore wealthy nations to aid states "which are in the process of development," without "any intention of political domination." Within their own states, government officials should "alert public opinion" about world needs, aid immigrants and seasonal workers from impoverished nations, and make citizens "accept the necessary taxes on their luxuries and their wasteful expenditures, in order to bring about development and to save the peace."[66]

Though cooperation between nation-states is necessary for international peace and justice, the popes do not consider it sufficient. Given the world's current political structure, the independent state's first priority, even while pursuing international cooperation, remains national self-interest. The papal solution to this problem is establishment of a world political authority. This new "public authority of the world community," says John XXIII, ". . . is not intended to limit the sphere of action of the public authority of the individual political community"; rather, "its purpose is to create, on a world basis, an environment in which the public authorities . . . can carry out their tasks, fulfill their duties and exercise their rights with greater security." As a step in this direction, the popes consistently support the United Nations and its international agencies.[67]

A dramatic difference between Leonine and post-Leonine period political teaching is the latter popes' silence on the topic of Church-state relations. Earlier encyclical discussions regarding distinctions between Church and state, areas of joint jurisdiction, and the institutional priority of the Church disappear. This papal silence anticipates and confirms the Second Vatican Council's reversal of Leonine period teaching on Church-state relations. According to Bryan Hehir, the conciliar declaration on religious freedom (*Dignitatis humanae*) "in fact restructured the conception of church-state relations which had prevailed in Roman Catholicism explicitly since Vatican I." In it, "freedom, not favoritism or special status, is the basic claim the church makes vis-à-vis the modern state."[68]

On the other hand, the popes' instructions on citizenship duplicate Leonine period teachings. Citizens must obey just laws, participate in state affairs, and resist compliance with civil orders "contrary to the will of God."[69] Regarding political resistance, post-Leonine period teaching mirrors the ambiguity apparent in prior papal letters. Like Leo XIII, John XXIII accepts resistance to unjust law through nonviolent participation in democratic government. "To proceed gradually," he says in *Pacem in terris*, 162, "is the law of life in all its expressions"; thus, "it is not possible to renovate" human institutions "except by working from within them." Contrariwise, Paul VI—like Pius XII—subtly suggests that citizen violence, in certain circumstances, cannot be absolutely condemned. In *Populorum progressio*, 31, he contends that "revolutionary uprising" produces new injustices "save where there is manifest, long-standing tyranny which would do great damage to fundamental personal rights and dangerous harm to the common good of the country."[70]

The post-Leonine period understanding of political freedom likewise mirrors earlier papal thought. Political freedom is not simply the exercise of unhindered, individual will, but the action of a human being imbued with "a consciousness of his obligations." Linking truth and goodness, John Paul II calls an "honest relationship with regard to truth" a "condition for authentic freedom."[71]

On the issue of human rights, the popes—like their predecessors—consider God the source of rights. "God," writes John XXIII in *Grata recordatio*, 18, ". . . is guarantor of the rights and dignity of the human person." Human nature can be identified as the source of rights only by virtue of its dependence on God. Consequently, the popes persist in the view that personal rights are inseparably connected with social duties. According to Ph. J. André-Vincent, the post-Leonine period popes look favorably upon the 1948 United Nations Universal Declaration of Human Rights because, unlike the 1789 French Declaration of the Rights of Man and the Citizen, it does not expressly adopt "l'idéologie individualiste de l'humanisme athée."[72]

The specific catalogue of human rights grows in post-Leonine period encyclicals. To the substantial list already gained in the pre-Leonine and Leonine period encyclicals, the popes add the rights to emigrate with just reason, preserve ethnic group identity, freely search for truth, receive true information, and express opinions (mindful of moral propriety), work, receive a just wage, work in safe surroundings, engage in occupations respecting individual competence, conduct a labor strike, receive employee benefits and pensions, choose vocations, rest, share in cultural benefits, receive respect as a human being, and enjoy juridical protection of all these rights.[73]

Beyond repeating and expanding the list of human rights, the popes reverse prior encyclical teaching in one area. Unlike previous encyclical teaching, the popes recognize that "every human being has the right to honor God according to the dictates of an upright conscience, and the right to profess his religion privately and publicly." This statement of John XXIII, from *Pacem in terris*, 14, anticipates section 19 of the conciliar declaration *Dignitatis humanae*. In his commentary on the Vatican II document, Pietro Pavan recognizes that the council's view is new, but insists that it represents an "intrinsic development in the sociopolitical teaching of the Catholic Church." Walter Burghardt, however, is "convinced that Vatican II's affirmation of religious freedom . . . is discontinuous with certain explicit elements within the Catholic tradition." Judging from the development of papal encyclical literature since the eighteenth century, Burghardt's position is affirmed.[74]

Family Ideas and Practices. The ambiguities created by juxtaposing Leonine period emphasis on human nature with a new stress on human experience are clearly indicated in post-Leonine period teaching concerning family life. While much instruction is adopted from the Leonine period, fresh emphasis on the affective dimension of family life generates novel recommendations.

Sustaining the view that marriage subsists in holiness and indissolubility, the popes place new focus on mutual love as a defining quality of married life. As the symbolic model for Christian marriage, Christ's relationship with the Church is one not only of grace and constancy, but also love. "Thus," writes Paul VI, "Christian couples walk together toward their heavenly fatherland in the exercise of mutual love."[75]

Regard for mutual love influences papal thought on the purpose of marriage. By stressing love, the popes abandon exclusive focus on procreation as a central goal of marriage. When the popes do note these latter goals, they typically set them within the context of the former. "Marriage," explains Paul VI, ". . . is the wise institution of the Creator to realize in mankind His design of love." He continues:

> By means of the reciprocal personal gift of self, proper and exclusive to them, husband and wife tend towards the communion of their beings in view of mutual personal perfection, to collaborate with God in the generation and education of new lives.[76]

Emphasis on mutual love also influences papal teaching on sexual intercourse in marriage. In *Humanae vitae*, 12, Paul VI introduces the notion that conjugal acts have two meanings: "the unitive meaning and the procreative meaning." The unitive meaning of conjugal relations represents the affective bond between husband and wife, while the procreative meaning denotes the act's capacity "for the generation of new lives." These two dimensions form an "inseparable connection, willed by God." According to John Noonan, this claim that "conjugal love is a purpose of conjugal intercourse is a development of doctrine."[77]

While introducing new emphasis on interpersonal love and affective sexuality, the popes maintain their predecessors' positions on the rhythm method of birth control and artificial contraception. Discussing "responsible parenthood," Paul VI says that parents must decide, based on "physical, economic, psychological and social conditions," whether to "raise a generous family" or avoid (by means of the rhythm method) "for the time being, or even for an indeterminate period, a new birth."[78] The rhythm method is acceptable because it entails the "legitimate use of natural disposition." Artificial birth control, on the other hand, impedes "the development of natural processes." In *Humanae vitae*, 11, Paul VI writes: "every marriage act must remain open to the transmission of life."[79] However, contraceptive use is licit if "truly necessary to cure diseases of the organism" and if the consequent infertility is not "directly willed" but accepted as a side effect of efforts to achieve normal health.[80]

Papal thought on family relations repeats Leonine period teaching. In *Ad Petri Cathedram*, 53-57, John XXIII says the father should "lead and guide . . . by his authority and the example of a good life." The mother must "form her children firmly and graciously." Together, they "should carefully rear their children . . . to an upright and religious life." For their part, children must "honor, obey, and love their parents," as well as give "concrete assistance if it is needed." In *Laborem exercens*, 42, John Paul II thinks such concrete assistance, or work, helps achieve "the purposes of the family, especially education." As in prior papal teaching, John XXIII holds up the "household at Nazareth" as a model Christian family.

Finally, like his forerunners, John XXIII considers families the "first and essential cell of human society." In *Ad Petri Cathedram*, 51, he asks rhetorically: "Unless peace, unity, and concord are present in domestic society, how can they exist in civil society?"

Economic Ideas and Practices. Encyclical teaching on markets, property ownership, economic relations, and the roles of Church and state in economic life continue developing in the post-Leonine period. New papal attention is focused on work, distribution of goods, agriculture, capital, worker solidarity, and global economics.

Like their predecessors, the popes accept the notions of profit, competition, private property, and wage labor if properly circumscribed by norms of social morality. Though John XXIII and Paul VI praised entrepreneurship and private initiative in business (*Mater et Magistra*, 51; *Populorum progressio*, 22), John Paul II is the first to acknowledge a person's "right of economic initiative."[81]

Throughout the post-Leonine period letters, property and labor receive particular attention. While earlier letters recognized—albeit with different emphases—the twofold character of property ownership, the popes after John XXIII raise the right of common use over the right of personal possession. In *Laborem exercens*, 64, John Paul II states: "The right to private property is subordinated to the right to common use." In *Populorum progressio*, 24, this new perspective legitimates state expropriation of "extensive, unused or poorly used" land when such properties "bring hardship to peoples or are detrimental to the interests of the country."[82] This understanding of property is consistent with what John Paul II's *Sollicitudo rei socialis*, 7, calls the "centuries-old tradition of the Church regarding the 'universal purpose of goods.'"

In *Laborem exercens*, John Paul II expands the Leonine period concept of the 'dignity of work.' On the basis of the period's theological juxtaposition of human nature and experience, John Paul II explores the phenomenon of work as a "fundamental dimension of human existence" (section 12). The popes' central message is the "pre-eminence of the subjective meaning of work over the objective one." "The basis for determining the value of human work is not primarily the kind of work being done [objective meaning]," writes John Paul II in sections 26–27, "but the fact that the one who is doing it is a person [subjective meaning]."

In his teaching on work, John Paul II draws two insights from Gen. 1:26–28. First, a human being is the image of God, "that is to say, a subjective being capable of acting in a planned and rational way, capable of deciding about himself and with a tendency to self-realization." God's recognition of humanity as the *imago dei* in the same breath as his command that they 'have dominion' over the earth, suggests the centrality of work for human self-realization.[83]

The link between self-realization and dominion prompts a second insight. According to John Paul II, humanity participates in God's creative activity through labor. "The word of God's revelation," insists the pope, "is profoundly marked by the fundamental truth that man, created in the image of God, shares by his work in the activity of the Creator."[84] On this basis, the pope makes the novel claim in section 11 that "human work is a key, probably the essential key, to the whole social question."

These teachings on property and work are reinforced by fresh perspectives on economic relations. In post-Leonine period letters the many recommendations brought forward from earlier encyclicals on relations between the rich and the poor, employers and employees, and capitalists and laborers are adjusted to highlight two values: equitable distribution and social solidarity.

Concerning the rich and the poor, the popes reverse their predecessors' Hermasian model wherein self-effacing indigents materially depend on the munificence of the rich, who themselves depend on the prayers of the poor. In post-Leonine period letters, almsgiving is no longer solely associated with munificence, but with justice. Retrieving Clement XIII's pre-Leonine period view, Paul VI writes: "No one is justified in keeping for his exclusive use what he does not need, when others lack necessities."[85]

Beyond providing for emergencies, the popes believe the rich should support programs working toward greater overall equity in the distribution of goods in society. In *Ad Petri Cathedram*, 45, John XXIII advances the idea that, since "many conveniences" have become "an integral part of everyday life," the poor should not be "excluded from the enjoyment of these advantages." Citing the Parable of the Rich Man and Lazarus in Lk 16:19-31, Paul VI writes: "It is not just a matter of eliminating hunger, nor even of reducing poverty"; rather, it is a question of "building a world where . . . the poor man Lazarus can sit down at the same table with the rich man."[86]

To build a more equitable world, John Paul II recognizes in *Dives in misericordia*, 148 that "justice must, so to speak, be 'corrected' to a considerable extent" by Christian love. Love promotes and binds authentic social solidarity. When imbued with a "spirit of solidarity," the rich are not content with impersonal aid; rather, they seek contact with the poor. Paul VI calls this "solidarity in action."[87] In *Populorum progressio*, 47, he hopes wealthy individuals will not only be willing to pay higher taxes for government aid to the poor and higher prices for imports from impoverished countries, but also consider leaving their country "in order to assist in this development of the young nations."

This emphasis on equitable distribution and social solidarity between the rich and the poor sparks new encyclical teaching on employer-employee relations. Regarding employers, John Paul II introduces the notion of direct and indirect employers. Concerning employees, the popes expand workers' rights and heighten support for employee participation in management.

John Paul II uses the concept of direct and indirect employers to identify the social agents responsible for creating and maintaining an "ethically correct labor policy." The direct employer "is the person or institution with whom the worker enters directly into a work contract." The indirect employer is the persons and institutions constituting "the whole socioeconomic system" outside the workplace. This latter concept, says John Paul II in *Laborem exercens*, 76-78, refers "in first place to the state." Both employers have distinct economic responsibilities.

While serving society through production of safe and helpful goods, direct employers must provide workers just remuneration and benefits. Like his predecessors, John Paul II supports wages "which will suffice for establishing and properly maintaining a family." He adds in *Laborem exercens*, 90, however, that direct employers need not pay a full family wage if the state provides "other social measures such as family allowances or grants to mothers." As outlined in section 93, employee benefits must include: health care, regular weekly rest ("comprising at least Sunday") and vacation ("once a year or possibly in several shorter periods"), accident insurance, and a pension.

As the primary indirect employer, the state must encourage regional and national balance of productive sectors, just and equitable distribution of social goods, and full employment. Several recommendations are made under each category throughout the post-Leonine period letters.

According to the popes, states must monitor social production. The state "should be present," says John XXIII in *Mater et Magistra*, 20, "to promote in a suitable manner the production of a sufficient supply of material goods." In section 151, he says the principal concern is that "progress in agriculture, industry, and services are made at the same time and in a balanced manner so far as possible." This assures that human beings working in one sector (or living in a region dominated by one sector) benefit by developments in another sector.

The popes' central worry is agriculture. John XXIII thinks the state should ensure that the agricultural sector "absorbs a larger share of industrial output" and a "higher quality of services." In this way, farmers can offer "to the industrial and service sectors of the economy, as well as to the community as a whole, those products which in kind and in quantity better meet consumer needs."[88] As in all its activities, however, the state must recognize the Leonine period principle of subsidiarity, which not only justifies "intervention of public authorities" for the sake of the common good, but also restrains the state from inordinate intervention "in order to allow private citizens themselves to accomplish as much as is feasible."[89]

Beyond production, the state's major responsibility is to establish just and equitable distribution of goods in society. John XXIII summarizes this repeated encyclical teaching in *Mater et Magistra*, 74: "The economic prosperity of any people is to be assessed not so much from the sum total of goods and wealth possessed as from the distribution of goods according to norms of justice." The popes tend to associate the term 'social justice' with this demand for distributional equity.[90]

In the popes' view, the state must facilitate full employment. The "fundamental issue," says John Paul II's *Laborem exercens*, 82, is "finding work, or, in other words, the issue of finding suitable employment for all who are capable of it." This includes, for the first time in encyclical literature, a government obligation to promote employment of emigrants and the disabled. For everyone entering the work force, the state "should see to it that labor agreements are entered into according to the norms of justice and equity."[91]

Employees are alerted to their economic rights and encouraged to participate in the economic affairs of the firm. In addition to the employees' right of association (already recognized in the Leonine period), the popes add rights to work, just wage, safe working conditions, occupations consistent with individual competence, strike, rest, benefits, and pensions. Regarding employee co-management, John XXIII writes in *Mater et Magistra*, 77: "It is very desirable that workers gradually acquire some share in the enterprise by such methods as seem appropriate." In *Laborem exercens*, 67, John Paul II lists such methods as "joint ownership of the means of work, sharing by the workers in the management and-or profits of businesses, so-called shareholding of labor, etc."[92]

Relations between groups representing the broader economic categories of capital and labor receive novel treatment in John Paul II's *Laborem exercens*. Central to this teaching is the pope's parallelization of the terms 'capital' and 'labor' with the concepts 'object' and 'subject.' According to John Paul II, the word 'labor' represents workers as subjective human beings, while the word 'capital' denotes "in the strict sense . . .only a collection of things."[93] On this basis, "we must emphasize and give prominence to the primacy of man in the production process, the primacy of man over things." This is the meaning of the "principle of the priority of labor over capital."[94]

The net of this principle is to merge capitalists and laborers through their shared identity as workers and to motivate mutual interest in economic change. Just as labor cannot "be opposed to capital or capital to labor," says John Paul II, ". . . still less can the actual people behind these concepts be opposed to each other."[95] Regarding motivation for change, the pope makes an unprecedented papal interpretation of history when he says in section 34 that it must be "frankly recognized" that the "impetuous emergence" of the nineteenth century labor movement "was justified from the point of view of social morality." Contemporary economic problems require similarly "daring creative resolves"—but by 'worker' movements of both laborers and capitalists.[96] Such "movements of solidarity," says the pope in section 36, must never be "closed to dialogue and collaboration."

A new feature of encyclical economic teaching during the post-Leonine period is emphasis on equitable distribution and social solidarity between nations. "On a world-wide scale," says John XXIII's *Mater et Magistra*, 37, "governments should seek the economic good of all peoples." According to the popes, developed countries must provide nonopportunistic emergency and infrastructural aid to underdeveloped countries.[97] In *Populorum progressio*, 51, Paul VI suggests establishing a 'world fund' "to be made up of part of the money spent on arms, to relieve the most destitute of the world."

Beyond aid, states and international organizations must promote "a certain equality of opportunity" in world trade between rich and poor nations. According to Paul VI's *Populorum progressio*, 61, "this equality is a long-term objective, but to reach it, we must begin now to create true equality in discussion and negotiations." Eventually, all nations must recognize they are "members of one and the same household."[98]

Finally, the popes introduce three new dimensions to the Church's positive role in economic life. First, they assert a new role for the Church as a global advocate for equitable world distribution and social solidarity. Second, adopting language from the Latin American bishops, John Paul II refers to the Church's "love of preference for the poor."[99] Third, in *Sollicitudo rei socialis*, 31, John Paul II insists that the Church around the world has an obligation to sell "superfluous church ornaments and costly furnishings" when people are in need of "food, drink, clothing, and shelter."

Cultural Ideas and Practices. In some cases, post-Leonine period teaching on cultural life adopts Leonine period instruction; in other instances earlier papal thought is abandoned. Papal recommendations regarding life-style, technology, and group relations follow the former course, while directives on communication, education, and the nature of civilization follow the latter.

Post-Leonine period teaching on communications abandons earlier papal emphasis on censorship and introduces fresh appreciation for open, pluralistic social dialogue. In *Pacem in terris*, 12, John XXIII gives the first encyclical recognition of a human being's right to freedom "in expressing and communicating his opinions."[100] This right entails obligations to maintain "just regard for another's opinions" and communicate "within the limits laid down by the moral order and the common good." The latter duty requires that public media provide "careful, exact, and prudent presentation of the truth." By these means, says John XXIII approvingly, "individuals are enabled to take part in events on a world-wide scale."[101]

On the matter of life-style, the popes repeat their predecessors' recommendations regarding sexuality and leisure. "Conjugal morals," writes Paul VI in *Humanae vitae*, 18, must be defended "in their integral wholeness." This means that sexual relations outside marriage, as well as imposed and artificially infecund marital sex, are prohibited. In *Laborem exercens*, 93, John Paul II makes the first encyclical claim for a worker's right to weekly rest and yearly vacations, though general recognition of the importance of leisure for all human beings occurs throughout post-Leonine period letters.

Papal instruction on both the quantity and the quality of education changes in post-Leonine period letters. In *Mater et Magistra*, 94-95, John XXIII says "advances in technology and science" require that workers develop "greater abilities and professional qualification." As a result, young people should receive "additional years to acquire a basic education and necessary skills."

Like their predecessors, the popes consider education a human right. But in describing this right, the popes reverse earlier encyclical teaching. In *Pacem in terris*, 12, John XXIII recognizes humanity's right to freedom "in searching for truth." In *Ecclesiam suam*, 28, Paul VI notes "the genius and mentality of our contemporaries, who like to explore their minds in depth." While this method sometimes leads to "abstruse, barren, absurd, and wholly fallacious conclusions," the pope considers it "an excellent thing" and "reckoned today as being the highest expression of modern culture."

Progress in science and technology receives ample praise and encouragement in post-Leonine period encyclicals. John XXIII writes: "Advances in science and technology and the prosperity resulting therefrom, are truly to be counted as good things and regarded as signs of the progress of civilization." All such progress, however, must respect not only "the norms of humanity and of the Gospel teaching," but also the "integrity and the cycles of nature" and the "limits of available resources."[102]

General directives concerning group relations in society grow during the post-Leonine period. Papal teaching concerning the social status of women follows Leonine period thought, while new recommendations are advanced concerning dissident groups, ethnic minorities, and socialization.

Though John XXIII's *Pacem in terris*, 41 defends a woman's rights and duties "in domestic and public life," the woman typically described in the encyclicals is a wife and mother. In *Laborem exercens*, 92, John Paul II acknowledges the reality of professional and nonprofessional working women, but warns that they should "fulfill their tasks in accordance with their own nature," without having to abandon "what is specific to them and at the expense of the family, in which women as mothers have an irreplaceable role."[103]

Concerning dissident groups in society, John XXIII borrows and expands an insight first offered by Leo XIII and Pius XI. In *Pacem in terris*, 158-59, the pope says that just as "one must never confuse error and the person who errs" (because the person always "retains his dignity"), "neither can false philosophical teachings regarding the nature, origin and destiny of the universe and of man be identified with historical movements." This is because, writes John XXIII in *Pacem in terris*, 16, "teachings, once they are drawn up and defined, remain always the same, while the movements, working in constantly evolving historical situations," are "subject to changes." Whereas Leo XIII introduced this distinction to lessen the moral culpability of individual freemasons for the errors of freemasonry as a whole (and Pius XI, to distinguish between the Russian people and Soviet communism), John XXIII uses it to permit collaboration between Christians and socialists on beneficial social projects.

The popes sustain Leonine period support for racial equality. "All men," says John XXIII's *Pacem in terris*, 44, "are equal by reason of their natural dignity." Recognition of racial or ethnic equality, however, does not require suppression of group identity. Rather, the pope writes in section 96, civil authorities should

> . . . promote the natural betterment of those citizens belonging to a minority ethnic group, particularly when that concerns their language, the development of their natural gifts, their ancestral customs, and their accomplishments and endeavors in the economic order.

Overall, the post-Leonine period popes encourage a heightened sense of local, national, and international interdependence among individuals and social groups. In what Jerome Kirwin calls the "key passage" of *Mater et Magistra*, John XXIII approvingly observes: "One of the principal characteristics of our time is the multiplication of social relationships, that is, a daily more complex interdependence of citizens."[104]

Finally, the popes abandon the Leonine period identification of high culture with Church-created Western civilization. According to Paul VI's *Populorum progressio*, 39, all nations possess "a civilization handed down by their ancestors." In *Pacem in terris*, 13, John XXIII first recognizes a people's right to enjoy the benefits of their culture. Dominant cultures cannot squash this right because, says Paul VI, no single civilization enjoys "a monopoly of valuable elements." Because "civilizations are born, develop, and die," the Church cannot be "identical with civilization."[105] "The goal," declares John Paul II in *Dives in misericordia*, 150, "toward which all efforts in the cultural and social fields as well as the economic and political fields should tend" is a "'civilization of love.'"

Summary Interpretation

As several contemporary commentators recognize, significant changes occur between the Leonine and post-Leonine period encyclicals. However, commentators frequently miss both the nature of these changes and the fact that this is not the first time a major shift has occurred in papal teaching.

Like the metaphor shift between the pre-Leonine and Leonine periods, repeated use of the dialogical journey metaphor in post-Leonine period letters signals a real shift in papal thought. Newly emphasized are God's features as a dialogical Spirit, the world's physical and cultural features as the context for dialogue in history, and human affective experience as the medium of the Spirit.

Concomitantly, several prior social teachings are reversed. In the area of religious ideas and practices, Roman Catholic laity are encouraged to initiate social action and cooperate in such activities with non-Catholics and non-Christians; in addition, ecumenical dialogue with these latter groups is encouraged. In political life, participatory democracy is granted preferred status, the nondenominational state is practically and theoretically accepted, and an individual's right to exercise freedom of conscience in religion (privately and publicly) is recognized. In economic life, the Hermasian model of relations between rich and poor is definitively abandoned by recognizing almsgiving as a matter of both charity and justice. In cultural life, the popes acknowledge an individual's right to learn through exposure to widely divergent viewpoints, the right to express opinions privately and publicly, and the intrinsic value of non-Western cultures.

Like their forerunners, the post-Leonine period popes are not always internally consistent. Equivocation persists, for example, in the area of civil disobedience. Similarly, the popes are not of one mind on the issue of overpopulation.

At the same time, commonalities persist between Leonine and post-Leonine period teaching. The double-pulsed method of issuing negative judgments and positive recommendations continues. However, Paul Cremona's observation concerning John XXIII's letters could be applied to the entire period: post-Leonine period encyclicals are comparatively less "censorious or pessimistic" than earlier letters.[106]

Regarding encyclical content, breakdown of the community still lies at the heart of papal concerns. In some cases, troublesome practices identified in earlier letters do not reappear, in part a function of the popes' new theological perspectives. For example, the encyclicals no longer explicitly decry intercreedal relations, mixed and civil marriages, public school education, socialist influence over youth, coeducation, or sex education. Other problematic social practices identified in earlier letters are repeated, with new ones added: defection from the priesthood, lack of a world political structure, imposed sexual relations, oppressive family structures, threats to the environment, consumerism, and generational conflict.

Like their predecessors, the popes consider mistaken concepts to be the solvent causing communal erosion. Again, Enlightenment atheism, naturalism, and rationalism are spurned and their varieties identified: the 'death of God' movement, the Enlightenment notion of progress, ethical hedonism. However, some social ideas considered troublesome in earlier periods are not repeated: freedom of conscience in religion, Roman Catholic collaboration with socialists, ecumenism, the religiously neutral state, the centrality of sentiment in marriage, socialism (as distinct from communism, or "Marxist collectivism"), freedom of speech and press, artistic verism and relativism, freedom of instruction, and pedagogical naturalism. Many other social ideas thought dangerous by prior popes are repeated, with new candidates offered: the superpower 'logic of blocs' and both liberal capitalist and Marxist theories of development.

The popes' positive recommendations begin with what Roberto Unger calls an "idea of community."[107] But unlike earlier encyclical forms of territorial and cosmological communitarianism, the post-Leonine period popes offer what can be called an 'affective' communitarian ethic. Here, earlier encyclical commitment to the communal character of self and society continues, but founded primarily on the affective experience of human beings on a dialogical journey, not on an appeal to the requirements of sheepfold survival or the universal design of nature.

The popes understand human identity and purpose as community-dependent. But unlike earlier periods, this dependence is linked to human affectivity. David B. Clark's approach is similar to that of the popes. According to Clark, "the two fundamental 'communal' elements of any social system are a sense of solidarity and a sense of significance." The "sense of solidarity" is the "we-feeling" which contributes to personal identity. The "sense of significance" is the "role-feeling" which contributes to a person's sense of purpose.[108]

In this view, the character of society as a community of mutual aid is less a product of territorial loyalties or cosmological nature than what Unger calls the "political realization of the ideal of sympathy."[109] Because the affective sense of solidarity and significance ultimately depends on personal conversion through the Spirit, the popes mute—but do not utterly destroy—the older encyclical view of society as a hierarchical order of deferential human beings. Thus, the social value of democratic participation is recogized in political, economic, and cultural relations; and recognized in religious and family relations to a greater (though not complete) extent than in earlier encyclical periods.

The popes' positive social recommendations include ideas which change, sustain, or expand on earlier teaching. Changes were identified above. Here, new ideas not overtly inconsistent with earlier papal teaching are listed. Concerning religious ideas and practices, the popes support greater episcopal collegiality, lay participation in the Church, experiential religious education, and Church enrichment through openess to non-Western cultures. In political life, world government and an expanded list of human rights are encouraged. In family life, the popes recognize the role of affectivity in marital relations and the unitive character of sexual relations. In economic life, the papal letters introduce a right to economic initiative, the universal purpose of goods, the subjective character of work, the direct and indirect employer, the priority of labor over capital, a fund for Third World relief, the Church as global advocate for the poor, and Church divestment for the poor. In cultural life, an individual's right to rest and cultural enjoyment is cited, as is the importance of environmental protection.

Finally, a few remarks are in order concerning various commentaries on the post-Leonine period letters. Several commentators observe that the popes generally shift the basis of their social recommendations away from a predominantly natural law moral theory. From the standpoint of this study, Ernest Bartell, John Coleman, J. Bryan Hehir, John Langan, Charles Murphy, and Drew Christiansen are correct in the view that Scripture and patristic sources play a new role in post-Leonine period social thought.[110] Two points, however, must be made.

First, these commentators think encyclical social thought has become more 'theological' with this change in sources. This view is incorrect. Pre-Leonine and Leonine period encyclical teaching is no less theological than post-Leonine period thought; their theologies are simply different. Second, the commentators imply that post-Leonine period changes in source material constitute the first crack in a heretofore stable encyclical teaching. This too is incorrect. By neglecting pre-Leonine period texts, the authors fail to note that encyclical teaching began without use of natural law moral theory and with copious (albeit literalist) reliance on Scripture and patristics.

Other commentators note a methodological shift with the post-Leonine period encyclicals. George Grima, Charles Curran, David Hollenbach, and Marie-Dominique Chenu claim that the post-Leonine period texts employ an inductive method open to the historical 'signs of the times.'[111] In broad terms, this is correct; but two points must be noted.

The Leonine period letters are not as deductively tight as these commentators suggest. A significant number of Leonine period teachings are simply asserted, the product of no syllogistic reasoning from stated premises. Second, contemporary commentators sometimes ascribe to the popes a more plebiscitary understanding of what it means to read the 'signs of the times' than is warranted by the encyclicals. Whatever the popes' new sensitivity to history means, it does not involve commitment to the idea that moral principles and policies are created by ascertaining the numerically predominant will of either the laity or theologians at a given historical moment.

A last group of commentators disagree over whether the conclusions of the post-Leonine period letters constitute a socialistic *apertura a sinistra*, or an overdue appreciation for political and economic liberalism.[112] It is the argument of the present work that the papal encyclicals have persistently offered a communitarian ethic linked to a critique of certain Enlightenment-based notions of God, the world, and humanity. Thus, a social ethic acknowledging the communitarian quality of the self and society and open to the religious dimension of human life would find linkages with papal thought. Conversely, a social ethic denying the communitarian character of self and society on atheistic, naturalistic, or rationalistic grounds would run counter to the encyclical tradition.

But not all commentators would agree that the coherence of encyclical social teaching is located in a shared communitarian social ethic. It is to this issue that the final chapter turns.

NOTES

1.   Dorr, *Option for the Poor*, p. 115.

2.   On catechesis, see John XXIII, *Princeps Pastorum*, 31 and Paul VI, *Ecclesiam suam*, 87, 104. On insubordination, see John XXIII, *Sacerdotii Nostri primordia*, 31. In *Ecclesiam suam*, 51, Paul VI decries the trend toward "emancipation from the authority of wise and lawful superiors" in the Church. In *Sacerdotalis caelibatus*, 1, 5-7, 9, 11, he also reproves clerical protests over celibacy. In *Mysterium Fidei*, 24, Paul VI warns priests against using language during the celebration of the Eucharist that does not follow "dogmatic formulas."

3. Citing findings of the Swiss Pastoral Sociological Institute, Norbert Trippen says that between 1963 and 1970, five percent of the Roman Catholic clergy resigned from the official priesthood. Norbert Trippen, "Developments in the Clergy since 1914," in Adriányi et al., *Modern Age*, p. 341.

4. See John XXIII, *Ad Petri Cathedram*, 99, 144 and Paul VI, *Ecclesiam suam*, 49, 51, *Sacerdotalis caelibatus*, 8, 99.

5. See John XXIII, *Ad Petri Cathedram*, 137, 139, 141, 147 and Paul VI, *Ecclesiam suam*, 42, 101, 103. In *Princeps Pastorum*, 6, 58, John XXIII deplores persecution of the Church in missionary lands.

6. Dunn, *Détente*, pp. 22-46. See also Eric O. Hanson, *The Catholic Church in World Politics* (Princeton, N.J.: Princeton University Press, 1987), pp. 9-13.

7. See John XXIII, *Ad Petri Cathedram*, 31, *Mater et Magistra*, 53, 57-58, *Pacem in terris*, 4, 48, 61, 83, 94-95, 104; Paul VI, *Christi Matri*, 1, *Populorum progressio*, 63, *Humanae vitae*, 17; John Paul II, *Redemptor hominis*, 61, 64-65, *Dives in misericordia*, 110-11, *Dominum et vivificantem*, 47, 60. The popes have in mind oppressive tactics of both communist states and capitalist-inspired military dictatorships. Regarding the latter, for example, Paul VI supports Archbishop Kim's criticism of South Korean President Park, rebukes South Vietnamese President Diem for the persecution of Buddhists, and excommunicates the Paraguayan Minister of the Interior and Chief of Police for torturing political prisoners. See J. Derek Holmes, *The Papacy in the Modern World* (New York: Crossroad, 1981), pp. 244-45.

8. John Paul II, *Redemptor hominis*, 66.

9. On violent excess, see John XXIII, *Princeps Pastorum*, 25 and Paul VI, *Populorum progressio*, 31. On 'principled' violence, see John Paul II, *Dives in misericordia*, 121; and 119. See also Paul VI, *Populorum progressio*, 11, 31. On terrorism, see Paul VI, *Mense maio*, 8 and John Paul II, *Dives in misericordia*, 57, *Sollicitudo rei socialis*, 16, 24. During the rise of international terrorism in the 1970s, Paul VI twice offered himself as a hostage substitute: once for eighty-six people held in a jetliner at Somalia's Mogadishu airport and again for his kidnapped personal friend, former Italian Premier Aldo Moro. Holmes, *Papacy*, p. 247.

10. On excessive nationalism, see Paul VI, *Christi Matri*, 1 and *Populorum progressio*, 62. On weapons production, see John XXIII, *Ad Petri Cathedram*, 27, *Mater et Magistra*, 203, *Pacem in terris*, 109-12, 127-28; Paul VI, *Mense maio*, 6, *Populorum progressio*, 53; John Paul II, *Redemptor hominis*, 57-58, *Dives in misericordia*, 111, 120, *Dominum et vivificantem*, 57, *Sollicitudo rei socialis*, 7, 24. On deterrence, see John XXIII, *Pacem in terris*, 128, and *Mater et Magistra*, 203.

11. John XXIII, *Pacem in terris*, 134; and 135, 140, 200, 202-3. In his commentary on post-Leonine period episcopal documents, Joseph Gremillion (first secretary of the Vatican's Justice and Peace Commission) says: "The age of the sovereign nation-state as principal actor on the world scene is over." *Peace and Justice*, p. 78. See also John Paul II, *Dives in misericordia*, 117.

12. Noonan, *Contraception*, p. 537.

13. Most post-Leonine period criticism of these injustices comes through recounting events which gave rise to Leo XIII's *Rerum novarum*, Pius XI's *Quadragesimo anno*, and Pius XII's various radio addresses. See John XXIII, *Mater et Magistra*, 11, 13, 18, 68, 70, 92, 252; Paul VI, *Populorum progressio*, 21; John Paul II, *Laborem exercens*, 33-34, 48, 91.

14. On exploitation of workers, see John XXIII, *Ad Petri Cathedram*, 133; Paul VI, *Populorum progressio*, 67, 69; and John Paul II, *Laborem exercens*, 81-84. "In certain developing countries," says John Paul II in *Laborem exercens*, 102, "millions of people are forced to cultivate the land belonging to others and are exploited by the big landowners." On employee input, see John XXIII, *Mater et Magistra*, 92 and John Paul II, *Laborem exercens*, 102. On the disabled, see John Paul II, *Laborem exercens*, 104.

15. See John XXIII, *Mater et Magistra*, 13, 35-36, 104, 235, *Pacem in terris*, 87; Paul VI, *Populorum progressio*, 18-19, 26, 49, 53; John Paul II, *Redemptor hominis*, 53, *Dives in misericordia*, 113. Usury is alluded to in Paul VI's complaint against the "overwhelming debts" of developing countries "whose repayment swallows up the greater part of the gain." Paul VI, *Populorum progressio*, 54. In *Mater et Magistra*, 11, John XXIII refers to Leonine period problems of "interest on capital . . . determined purely mechanically by the laws of the marketplace," but suggests nothing regarding the issue's contemporary relevance.

16. On worker violence, see John XXIII, *Mater et Magistra*, 23; and, *Ad Petri Cathedram*, 38. See also John Paul II, *Laborem exercens*, 49. On the precipitation of worker violence, see John XXIII, *Ad Petri Cathedram*, 43; Paul VI, *Populorum progressio*, 30-31, 49; John Paul II, *Laborem exercens*, 48.

17. In *Mater et Magistra*, John XXIII laments abandonment of Sunday labor laws (section 252), the economics of weapons production (section 69), unjust expropriation of property (section 19), and government neglect of workers (section 20). On unemployment, see John XXIII, *Ad Petri Cathedram*, 44, *Mater et Magistra*, 13; John Paul II, *Laborem exercens*, 36-37, 82.

18. On capitalist individualism, see John XXIII, *Mater et Magistra*, 58 and Paul VI, *Populorum progressio*, 33. On capitalist distribution, see John XXIII, *Mater et Magistra*, 68-69, *Pacem in terris*, 63; Paul VI, *Populorum progressio*, 26. In *Mater et Magistra*, 70, John XXIII bemoans the fact that "in the economically developed countries, it frequently happens that great, or sometimes very great, remuneration is had for the performance of some task of lesser importance or doubtful utility." On the devaluation of agriculture, see John XXIII, *Mater et Magistra*, 124.

19. On communist collectivism, see Paul VI, *Populorum progressio*, 33. See also John XXIII, *Mater et Magistra*, 118 and John Paul II, *Laborem exercens*, 50, 71, 83. On communist restriction of liberty, see John XXIII, *Mater et Magistra*, 34; and 57, 69, 83. See also John Paul II, *Laborem exercens*, 41, 50, 68-69.

20. On pollution, see John Paul II, *Redemptor hominis*, 45, 52, *Laborem exercens*, 4, *Sollicitudo rei socialis*, 34. On work, see John Paul II, *Laborem exercens*, 19, 36. See also John XXIII, *Mater et Magistra*, 92. On the threat of technology, see John Paul II, *Redemptor hominis*, 44; and 50. See also John XXIII, *Mater et Magistra*, 198, 204.

21. On agribusiness surplus, see John XXIII, *Mater et Magistra*, 154; and 48, 94, 125. See also John Paul II, *Laborem exercens*, 35. On destruction of produce, see John XXIII, *Mater et Magistra*, 161.

22. On the imbalance between land and citizens, see John XXIII, *Mater et Magistra*, 153 and *Pacem in terris*, 101. See also John Paul II, *Laborem exercens*, 87. On migration, see John XXIII, *Mater et Magistra*, 127; and 140. See also Paul VI, *Populorum progressio*, 9 and John Paul II, *Laborem exercens*, 102.

23. John XXIII, *Mater et Magistra*, 244; and 242-43. On the problem of environmental pollution, see John XXIII, *Pacem in terris*, 111; John Paul II, *Redemptor hominis*, 21, 45, *Laborem exercens*, 4, *Sollicitudo rei socialis*, 34. Some commentators consider the popes' environmental complaints too feeble. Miroslav Volf directs this charge against John Paul II's repeated emphasis in *Laborem exercens* on humanity's duty to "dominate" nature. "On Human Work: An Evaluation of the Key Ideas of the Encyclical 'Laborem Exercens,'" *Scottish Journal of Theology* 37 (1984): 74. See also Stanley Hauerwas, "Work and Co-Creation: A Critique of a Remarkably Bad Idea," in John W. Houck and Oliver F. Williams, eds., *Co-Creation and Capitalism: John Paul II's 'Laborem Exercens'* (Washington, D.C.: University Press of America), pp. 46-47; and Pierre Vallin, "Laborem Exercens," *Etudes* (November 1981): 547. In seeming response to these charges, John Paul II writes in *Sollicitudo rei socialis*, 34: "the dominion granted to man by the Creator is not an

absolute power, nor can one speak of a freedom to 'use and misuse,' or to dispose of things as one pleases."

24. On racism, see Paul VI, *Christi Matri*, 1 and *Populorum progressio*, 66, 72. On abuse of women, see John XXIII, *Pacem in terris*, 41.

25. On the repression of minorities, see John XXIII, *Ad Petri Cathedram*, 133 and *Pacem in terris*, 94-95. On conflict between traditional and industrial cultures, see Paul VI, *Populorum progressio*, 10. On minority backlash, see John XXIII, *Pacem in terris*, 97. On generational conflict, see Paul VI, *Populorum progressio*, 10; and 68.

26. John Paul II, *Redemptor hominis*, 28; Paul VI, *Ecclesium suam*, 99, 104. *Gaudium et spes*, 19-20 differentiates a philosophically systematic atheism from more provisional political, economic, scientific, humanistic, and linguistic forms. The text also includes agnosticism and indifference as forms of atheism. See Walter M. Abbott, ed., *The Documents of Vatican II* (New York: Guild Press, 1966), pp. 215-20.

27. Paul VI, *Ecclesiam suam*, 104. According to *Gaudium et spes*, 19, Christians "can have more than a little to do with the birth of atheism" by neglecting "their own training in religious faith," teaching "erroneous doctrine," and exhibiting deficiencies "in their religious, moral, or social life." Abbott, *Documents of Vatican II*, p. 217.

28. David Tracy, *Blessed Rage for Order: The New Pluralism in Theology* (New York: Seabury Press, 1975), p. 31.

29. On the continuation of earlier diatribes against dissolute moral theories, see John XXIII, *Mater et Magistra*, 205; Paul VI, *Ecclesiam suam*, 48-49; John Paul II, *Dives in misericordia*, 123. On hedonism, see John XXIII, *Mater et Magistra*, 229; and 235. See also John XXIII, *Grata recordatio*, 18. On conscience, see John Paul II, *Dominum et vivificantem*, 43. On abandoning the world, see John XXIII, *Mater et Magistra*, 255.

30. See also John XXIII, *Ad Petri Cathedram*, 18. Consistent with this encyclical development, Jacques Sommet identifies modern religious indifference in this period as, in part, "an experience of emptiness and absence." "Religious Indifference Today," pp. 8-9.

31. On the principle of totality, see Charles, *Social Teaching of Vatican II*, p. 82.

32. On self-interest, see Paul VI, *Populorum progressio*, 26; and 18, 34. John Paul II calls this the "principle of maximum profit" in *Laborem exercens*, 48; and 34. Also see his *Sollicitudo rei socialis*, 37. On automatic justice, see John Paul II, *Laborem exercens*, 34. See also John XXIII, *Mater et Magistra*, 11-12, 23 and Paul VI, *Populorum progressio*, 26.

33. Paul VI, *Populorum progressio*, 58. In *Laborem exercens* 49, John Paul II calls 'liberalism' the "ideology of capitalism" and in *Sollicitudo rei socialis*, 20 refers negatively to "liberal capitalism."

34. On collectivism, see John Paul II, *Laborem exercens*, 64; and 29, 49. On class struggle, see John XXIII, *Mater et Magistra*, 23; and John Paul II, *Laborem exercens*, 49.

35. On the dictatorship of the proletariat, see John Paul II, *Laborem exercens*, 50; and 68-69, 83. See also John XXIII, *Mater et Magistra*, 34, 71 and John Paul II, *Redemptor hominis*, 55. On improper socialization, see John Paul II, *Laborem exercens*, 68; and 71. See also John XXIII, *Mater et Magistra*, 83 and 104.

36. John XXIII, *Mater et Magistra*, 209. On desacralization, see John Paul II, *Dives in misericordia*, 123; and, 109. See also Paul VI, *Ecclesiam suam*, 49, *Populorum progressio*, 41-42; John Paul II, *Dominum et vivificantem*, 56-57.

37. John Paul II, *Dominum et vivificantem*, 2. In section 26 of the same letter, John Paul II describes the teaching of Vatican II as "essentially 'pneumatological.'" See also *Dominum et vivificantem*, 53 and *Redemptor hominis*, 6, 8, 15. The theological importance of the Holy Spirit for Vatican II is most conspicuous in the conciliar documents on ecclesiology (*Lumen gentium*, 9-17, 25), revelation (*Dei verbum*, 9), the world (*Gaudium et spes*, 11, 45), and ecumenism (*Unitas redintegratio*, 2-4). It can be argued that the content

of the council's teaching remained true to its form; that is, the idea of conducting a council was more a consequence of John XXIII's personal "inspiration of the Holy Spirit" than "the implementation of a long prepared plan." See Hubert Jedin, "The Second Vatican Council," in Adriányi et al., *Modern Age*, p. 99. Though the image of God as a dialogue partner predominates in post-Leonine period letters, pastoral and cosmological portraits are not completely abandoned. On Christ as the Good Shepherd, see John Paul II, *Redemptor hominis*, 38. On God as the cosmological "first and final cause of all things," see John XXIII, *Mater et Magistra*, 215, *Grata recordatio*, 18, *Pacem in terris*, 3; Paul VI, *Ecclesiam suam*, 104; John Paul II, *Redemptoris Mater*, 7.

38.   According to Donal Dorr, a "new theology of the world" entered encyclical literature through John XXIII's confident openness to God's spiritual presence in history. *Option for the Poor*, p. 89. George Grima argues that John XXIII was the first pope to "let history speak for itself," rather than "reading history with the aid of a pre-formed historical model." "Method in Social Teaching," *Melita Theologica* 33 (1982): 22. Chenu thinks John XXIII's worldview was more the product of "le sens de l'histoire" than an intellectually developed "théologie de l'histoire." "Ses intuitions," says Chenu, "étaient commandée par une perception réaliste des situations concrètes qui décident de l'aggiornamento' de l'Eglise dans le développement et la variété des civilisations." Chenu, "Les signes des temps: réflexion théologique," in Y. M.-J. Congar and M. Peuchmaurd, eds., *L'église dans le monde de ce temps*, 3 vols. (Paris: Les editions du Cerf, 1967), 2:207. Though this new historical perspective on the world begins and grows during the post-Leonine period, allusions to the Leonine period's architechtonic worldview occasionally recur. See John XXIII, *Pacem in terris*, 2; Paul VI, *Ecclesiam suam*, 104, *Populorum progressio*, 16; John Paul II, *Redemptor hominis*, 23, *Dominum et vivificantem*, 33.

39.   Paul VI, *Ecclesiam Suam*, 50; John Paul II, *Redemptor hominis*, 49, *Sollicitudo rei socialis*, 7. According to Chenu, John XXIII first suggested monitoring the "signs of the times" (Mt 16:3) in his 1961 apostolic constitution *Humanae salutis*, which convoked the Second Vatican Council. Though only appearing as a subtitle in some translations of John XXIII's 1963 *Pacem in terris*, Chenu thinks the encyclical advances interest in the "signs of the times" by stressing the theological importance of analyzing "traits qui caractérisent notre époque." After occurring in Paul VI's 1964 *Ecclesiam suam*, the phrase enters widespread theological use through its appearance in section 4 of Vatican II's pastoral constitution *Gaudium et spes*. Marie-Dominique Chenu, "Les signes des temps," pp. 206-10. Drew Christiansen thinks "discernment of the signs of the times was one of the singular contributions of John's pontificate to modern Roman Catholic social ethics." Drew Christiansen, "On Relative Equality: Catholic Egalitarianism after Vatican II," *Theological Studies* 45 (December 1984), p. 651.

40.   On the Kingdom of God, see Paul VI, *Populorum progressio*, 79, and *Sacerdotalis caelibatus*, 33. See also John XXIII, *Ad Petri Cathedram*, 68, *Pacem in terris*, 168; John Paul II, *Dominum et vivificantem*, 67, *Sollicitudo rei socialis*, 48. Because the world is impaired by sin, neither social stability nor change can be blindly interpreted as expressions of the Spirit; only careful scrutiny discloses God's will in history. In *Ecclesiam suam*, 50, Paul VI cites the 1 Thes 5:21 advice to "test everything." On the world's imperfection, see Paul VI, *Ecclesiam suam*, 58-60; John Paul II, *Redemptor hominis*, 21, *Dominum et vivificantem*, 55. On the world's movement toward God, see John XXIII, *Grata recordatio*, 19, *Mater et Magistra*, 211; John Paul II, *Redemptor hominis*, 69.

41.   Margaret Miles, "Pilgrimage as Metaphor in a Nuclear Age," *Theology Today* 45 (July 1988): 179.

42.   Grima, "Method in Social Teaching," p. 26.

43.   John Paul II, *Dives in misericordia*, 136; *Redemptoris Mater*, 6. The popes do not suggest that emphasis on the role of affectivity and conversion in the act of faith

challenges the Leonine period principle that faith and reason cannot conflict; instead, it highlights the "dialectical nature of human knowledge." John Paul II, *Redemptor hominis*, 48. Wilhelm Weber cites *Pacem in terris*, 36 as evidence that John XXIII made a "genuine breakthrough to new shores" by appreciating the affective and historical dimensions of human knowing. In John XXIII, writes Weber, "truth is no longer a merely possessed, guarded, and authoritatively interpreted objective 'Depositum'"; rather, "truth occurs in the freedom of mankind as a process of truth finding." Wilhelm Weber, "Society and State as a Problem for the Church, " in Adriányi, *Modern Age*, p. 235. This new view of knowledge and truth—profoundly influential at Vatican II—was prepared in post-World War II Europe by 'transcendental Thomists' (e.g. Rahner) and historical theologians (e.g. Chenu and Congar). For these theologians, observes Schoof, "the part played by the Spirit of God, who manifests himself humanly in the grace of the light of faith, is fundamental." Schoof, *Survey of Catholic Theology*, p. 214. See also Gerald A. McCool, "Twentieth-Century Scholasticism," *The Journal of Religion* Supplement 58 (1978): S198-S221.

44. John Paul II, *Dominum et vivficantem*, 59.

45. Ibid., 45. The Latin American bishops' treatment of sin occurs in the Medellín documents on "Justice," 2, "Peace," 1, "Poverty of the Church," 4-5, and in the Puebla document "Evangelization in Latin America's Present and Future," 28, 73, 487. The Medellín documents can be found in Gremillion's *Gospel of Peace and Justice*, pp. 445-76. The Puebla document is in John Eagleson and Philip Scharper, eds., *Puebla and Beyond: Documentation and Commentary*, trans. John Drury (Maryknoll, N.Y., 1979), pp. 123-285. The post-Leonine period view of sin combines Leonine period emphasis on discrete acts of disobedience and Latin American focus on structural sin, with stress on sin as a more general human disposition against the "saving action of the Holy Spirit." See John Paul II, *Dominum et vivificantem*, 36 and 55-56. Leonine period reference to 'intrinsic evil' recurs in Paul VI, *Humanae vitae*, 14. On "physical and moral evil," see John Paul II, *Dives in misericordia*, 100, 115, 125.

46. The popes' association of conscience with the human heart and conversion is juxtaposed with the older, Leonine period association of conscience with reason and law. On conscience, heart, and conversion, see John Paul II, *Redemptor hominis*, 27 and *Dominum et vivificantem*, 31-32, 44-45, 55. On conscience, reason, and law, see John XXIII, *Grata recordatio*, 19, *Pacem in terris*, 5, *Mater et Magistra*, 211, 215; and Paul VI, *Humanae vitae*, 10. The popes' new view of conscience includes "discovery of the way in which the conscience has been conditioned in the course of history." John Paul II, *Dominum et vivificantem*, 44. With regard to moral values, Paul VI makes frequent reference to their "order," "scale," or "hierarchy." These values include "the brotherhood of man, mutual aid, and human compassion." See Paul VI, *Ecclesiam suam*, 104; and 97, 108. See also his *Populorum progressio*, 18 and *Humanae vitae*, 10. On general use of the term 'value,' see John XXIII, *Mater et Magistra*, 176, 245, *Pacem in terris*, 57, John Paul II, *Redemptor hominis*, 29, *Slavorum apostoli*, 18.

47. John Paul II, *Dominum et vivificantem*, 60. Nowhere do the popes suggest a theoretical discordance in joining this new emphasis on affectivity and value with the earlier papal focus on reason and law. In the mind of John Paul II, writes George Hunston Williams, "value is an objective ethical and aesthetic standard grounded in reality," no less than the natural law. George Huntston Williams, *The Mind of John Paul II: Origins of His Thought and Action* (New York: Seabury Press, 1981), p. 69. On moral objectivity, see Paul VI, *Ecclesiam suam*, 41, *Humanae vitae*, 10, 16 and John Paul II, *Dominum et vivificantem*, 43. Post-Leonine period references to the natural and eternal law occur in John XXIII, *Pacem in terris*, 28, 81, 160; Paul VI, *Humanae vitae*, 4, 12; and John Paul II, *Dominum et vivificantem*, 36.

48.   See Paul VI, *Ecclesiam suam*, 41, *Christi Matri*, 9, *Sacerdotalis caelibatus*, 18, 41, 44-45, 57-59, 96; John Paul II, *Dives in misericordia*, 94, *Slavorum apostoli*, 16, *Redemptoris Mater*, 5-6, 25, 27, 37. Though current in post-World War II theological discussion, the concept of the Church as the 'pilgrim People of God' entered general religious discourse through its appearance in *Lumen gentium*, the Second Vatican Council document on the Church. Here, John Paul II (then Cardinal Wojtyla) made a decisive contribution by suggesting that the document introduce the ecclesiological concept of the 'People of God' before treating the hierarchical nature of the Church. See Williams, *Mind of John Paul II*, p. 169.

49.   John Paul II, *Redemptoris Mater*, 6.

50.   Patrick Granfield, *The Limits of the Papacy: Authority and Autonomy in the Church* (New York: Crossroad, 1987), p. 175. In sections 15 and 16 of Vatican II's *Lumen gentium* (under the chapter entitled 'The People of God'), the council fathers discuss the Spirit's presence within both Christian communities outside the Roman Catholic Church and non-Christian communities. This discussion is theologically dependent on the prior section 8 which states that the Church of Christ "subsists in the Catholic Church . . . although many elements of sanctification and of truth can be found outside her visible structure." Responding to controversy over the words *subsistit in*, Cardinal Johannes Willebrands (architect and later director of the Vatican Secretariat for Promoting Christian Unity) says this phrase was self-consciously chosen by the council fathers to broaden the older, Leonine period claim, which held that "the church of God in this world 'est' the Catholic Church." Johannes Willebrands, "Vatican II's Ecclesiology of Communion," *Origins* 17 (28 May, 1987): 30. " 'Subsistit in' thus allows emphasizing," Willebrands says, "both the conviction that the one and genuine church of God is found in the Catholic Church and the certitude that it nonetheless extends, though lacking its fullness, beyond the Catholic Church." Ibid., p. 32. Also see the conciliar document on ecumenism, *Unitas Redintegratio*, 3-4.

51.   On papal authority, see John XXIII, *Aeterna Dei sapientia*, 43-44. Beyond its juridical authority, the popes stress the symbolic value of the papal office as "the visible center of the church's unity." John Paul II, *Slavorum apostoli*, 13. See also Paul VI, *Ecclesiam suam*, 110. On clerical obedience, see John XXIII, *Aeterna Dei sapientia*, 103; Paul VI, *Ecclesiam suam*, 114, and *Humanae vitae*, 28. In *Sacerdotalis caelibatus*, 13-14, Paul VI insists on clerical obedience of celibacy regulations.

52.   On lay participation, see John Paul II, *Redemptor hominis*, 12. On the gift of the Spirit, see John Paul II, *Dominum et vivificantem*, 25. John Paul II's association of charismatic gifts with the laity is taken from Vatican II's *Lumen gentium*, 12. In a related conceptual shift, the popes consider the "living heritage of the original apostolic tradition" preserved within both the papal magisterium and the Church as a whole. Paul VI, *Ecclesiam suam*, 46; John Paul II, *Redemptor hominis*, 34.

53.   John XXIII, *Ad Petri Cathedram*, 116; and 121. See also John XXIII, *Princeps Pastorum*, 28, 43-45. The last mention of Catholic Action in encyclical literature occurs in Paul VI's *Ecclesiam suam*, 116. For general remarks on social activity, see John XXIII, *Mater et Magistra*, 241, 256-57. In section 259, the pope encourages clerical involvement in social action. In *Ad Petri Cathedram*, 111-14, John XXIII praises the social work of religious women.

54.   John XXIII, *Pacem in terris*, 160. Consistent with Leonine period teaching, the hierarchical magisterium reserves the right to intervene as the authentic interpreter of "all the moral law, not only that is, of the law of the gospel, but also of the natural law." Paul VI, *Humanae vitae*, 4; and 18. In *Redemptor hominis*, 76, John Paul II defines the magisterium as "the bishops joined by the bond of hierarchical communion with Peter's successor."

55. On passivity, see John XXIII, *Princeps Pastorum*, 31. On the teaching of Catholic social thought, John XXIII, *Mater et Magistra*, 222-23.

56. Prior to Vatican II, John XXIII's *Ad Petri Cathedram*, 71 repeated Pius XII's statement that matters defined by the episcopal magisterium as "absolutely certain" are closed to theological discussion. After Vatican II, this claim does not reappear.

57. On missionary social work, see John XXIII, *Princeps Pastorum*, 22 and Paul VI, *Populorum progressio*, 12. On indigenous cultures, see John XXIII, *Ad Petri Cathedram*, 109, *Princeps Pastorum*, 16, 18, 23, *Mater et Magistra*, 181; John Paul II, *Redemptor hominis*, 3, *Slavorum apostoli*, 11-13, 26. On native clergy, see John XXIII, *Princeps Pastorum*, 13-15, 17.

58. *Catholic Encyclopaedia*, Supplement, vol. 16, s.v. "Missionary Adaptation," by J. Boberg. See the conciliar documents *Ad gentes*, 22, *Lumen gentium*, 13, *Gaudium et spes*, 58.

59. Paul VI, *Ecclesiam suam*, 109; and 112. See the Vatican II document on ecumenism, *Unitas redintegratio*, 3-6. Encouraging Christian ecumenism and dialogue with non-Christians, the Vatican established the Secretariat for Promoting Christian Unity in 1960 and the Secretariat for Non-Christians in 1964. The Secretariat for Unbelievers was established in 1966.

60. John Paul II, *Redemptor hominis*, 38. In section 15, the pope notes, however, that these activities cannot involve "giving up or in any way diminishing the treasures of divine truth that the church has constantly confessed and taught."

61. In section 76 of *Pacem in terris*, John XXIII says "the governing powers are to be *designated*" (italics mine). This recalls the Leonine period concern that popular elections be understood as the citizen's identification of God's power in the chosen ruler and not a transfer of power possessed by the citizenry itself. In this way, the popes distinguish their understanding of participatory democracy from majoritarian interpretations which hold that "the power of bare popular majorities to take any government action that they choose be subject to no limitations other than those imposed—and removable—by such majorities." Austin Ranney, *The Governing of Men*, 3d ed. (New York: Holt, Rinehart and Winston, 1971), p. 81. In sections 68-69, the pope says "it is in keeping with the innate demands of human nature that the state should take the form which embodies the threefold division of powers corresponding to the three principal functions of public authority." This constitutes the first recognition of the principle of separation of powers in encyclical literature (during the pre-Leonine period, Montesquieu's *L'esprit des lois*—the most authoritative and thorough discussion of this theory—was placed on the Index of Forbidden Books).

62. John XXIII, *Pacem in terris*, 67. It is the model of the "democratic-social state founded on law," comments Pietro Pavan, toward which John XXIII "turns all his social-political thinking." Pietro Pavan, "Ecumenism and Vatican II's Declaration on Religious Freedom," in Walter J. Burghardt, ed., *Religious Freedom: 1965 and 1975, A Symposium on a Historic Document* (New York: Paulist Press, 1977), p. 29. In an astute observation, Walter Burghardt considers this preference for participatory democracy a "fascinating turnabout from the Catholic vision before 1965." At that time, "the Catholic state was the ideal, was doctrine, a secular or a democratic-social state was the contingently historical"; now, "the democratic-social state is 'doctrine,' the confessional state at best tolerable." Walter Burghardt, "Critical Reflections," in ibid., p. 70. George Weigel's claim that John Paul II's defense of democracy takes papal thought in a "significantly different direction" misses the fact that John XXIII already effected this change. George Weigel, "The Democracy Connection," in Kenneth A. Myers, ed., *Aspiring to Freedom: Commentaries on John Paul II's Encyclical 'The Social Concerns of the Church'* (Grand Rapids, Mich.: William B. Eerdmans Pub., 1988), p. 123.

63. Weber, "Society and State," p. 240.

64. Paul VI, *Populorum progressio*, 37; and *Humanae vitae*, 23. In "The Church and the Population Year: Notes on a Strategy," *Theological Studies* 35 (March 1974) :75-81, Bryan Hehir says Paul VI's *Humanae vitae* condemnation of artificial contraception should be distinguished from his discussion of population control in *Populorum progressio*. On this basis, while papal condemnation of contraception is unequivocal with regard to the personal morality of Roman Catholics, Hehir thinks an opening exists in papal thought for support of contraception as a state policy addressing overpopulation. However, the popes' repeated appeals for government "conformity with the moral law" (meaning, no encouragement of artificial contraception) makes Hehir's interpretation of encyclical teaching untenable. See John XXIII, *Mater et Magistra*, 193; Paul VI, *Populorum progressio*, 37, and *Humanae vitae*, 17, 23.

65. See also John XXIII, *Grata recordatio*, 16, *Pacem in terris*, 114, 126; Paul VI, *Christi Matri*, 5. In "*Pacem in Terris*: An Analysis," *World Justice* 6 (September 1964): 34, Peter Riga thinks the claim that John XXIII banned nuclear war is a "misrepresentation of the Pope's thought." "In theory," he says, "there could conceivably be a moral use of nuclear weapons in certain circumstances." By assuming John XXIII accepts the just war theory, Riga imports it into his interpretation of *Pacem in terris*. However, no explicit reference to the just war theory is ever made in this or any other papal encyclical. Yoder is correct when he writes: "There has never been a normative proclamation or promulgation by a synod or a pope, speaking 'ex cathedra' or otherwise, to make the acceptance of this doctrine [just war theory] necessary for Catholics." John Howard Yoder, *When War Is Unjust: Being Honest in Just-War Thinking*, with an introduction by Charles P. Lutz (Minneapolis, Minn.: Augsburg Publishing House, 1984), pp. 33-34.

66. On state aid, see John XXIII, *Pacem in terris*, 121; and 101. See also John XXIII, *Mater et Magistra*, 157, 161, 174; Paul VI, *Populorum progressio*, 35, 54; John Paul II, *Sollicitudo rei socialis*, 19, 32. On political domination, see John XXIII, *Pacem in terris*, 125; and 92. See also John XXIII, *Mater et Magistra*, 171, and Paul VI, *Populorum progressio*, 65. On citizen awareness, see John XXIII, *Pacem in terris*, 84; and *Ad Petri Cathedram*, 136. See also Paul VI, *Populorum progressio*, 67, 69, 83.

67. John XXIII, *Pacem in terris*, 141-42; and 137-39, 144-45. In section 137, John XXIII says the moral order of the world "demands that such a form of public authority be established." According to Riga, the pope makes support for the United Nations "a matter of conscience" for Roman Catholics. Riga, "*Pacem in Terris*: An Analysis," p. 41. See also Paul VI, *Populorum progressio*, 64, 78, *Humanae vitae*, 23; John Paul II, *Sollicitudo rei socialis*, 43. The popes still acknowledge an individual state's right of sovereignty. See John XXIII, *Ad Petri Cathedram*, 30, *Grata recordatio*, 15, *Mater et Magistra*, 174, *Pacem in terris*, 42, 51, 80, 86, 92; Paul VI, *Populorum progressio*, 54; John Paul II, *Redemptor hominis*, 59, 64.

68. Bryan Hehir, "Church and State: Basic Concepts for an Analysis," *Origins* 8 (30 November 30 1978): 377-79. Williams notes that John Paul II supported the work of John Courtney Murray (architect of *Dignitatis humanae*) during the council. *Mind of John Paul II*, pp. 176-77. See also Jedin, "Second Vatican Council," p. 128. A single reference to the distinction between Church and state occurs in Paul VI's *Populorum progressio*, 13: "The two realms are distinct, just as the two powers, ecclesiastical and civil, are supreme, each in its own domain."

69. See John XXIII, *Pacem in terris*, 50-51, 61, 73. See also Paul VI, *Populorum progressio*, 30. Gudorf suggests John XXIII's *Pacem in terris*, 53 citation of Aquinas' *Summa Theologica* I, II, q. 93, a. 3 ("a wicked law . . . is rather a kind of violence") constitutes a "milestone in the social teaching" because it signals papal recognition of "structural or institutionalized violence." *Liberation Themes*, p. 223. John Paul II employs the phrase 'unjust structures' with regard to economic life in *Laborem exercens*, 9.

70. See also Paul VI, *Populorum progressio*, 51. Though the pope's remarks are descriptive rather than prescriptive, "the parenthesis is clearly meant to suggest that in certain extreme situations a revolution might be justified." Dorr, *Option for the Poor*, p. 147. "Faced with the same ultimate choice as that which faced Leo XIII," says Dorr, "Pope Paul [like Pius XII] refused to take the same position." Ibid., p. 148. Gudorf claims Paul VI's approach "assumes much more importance" than Pius XII's because the former pope's "implicit approval of violence in some limited situations" is "on the side of *leftist* movements," whereas the latter pope's approval was given to a "rightist, anti-revolutionary movement." *Liberation Themes*, p. 189.

71. On freedom and obligation, see John XXIII, *Pacem in terris*, 34; and 35. On freedom and truth, see John Paul II, *Redemptor hominis*, 35; and 36, 39.

72. Ph. J. André-Vincent, 'À propos de l'enseignement pontifical et des droits de l'homme," *La pensée catholique* 185 (March-April 1980): 92. Also see his "Les droits de l'homme condamné en 1789," in the same number, pp. 84-90. For papal support of the UN Declaration, see John XXIII, *Pacem in terris*, 143-44 and John Paul II, *Redemptor hominis*, 62-63. On rights and human nature, see John XXIII, *Pacem in terris*, 143-44 and John Paul II, *Laborem exercens*, 72. For general acknowledgments of "fundamental human rights," see John XXIII, *Ad Petri Cathedram*, 40, *Mater et Magistra*, 55, 211, *Pacem in terris*, 75, 79; Paul VI, *Mense maio*, 12, *Christi Matri*, 6, *Populorum progresso*, 33; John Paul II, *Redemptor hominis*, 61, 63, *Dives in misericordia*, 121, *Laborem exercens*, 81. In *Redemptor hominis*, 65, John Paul II notes that, historically, human rights "reached formulation on the international level in the middle of our century."

73. The popes repeat earlier papal claims for rights to property (John XXIII, *Pacem in terris*, 21), necessary goods (sections 11, 29), education (sections 13, 17), life and bodily integrity (sections 11, 29), association (sections 23, 27; and John Paul II, *Laborem exercens*, 94, 99), political participation (John XXIII, *Pacem in terris*, 26; and John Paul II, *Redemptor hominis*, 64), work (John XXIII, *Mater et Magistra*, 55, *Pacem in terris*, 18; and John Paul II, *Laborem exercens*, 82, 84-85, 102, 105—including the disabled), and marriage (John XXIII, *Pacem in terris*, 15; Paul VI, *Populorum progressio*, 37, and John Paul II, *Laborem exercens*, 42). Compared with the Leonine period, the popes expand the meanings of 'necessary goods' and the right to education. For John XXIII, goods necessary for a humane life include: food, clothing, shelter, rest, medical care, social services, and security in case of illness, work-related injury, widowhood, old age, and unemployment. John XXIII, *Pacem in terris*, 11. The right to education includes not only adolescent instruction, but also technical and professional training of qualified adults. Ibid., 13. On the new rights recognized by the popes, see John XXIII, *Pacem in terris*, 12-13, 15, 18-20, 25, 27, 29, 62-63, 77, 100, 106, 144; John Paul II, *Laborem exercens*, 71, 93, 100, 107. Though it can be inferred, the Leonine period popes never explicitly say the worker has a 'right' to a just wage. What the popes insist on is the employer's moral obligation to pay a just wage consistent with company survival. Similarly, the post-Leonine period popes are the first to state good working conditions as an explicit 'right,' beyond earlier papal exhortations on the employer's moral obligation to provide such conditions.

74. Pavan's view is stated in "Ecumenism and Vatican II," 13-14. Burghardt's position is in "Critical Reflections" p. 72. Pavan's approach is maintained in Brian W. Harrison, "Vatican II and Religious Liberty: Contradiction or Continuity?," *Social Justice Review* (July-August 1989): 104-12 and Thomas Storck, "The Problem of Religious Liberty," *Faith and Reason* 15 (Spring 1989): 59-67. On papal recognition of the right to freedom of conscience in religion, see also John Paul II, *Redemptor hominis*, 66 and *Sollicitudo rei socialis*, 33.

75. Paul VI, *Sacerdotalis caelibatus*, 20; and *Humanae vitae*, 8. See also John Paul II, *Dives in misericordia*, 149. On holiness and indissolubility as fundamental marks of

marriage, see John XXIII, *Ad Petri Cathedram*, 52, *Mater et Magistra*, 193, *Pacem in terris*, 16; Paul VI, *Populorum progressio*, 36; John Paul II, *Dives in misericordia*, 123. Theodore Mackin thinks the conciliar document *Gaudium et spes* and Paul VI's *Humanae vitae* elevate mutual love to a *pars essentialis* of Christian marriage, beyond its previous status as a *pars integrans* (recognized since Pius XI's *Casti connubii*). Theodore Mackin, "Conjugal Love and the Magisterium," *The Jurist* 36 (1976): 286.

76. Paul VI, *Humanae vitae*, 8. See also John XXIII, *Mater et Magistra*, 195. According to Mackin, the "rejection of the hierarchy of ends" and the association of mutual love with procreation and education of children first occurred on the episcopal level in Vatican II's *Gaudium et spes*, 50. Conciliar debate over this change was "deservedly bitter because it meant rejection of the definition of marriage in *Casti connubii.*" "Conjugal Love," p. 270.

77. Noonan, *Contraception*, p. 537. Noonan correctly observes that "never before had it [expression of love as a purpose of sexual intercourse] been taught by an ecumenical council or by a papal encyclical."

78. Paul VI, *Humanae vitae*, 10. Noonan claims this overt focus on the couple's prerogatives concerning parenthood "was new." *Contraception*, p. 538-39.

79. See also John XXIII, *Mater et Magistra*, 193. Post-Leonine period letters are the first to claim the sacred "life of man" begins "from its inception." See John XXIII, *Mater et Magistra*, 194; and John Paul II, *Dives in misericordia*, 123. According to Paul VI, avoiding artificial contraception preserves not only the procreative meaning of conjugal love, but also the unitive meaning. By pursuing the "honest practice of regulation of birth," couples acquire "solid convictions concerning the true values of life," "self-mastery," "attention for one's partner," and "a deeper and more efficacious influence in the education of their offspring." Paul VI, *Humanae vitae*, 21. Citing Lk 2:34 ("a sign of contradiction"), the pope acknowledges this teaching is countercultural. Ibid., 18.

80. Paul VI, *Humanae vitae*, 14. Preoccupied with the papal discussion of artificial contraception, Richard McCormick thinks no development has occurred "in the area of the Church's approach to familial and sexual morality." This is incorrect; significant developments occur in the post-Leonine literature regarding the nature and purpose of marriage and the meaning of sexual love. Richard A. McCormick, *Notes on Moral Theology 1981 through 1984* (Lanham, Md.: University Press of America, 1984), p. 80. Kenneth R. Overberg has a better grasp of the issue when he points out the "dichotomy" in contemporary encyclical teaching between, on the one hand, an appreciation for the role of human experience and affectivity in moral reasoning and, on the other hand, an insistence that sexual morality be governed by "the essential order of nature and the physical structure of sexuality." Kenneth R. Overberg, *An Inconsistent Ethic?: Teachings of the American Catholic Bishops* (Lanham, Md.: University Press of America, 1980), p. 177.

81. John Paul II, *Sollicitudo rei socialis*, 15. Peter L. Berger is incorrect when he says John Paul II's discussion of economic initiative is "the first time that a papal encyclical has . . . come close to affirming the value of free enterprise." Peter L. Berger, "Empirical Testings," in Myers, *Aspiring to Freedom*, p. 112. In his enthusiasm over John Paul II's "right of economic initiative," Michael Novak claims this is "the linchpin of John Paul II's theological vision of a good economic order." Michael Novak, "The Development of Nations," in Myers, *Aspiring to Freedom*, p. 84. However, careful reading of John Paul II's encyclical corpus does not bear this out.

82. See also Paul VI, *Populorum progressio*, 23; and John Paul II, *Laborem exercens*, 65. In "The Problem of Poverty and the Poor in Catholic Social Teaching: A Marxist Perspective," in Curran and McCormick, *Readings in Moral Theology No. 5*, p. 308, József Lukàcs says Paul VI's "statement of the possibilities of expropriation is certainly something new."

83.   John Paul II, *Laborem exercens*, 23; and 13, 24, 40, 46, 73. See also John XXIII, *Mater et Magistra*, 125. John Paul II considers work a duty "both because the Creator has commanded it" and because humanity "requires work in order to be maintained and developed." John Paul II, *Laborem exercens*, 73; and 72. In his study of the relationship between the thought of Karl Marx and John Paul II, Gregory Baum observes that "it was Karl Marx . . . who introduced man's self-definition through labor into European philosophy." Gregory Baum, *The Priority of Labor: A Commentary on "Laborem exercens," Encyclical Letter of Pope John Paul II* (New York: Paulist Press, 1982) p. 12. Dorr notes, however, that John Paul II "takes a much broader view of what is meant by 'work' than is common in the Marxist tradition." Beyond manual activity in industry, the pope's conception "is one of *homo faber*—the human person as a 'maker,' " in all areas of life. *Option for the Poor*, p. 267.

84.   John Paul II, *Laborem exercens*, 113; and 13, 15, 42-44, 114-15, 117. See also Paul II, *Populorum progressio*, 22. Miroslav Volf says "contrary to LE [*Laborem exercens*], the Bible does not see man's work in correspondence to God's work." "Human work," p. 68, n. 17. Stanley Hauerwas registers the same complaint in "Work as Co-Creation," pp. 44-47.

85.   Paul VI, *Populorum progressio*, 23; and 49. See also, John Paul II, *Sollicitudo rei socialis*, 28, 39. Valentine N. Handwerker notes this change in papal interpretation of almsgiving in " 'Take of your substance, and not just of your abundance'; The Modern Catholic Social Tradition on the Distribution of Surplus Wealth" (Ph.D. dissertation, Lateran University, Rome, 1981), p. 46.

86.   Paul VI, *Populorum progressio*, 47; and *Ecclesiam suam*, 55. See also John XXIII, *Ad Petri Cathedram*, 127-28 and *Mater et Magistra*, 79. In *Ad Petri Cathedram*, 42, John XXIII states approvingly that "the distances which separate the classes of society are shrinking." He also thinks "anyone who is diligent and capable has the opportunity to rise to higher levels of society." Drew Christiansen claims the popes' new emphasis on social equality represents a change from Leonine period thought. "On Relative Equality," pp. 651-52. Gudorf makes the same point in *Liberation Themes*, p. 44. A remnant of the Leonine period notion of natural inequality occurs in John XXIII, *Ad Petri Cathedram*, 37.

87.   On the spirit of solidarity, see Paul VI, *Populorum progressio*, 43; and John XXIII, *Mater et Magistra*, 211. Baum's remark in *Priority of Labor*, p. 70, captures the pope's sentiment: "It seems to me that there is no wholly secular reason for universal solidarity . . . it is only out of faith in the unity of man, out of a sacred sense of solidarity, out of a religious awareness that we are all brothers and sisters, that people commit themselves to justice on a world scale." On solidarity in action, see Paul VI, *Populorum progressio*, 1; and 43. See also John XXIII, *Ad Petri Cathedram*, 45 and *Pacem in terris*, 32. "There is a unity and focus to postconciliar social teaching," says Christiansen, "which can only be appreciated if solidaristic equality is seen to lie at the center of the teaching." "Relative Equality," p. 653. Christiansen identifies the source of this new encyclical thinking in the Vatican II retrieval of "the patristic conception of human solidarity." Ibid., p. 661. But because patristic texts are not uniform on this point (see *Shepherd of Hermas*), the source (such as John Chrysostom or Ambrose) should be specified.

88.   John XXIII, *Mater et Magistra*, 129. In this letter, John XXIII draws a long list of rural needs: roads, transportation, marketing centers, water, housing, medical care, education, recreational facilities, religious care, home furnishings, improvement in productive technology, just taxes, insurance, financing, price protection, farmer associations and cooperatives. Ibid., 127-28, 132-35, 137, 140-43, 146. See also John Paul II, *Laborem exercens*, 101, 103.

89.   On state intervention, see John XXIII, *Mater et Magistra*, 53; and 99, 117, 147. On state restraint, see ibid., 152; and 117, 144, 151. See also John XXIII, *Pacem in terris*, 65;

Paul VI, *Populorum progressio*, 33. In *Liberation Themes*, pp. 27-29 and 126, Gudorf thinks John XXIII shifts the principle of subsidiarity from its Leonine period meaning as a brake on state activity to a justification for state intervention. Gudorf's view unduly downplays both the degree to which the Leonine period popes understood subsidiarity as a warrant for state intervention and the repeated emphasis in post-Leonine period letters on subsidiarity as protecting local, nongovernmental initiative.

90.   See John XXIII, *Mater et Magistra*, 73; John Paul II, *Laborem exercens*, 37, 96. In *Populorum progressio*, Paul VI reserves the term 'social justice' for equity between nations. In "Uses and Misuses of the Term 'Social Justice'," Paulus complains that melding social and distributive justice obfuscates the authentic meaning of the former term, which—in his view—is equivalent with Aquinas' notion of general justice. As such, social justice should not be employed as a "principal ethical tool when dealing with specific moral issues in the realm of the economy," but "used exclusively to relate issues directly to the common good [which concerns not only economic life, but also religious, political, family, and cultural affairs]." John XXIII's association of social justice with international "juridical order" in *Mater et Magistra*, 40 is closer to Paulus' understanding of the term.

91.   On migrants and disabled, see John Paul II, *Laborem exercens*, 104-5, 107-9. On labor agreements, see John XXIII, *Mater et Magistra*, 21.

92.   In *Laborem exercens*, 4, John Paul II calls for a "reordering and adjustment of the structures of the modern economy." The pope's vision of a just economic system entails workplace decentralization and national planning, with intermediate associations linking the two. For a description of John Paul II's economic model, see Baum, *Priority of Labor*, pp. 86-87. Though specifically referring to John XXIII, George Higgins is correct when he observes that Pius XI's vocational group theory of economic organization still has a lingering influence over papal thought in the post-Leonine period. George G. Higgins, "Issues of Justice and Peace," *Chicago Studies* 20 (Summer 1981): 200-202. See John XXIII, *Ad Petri Cathedram*, 40, *Mater et Magistra*, 37, 67, *Pacem in terris*, 24; Paul VI, *Populorum progressio*, 32-33, 44.

93.   John Paul II, *Laborem exercens*, 57; and 52, 55-56, 59, 66. In his commentary on *Laborem exercens*, Michael Novak claims John Paul II's definition of capital "is severely limited." "Capital, too," Novak insists, "has its subjective, moral, and humanistic dimension." Michael Novak, "Creation Theology," in Houck and Williams, eds., *Co-Creation and Capitalism*, pp. 23-25.

94.   On the primacy of humanity, see John Paul II, *Laborem exercens*, 57; and 60. On the priority of labor over capital, see section 52; and 55, 58, 62, 70, 109. There is nothing in prior encyclical literature directly supporting John Paul II's claim in section 52 that the principle of the priority of labor over capital "has always been taught by the church."

95.   Ibid., 58. This statement recalls Leo XIII's words in *Rerum novarum*, 19: "Capital cannot do without labor, nor labor without capital." Unlike John Paul II, however, Leo XIII uses the word 'capital' to signify a social class. Leo XIII's point is not to amalgamate the classes, but to counsel patience that all may "dwell in harmony and agreement, so as to maintain the balance of the body politic."

96.   Based on the pope's support for labor unrest and movements of worker solidarity in the nineteenth century, Baum concludes: "The conflictual view of modern society . . . was fully endorsed by Pope John Paul II in his *Laborem exercens* (1981)." Gregory Baum, "Class Struggle and the Magisterium: A New Note," *Theological Studies* 45 (December 1984): 693. Baum goes on to suggest four elements which differentiate John Paul II's notion of social action from the Marxist theory of class struggle. The pope supports (1) success through cooperation, not class victory, (2) motivation through neighbor love, not resentment, (3) tactics of dialogue and honest confrontation, not violence,

(4) change as a way to correct specific problems, not as a self-justifying dynamic behind a world-historical movement. Ibid., pp. 697-701.

97.   On emergency aid, see John XXIII, *Mater et Magistra*, 80, 158, 161, *Pacem in terris*, 121; Paul VI, *Populorum progressio*, 49. On infrastructural aid, see John XXIII, *Mater et Magistra*, 163; Paul VI, *Populorum progressio*, 48; John Paul II, *Sollicitudo rei socialis*, 9, 26, 39. On the importance of nonopportunistic aid, see John XXIII, *Mater et Magistra*, 170-71, 173.

98.   John XXIII, *Mater et Magistra*, 157; and 155. See also John XXIII, *Ad Petri Cathedram*, 23, 27, 40, *Grata recordatio*, 12, John Paul II, *Redemptor hominis*, 54.

99.   John Paul II, *Redemptoris Mater*, 37; and *Laborem exercens*, 37, *Sollicitudo rei socialis*, 42. The Latin American bishops use the language of "preferential option" in their Medellín documents ("Poverty of the Church," 9) and Puebla document (section 1134). See Gremillion, *Gospel of Peace and Justice*, p. 474; and Eagleson and Scharper, *Puebla and Beyond*, p. 264. From these documents and the theological discussion they have generated in Central and South America, it is fair to claim that the Latin American "option for the poor" means at least the following five things in a descending order of priority: (1) a commitment to radical social change founded on an unqualified rejection of the structural injustices perpetuated by liberal capitalists and totalitarian Marxists; (2) an anticipation of social conflict in view of this commitment; (3) an adoption of lifestyles in solidarity with the poor; (4) a commitment to working and living with the poor with the primary goal of *concientización*; (5) an experience of personal religious conversion through direct action with the poor. See Michael J. Schuck, "The Bishops' Letter, Loyola University, and the Urban Poor," in James D. Barry, ed., *The Catholic University and the Urban Poor: The 1987 Loyola Symposium on Values and Ethics* (Chicago: Loyola University Press, 1988), pp. 59-68. John Paul II refers to both a "preferential option for the poor" and a "love of preference for the poor." The latter phrase first appeared in the Congregation for the Doctrine of the Faith's document "Instruction on Christian Freedom and Liberation," 66-70, in *Origins* (17 April 1986): 723-24. Though it meant to signal the Congregation's difficulties with certain interpretations of the Latin American concept of "preferential option," there is nothing in John Paul II's encyclical corpus suggesting his disagreement with the five points noted above.

100.   See also John XXIII, *Pacem in terris*, 29 and 144. This right to freedom of expression also includes "pursuit of art." Ibid., 12. In a related development, the Congregation for the Doctrine of the Faith declared on June 14, 1966 that the Index of Forbidden Books and its penalties of excommunication no longer had the force of law in the Church.

101.   On regard for others' opinions, see John XXIII, *Ad Petri Cathedram*, 29. On moral limits, see John XXIII, *Pacem in terris*, 12. On public media, see John XXIII, *Ad Petri Cathedram*, 12. See also Paul VI, *Populorum progressio*, 83. On world events, see John XXIII, *Mater et Magistra*, 61.

102.   On the norms of humanity, see John XXIII, *Mater et Magistra*, 256. See also Paul VI, *Populorum progressio*, 19; John Paul II, *Redemptor hominis*, 46, *Dives in misericordia*, 103-4, *Laborem exercens*, 21, *Dominum et vivificantem*, 60. On the limits of nature, see John Paul II, *Sollicitudo rei socialis*, 26.

103.   See also John XXIII, *Pacem in terris*, 19; John Paul II, *Laborem exercens*, 91. In their commentary on *Laborem exercens*, Andrea Lee and Amata Miller say "the Pope's idea that, in most cases, quality of life for women is attained by being wife and mother is resisted by feminists." Andrea Lee and Amata Miller, "Feminist Themes and 'Laborem Exercens,' " in Curran and McCormick, eds., *Readings in Moral Theology No. 5*, p. 427. It is noteworthy, however, that the post-Leonine period letters—unlike the Leonine period texts—contain no explicit criticism of the women's emancipation movement.

104.   Jerome R. Kirwin, "*Mater et Magistra,*" *The Wiseman Review* 489 (1961): 205. John XXIII, *Mater et Magistra,* 59; and 60-67. The Italian version of *Mater et Magistra* (widely used in Europe and Latin America) translates the Latin phrase "socialium rationum incrementa" in section 59 as "sozializzazione." However, the version accepted by the German hierarchy and most English editors translates the Latin phrase as "die wachsende Zahl gesellschaftlicher Verflectungen," or "the increasing number of social interrelationships." When English editors use the Italian version, "sozializzazione" becomes "socialization." This translation leads some commentators to conclude mistakenly that John XXIII is advocating socialism, rather than commending increased human relationships in society. On these translation problems, see J[erome] R. Kirwin, "Christianising the New Society: A New Translation of *Mater et Magistra,*" in Catholic Social Guild, *The Social Thought of John XXIII* (Hinckley, England: Samuel Walker, 1964), pp. 90-93. On misunderstandings of this passage, see Higgins, "Justice and Peace," pp. 197-200.

105.   On the richness of cultural diversity, see Paul VI, *Populorum progressio,* 72. See also John XXIII, *Pacem in terris,* 36; John Paul II, *Laborem exercens,* 44. In "Understanding Culture: The Ultimate Challenge of the World-Church?," in Joseph Gremillion, ed., *The Church and Culture since Vatican II: The Experience of North and Latin America* (Notre Dame, Ind.: University of Notre Dame Press, 1985), p. 18, Hervé Carrier argues that Paul VI dropped an exclusively "classical view" of culture (fine arts, humanism, education) common during the Leonine period, and brought into papal literature a "modern view about culture which incorporates . . . the classic as well as the anthropological dimension of culture." On the value of all cultures, see Paul VI, *Populorum progressio,* 40 and *Ecclesiam suam,* 98. Reflecting the popes' new attitude toward cultural diversity, John Paul II established the Pontifical Council for Culture in 1982.

106.   Paul Cremona, *The Concept of Peace in Pope John XXIII* (Malta: Dominican Publication, 1988), p. 159.

107.   Roberto Mangabeira Unger, *Knowledge and Politics* (New York: The Free Press, 1975), p. 220.

108.   David B. Clark, "The Concept of Community: A Re-examination," *The Sociological Review* 21 (August 1973): 404.

109.   Unger, *Knowledge and Politics,* p. 221.

110.   See Ernest Bartell, "Private Goods, Public Goods and the Common Good: Another Look at Economics and Ethics in Catholic Social Teaching," in Oliver F. Williams and John W. Houck, eds., *The Common Good and U. S. Capitalism* (Lanham, Md.: University Press of America, 1987), p. 189; Christiansen, "On Relative Equality," p. 652; Coleman, "Church Social Teaching," p. 176; Bryan Hehir, "Religion and International Human Rights: A Catholic Perspective," in Eugene J. Fisher and Daniel F. Polish, eds., *Formation of Social Policy in the Catholic and Jewish Traditions* (Notre Dame, Ind.: University of Notre Dame Press, 1980), p. 113; John Langan, "Human Rights in Roman Catholicism," in Curran and McCormick, *Readings in Moral Theology No. 5,* p. 122; Charles Murphy, "Action for Justice as Constitutive of the Preaching of the Gospel: What Did the 1971 Synod Mean?," in ibid., pp. 161-62.

111.   See Marie-Dominique Chenu, "The Church's 'Social Doctrine,'" in Dietmar Mieth and Jacques Pohier, eds., *Christian Ethics and Economics: The North-South Conflict, Concilium,* vol. 140 (Edinburgh: T. & T. Clark, 1980), pp. 73-74; Charles E. Curran, "The Changing Anthropological Bases of Catholic Social Ethics," in Curran and McCormick, *Readings in Moral Theology No. 5,* p. 198; Grima, "Method in Social Teaching," pp. 22-23; David Hollenbach, *Claims in Conflict: Retrieving and Renewing the Catholic Human Rights Tradition* (New York: Paulist Press, 1979), p. 131.

112.   Some commentators applaud the purported socialist-leaning 'radicalization' of papal social thought. Others oppose it. Among the former group are Christiansen,

"Relative Equality," pp. 654-55; and Dorr, *Option for the Poor*, pp. 112-16. The latter group includes Andrew Greeley, *No Bigger than Necessary: An Alternative to Socialism, Capitalism, and Anarchism* (New York: Meridian, 1977), p. 12; and Michael Novak, *The Spirit of Democratic Capitalism* (New York: Simon & Schuster, 1982), p. 248. In "Popes, Peace and People: Marxist Comment on Three Encyclicals," *Una Sancta* 25 (1968) : 64-70, Douglas Stange cites over fifty favorable reviews of post-Leonine period social encyclicals in socialist and communist periodicals between 1963 and 1968. Other commentators think papal social teaching has finally 'baptized' notions of freedom and human rights first articulated during the Enlightenment and actualized by the liberal, *Girondins* wing of the French Revolution. See Oscar L. Arnal, "Why the French Christian Democrats Were Condemned," *Church History* 49 (June 1980): 202; David J. O'Brien and Thomas A. Shannon, *Renewing the Earth: Catholic Documents on Peace, Justice and Liberation* (Garden City, N.Y.: Image Books, 1977), p. 40; François Perroux, " 'Populorum progressio': l'encyclique de la résurrection," in Congar and Peuchmaurd, *L'église dans le monde*, 1:204; Stephen H. P. Pfürtner, "Human Rights in Christian Ethics," in Alois Müller and Norbert Greinacher, eds., *The Church and the Rights of Man, Concilium*, vol. 124 (Edinburgh: T. & T. Clark, 1979), p. 60; François Refoule, "L'église et les libertés de Léon XIII à Jean XXIII," *Le supplément* 125 (May 1978): 259; Charles Wackenheim, "The Theological Meaning of the Rights of Man," in Muller and Greinacher, *Church and the Rights of Man*, p. 51. Regarding economics, A. F. McKee says John XXIII "reset the balance" of papal teaching "in favour of the neo-liberal [private enterprise] trend." A. F. McKee, "The Market Principle and Roman Catholic Thought," *Kyklos* 17 (1964): 65-66.

4

THEORIES OF COHERENCE

The Roman Catholic popes have generated a substantial body of social teaching since inaugurating the modern encyclical genre of papal communication in 1740. When located, assembled, and analyzed, this teaching exhibits a wide-ranging interest in ideas and practices directly affecting religious, political, family, economic, and cultural life, as well as the theological and philosophical concepts underlying these social relations.

But do the encyclical teachings of the Roman Catholic papacy form a coherent social ethic? This is an important question for three reasons. First, "justification of our views or our principles of morality, justice, law, and society," writes Barry Gross, "ultimately rest upon argument." And since "inconsistent arguments can prove anything we want," an incoherent social ethic invariably loses its rationale and "falls away." Second, "a major feature of laws, customs, and social practices is that they announce in advance what is or is not permitted." If reasonable foreknowledge of the moral and legal ramifications of one's actions is destroyed through incoherent or inconsistent statements by otherwise respected authorities, "planning, safety, and security are gone."[1] In other words, "social teaching has to be internally coherent if it is to be credible."[2] Third, the popes frequently claim possession of a coherent social 'doctrine,' or 'teaching.' If, in fact, such does not exist, the papal claim is mistaken.

Since the question of coherence has surfaced in the postconciliar period, two coherence theories have emerged in English-language commentary literature. Both are flawed. This chapter describes and examines these theories and, in the light of findings from chapters 1-3, offers an alternative theory.

Two Current Coherence Theories

Two theories of encyclical coherence presently dominate English-language commentary literature. The first is referred to here as the 'natural law' theory, the second is the 'human dignity' theory. To analyze these theories, representative samples of both are scrutinized. Roger Charles' work is investigated as a representative of the natural law approach, David Hollenbach's work is studied as a representative of the human dignity approach.

Natural Law Theory

In *The Social Teaching of Vatican II: Its Origin and Development*, Roger Charles outlines what he calls the "coherent framework" of Roman Catholic episcopal social teaching. He obtains this framework by analyzing teachings from fourteen papal encyclicals and the Vatican II documents *Gaudium et spes* and *Dignitatis humanae*.[3] In Charles' view, the coherence of Roman Catholic social teaching is shown in the letters' shared moral theory and derived principles guiding family, political, and economic life.

According to Charles, encyclical social teaching is wholly linked to a natural law moral theory. Here, "God's eternal law, objective and universal" is the "ultimate and objective ethical norm" of the moral life. "This law is true and unchanging," he explains, "precisely because it is founded in the nature of God." By possessing a nature "created by God and for him," human beings can participate in eternal law through the natural law. This natural law abides in human conscience. A complementary "divine positive law" (Ten Commandments, teachings of Christ, precepts of the Church) also exists because "human judgement on moral matters is wayward" due to sin. Ultimately, the moral directives of eternal, natural, and divine positive law are "authoritatively interpreted by the Church."[4]

The principles of natural law moral theory guide family, political, and economic relations. For Charles, these principles have been continuously and uniformly conveyed in papal teaching. Regarding family life, Charles says its origin lies in a sacred, indissoluble marriage "based on the equal love of the partners." The "fundamental orientation" of this union is to "begin and foster new life." Spousal relations are complementary. As "head of the family," husbands possess ultimate authority while financially supporting the family through careers "outside the home." A wife's primary responsibility is "home-making and child-rearing." Spousal sexual relations are "both unitive and potentially procreative," making artificial contraception (though not periodic continence) "intrinsically wrong." A primary responsibility of both parents is the education of children.

Well-ordered families are the foundation of society.[5]

Stable political life requires just exercise of state power and authority—a prerogative ultimately granted by God through the citizenry of the state. Correlatively, the best form of state organization is "representative government." The state's purpose is to serve the common good. The Church supports this endeavor, seeking no privileged status beyond freedom to exercise its religious ministry. The theory of the separation of the two powers—wherein the Church is "indifferent to political systems as such"—was "reaffirmed at Vatican II." Citizens must obey just authority, though active dissent is appropriate against unjust law. In Charles' view, Paul VI's *Populorum progressio* "reasserted the traditional teaching that violence may in extreme cases be an option open to the individual." The "patterns of freedom embodied in the modern constitutional state" are acceptable with the understanding that authentic freedom means "freedom under the law of God." Citizens should recognize their "full human rights and accept the responsibilities attached to them." Included among these rights is the right of individuals to profess their religion publicly, be they Roman Catholic or not. Finally, people should "search for a better world order and an effective means of supra-national government."[6]

According to Charles, the popes consider a "modified" market system the best economic organization for providing people's material needs. This system protects the private right to own productive property, while monitoring its exercise for the good of the community. Though not absolute, an individual's right to possess private property is "central to the Church's social teaching" because it protects economic freedom—"the essential bulwark of all other freedoms." Mindful of the account they must give God in heaven, the rich must give charitable alms to the poor. Egalitarianism, however, "is not a Christian ideal." Because labor is an expression of the human person, it possesses a unique dignity. This dignity is reflected in the worker's rights to a family wage, association, and strike, as well as in efforts to involve workers in business management. The economy benefits through cooperation of labor and management on the shop floor and in regional and national councils. States must oversee their national economies while observing the restraining influence of the principle of subsidiarity. "To prefer to have people do things for themselves," writes Charles, ". . . is the essential import of the [sic] subsidiarity." Developed nations should give aid to underdeveloped nations and maintain open trade relations. Improvement of agriculture is a global economic priority.[7]

Charles does not offer a complete discussion of papal teaching on religion and culture, but he does make two observations. Regarding religious ideas and practices, Charles believes papal teaching since Vatican II has not contradicted itself by claiming "there is salvation outside the Church." Concerning cultural life, he suggests that an individual's right to "seek the truth" in any manner consistent with public order (as defined by the state) is a long-standing papal directive.[8]

In Charles' view, the coherence of papal social teaching rests in these several religious, political, family, economic, and cultural principles drawn from a shared moral theory of natural law. He counters the "frequently made objection" that Church teaching has changed by arguing that while expressions may change, the substance remains the same.[9]

The findings of this study do not support Charles' 'natural law' theory of encyclical coherence. Problems exist for this approach on the levels of both general moral theory and specific social principles. At the level of moral theory, this study shows that natural law moral theory is not utilized throughout the papal encyclical literature. Pre-Leonine period letters make no appeal to this theory; instead, moral recommendations are drawn from an eclectic assortment of scriptural statements, patristic teachings, and customary practices. The post-Leonine period letters utilize the natural law theory, but not exclusively. Here, a new appreciation of history and affectivity is placed alongside the natural law approach. Only the Leonine period letters unequivocally employ the moral theory of natural law.

This study also shows that several moral principles cited by Charles have not been uniformly held in papal letters. Despite Charles' protestations to the contrary, contradictions have occurred in encyclical teaching. Concerning religious ideas and practices, the popes' interest in religious education begins with a literalistic emphasis on Scripture and patristics, moves to the philosophical and theological premises of neo-Thomism, and arrives at an appreciation of affective religious conversion enhanced by modern methods of Scripture and patristic study. In the missionary field, the popes move from a missiology of saving and remaking non-Western 'savages' to the view that the Church itself is reformed and taught by contact with non-Western peoples. In post-Leonine period letters, the laity are no longer expected to wait for hierarchical initiative or approval before undertaking social action; and such action may be pursued in cooperation with non-Roman Catholic Christians and non-Christians. Because both Spirit and salvation can exist outside the Roman Catholic Church, open ecumenical dialogue is not only acceptable, but required.

Several reversals also occur in papal political teaching. Participatory democracy is not considered the 'best' form of government prior to the post-Leonine period; indeed, the contrary is nearer the truth. Similarly, contemporary papal approval of Church and state separation on the model of Western democracy does not correspond with the political recommendations of either pre-Leonine or Leonine period encyclicals. Nor is Pius XII and Paul VI's oblique and guarded acceptance of violent citizen resistance to unjust governments a 'traditional' encyclical teaching. Finally, the right of non-Roman Catholics publicly to profess their religion is denied by the popes until the post-Leonine period.

Of all the discussions on social relations, the papal treatment of family life contains the fewest overt contradictions. Nevertheless, Charles' claim that the popes consistently consider spousal love the fundamental basis of marriage is inaccurate. Nor do the popes uniformly teach that procreation is the primary purpose of married life.

In their economic teachings, the popes offer different views on the relationship between the rights of possession and use of property. Contrary to Charles' opinion, the popes do not continually teach that the individual's right to possess private property is the 'essential bulwark' of every human freedom. Nor is the economic relation between rich and poor uniformly understood. The popes do not consistently understand almsgiving as an obligation solely of charity; rather, greater egalitarian sharing is a primary desideratum of justice in pre-Leonine and post-Leonine period thought. Nor do all the popes interpret the principle of subsidiarity as simply a brake on state involvement in social affairs. Finally, John Paul II's assessment of the aggressive factions within the nineteenth century labor movement does not correspond with Leonine period thought.

In the area of cultural relations, post-Leonine period thought profoundly alters earlier papal teaching on individual rights to freedom of expression, pursuit of truth, and teaching. Earlier popes do not recognize a person's right to 'seek the truth' through a public airing of all opinions. Post-Leonine teaching also reverses prior papal recommendations on treatment of the Jews and relations with individuals and groups holding disagreeable ideologies. In addition, recent popes no longer offer Western civilization as the best model of human civilization; nor do they persist in the view that Roman Catholicism is linked by necessity with Western culture.

Though much of Roger Charles' research on Roman Catholic social thought is enlightening and useful, his natural law theory of encyclical coherence fails. This failure is due to a textually limited and topically

narrow reading of the encyclical literature, resulting in an overexten-
sion of natural law moral theory and a universalization of moral principles not uniformly held by the popes. No amount of verbal circumlo-
cution can mask the reversals which have occurred in encyclical
teaching.

Human Dignity Theory

David Hollenbach's work represents a second approach to encyclical
coherence. In *Claims in Conflict: Retrieving and Renewing the Catholic
Human Rights Tradition*, Hollenbach locates coherence in the concept of
human dignity. "The dignity of the human person," he writes, is "the
thread that ties all these [papal and conciliar] documents together."[10]
According to Hollenbach, Leo XIII assumes the moral norm of
human dignity when he says "man precedes the state." In *Quadragesimo anno* and *Divini Redemptoris*, Pius XI "continued to give major
emphasis to the centrality of human dignity." In Pius XII's speeches
and writings, "the dignity of the human person was lifted from the
level of a basic but frequently implicit first principle of Roman Catholic social morality to the level of explicit and formal concern." John
XXIII clearly states the importance of this norm in *Pacem in terris*: "The
cardinal point of this teaching is that individual men are necessarily
the foundation, cause, and end of all social institutions." The encyclicals of Paul VI sustain this emphasis on human dignity.[11]
The papal concept of human dignity connotes an understanding of
human life as transcendental. This valuation is anchored in an interpretation of Gen 1:26, wherein God says: "Let us make man in our
image and likeness." Hollenbach argues that pre-Vatican II writings
locate the *imago dei* in humanity's power of discursive reason, while
post-Vatican II writings focus on humanity's multiform cultural
expressions. Despite this shift, Hollenbach thinks all popes agree:
human dignity is the "fundamental norm" of social morality.[12]
The popes gradually devolve a list of human rights as a way of
socially concretizing the moral norm of human dignity. Hollenbach
writes: "The history of the papal teaching has been a process of dis-
covering and identifying these conditions of human dignity. These
conditions are called human rights." Leo XIII begins by formulating "a
number of quite specific rights and duties in the economic sphere." In
"continuity with Leo XIII," Pius XI offers an enlarged list of human
rights, though in an "incomplete and unsystematic" way. Pius XII
follows in his predecessor's footsteps. In John XXIII's *Pacem in terris*,

human rights are given their first systematic treatment. "The single foundational norm of respect for human dignity," writes Hollenbach, "led John XXIII to understand both civil-political rights and social-economic rights within a single integrated theoretical framework."[13]

Hollenbach shows the "logic operating throughout the development of the tradition" by using the image of a wheel.[14] At the wheel's hub is the concept of human dignity. Extending out from the hub are eight spokes linked by three concentric circles. Each spoke represents a distinct category of human rights: bodily, political, movement, associational, economic, sexual and family, religious, and communication. Each circle radiating from the hub represents a distinct type of relationship governed by human rights: personal, social, and instrumental. In total, Hollenbach lists twenty-seven human rights covering the various categories and relationships of human life.

In Hollenbach's view, the coherence of encyclical social teaching lies in the concept of human dignity and its associated collection of human rights. Recognition of "historicity and the problem of ideological pluralism" in papal thought does not destroy this coherence because "the norm of personal dignity remains central."[15]

This study does not find enough evidence in the papal letters to support Hollenbach's human dignity theory of encyclical coherence. Problems exist on the issues of human dignity and human rights. As this study shows, the concept of human dignity is not used throughout the papal encyclical literature. Pre-Leonine letters make no reference to this concept. During the Leonine period the phrase is used sparingly. Though Leo XIII, Pius X, and Benedict XV acknowledge the elevated status of human beings as the *imago dei*, this is not a claim around which their social teaching revolves. Rather, the Leonine period popes' controlling moral insight is a cosmological vision of a communal hierarchy of being (within which human beings are one of many members) proceeding from God and striving toward God under the influence of formal, material, efficient, and final causes. Within this vision God's eternal, natural, and divine laws function to guide human moral action. Though the incidence of the phrase 'human dignity' increases in the letters of Pius XI and Pius XII, it does not acquire the status of a virtually free-standing moral concept until the post-Leonine period.[16]

The present study also shows that the encyclical discussion of human rights neither evolved out of a prior concept of human dignity, nor followed a self-conscious plan or 'logic.' Papal interpretation and recognition of specific rights predates encyclical discussion of human dignity and develops on an ad hoc basis for 223 years before John XXIII 'systemizes' these claims in *Pacem in terris*.

Though Hollenbach presents masterful research on episcopal social teaching, his approach to the specific question of encyclical coherence is flawed. The failure of the 'human dignity' theory is due to an over-emphasis on both the role of the concept of human dignity in encyclical teaching and the logical derivation of human rights therefrom.

According to Deny Turner, "an excessively narrow concept of something is a concept whose coherence is bought at the price of insufficient difference." On the other hand, "an excessively diffuse concept is one whose definition is incoherently constructed."[17] Based on the findings of the present study, Turner's statement compactly identifies the respective problems of the natural law and human dignity theories of encyclical coherence.

An Alternative Coherence Theory

Analyzing the complete encyclical corpus uncovers not only contradictions in papal thought, but also commonalities. Properly construed, the shared features of papal teaching constitute an alternative theory of encyclical coherence. This theory holds that papal teaching coheres around a theologically inspired communitarian social ethic which has yielded a cluster of shared, double-pulsed insights concerning religious, political, familial, economic, and cultural relations in society. Common features of the popes' theological perspectives, social recommendations, and understandings of self and society support this claim.

Theological Perspective

The intersection of encyclical teaching on the idea of community appears in papal discussions of God, the world, and humanity. Although their respective controlling images—or root metaphors—shape significantly different theological perspectives, the popes' emphasis on community perdures.

The central influence, or "prime analogue," behind this concentration on community is the popes' image of God.[18] On one level, the conceptions are diverse: pre-Leonine period letters focus on Christ the Good Shepherd, Leonine period texts stress the Father-Creator, and post-Leonine period encyclicals emphasize the dialogical Spirit. On another level, however, the perspectives are linked. The Shepherd's ingathering, the unity of creation, the Spirit's dialogic invitation—all communicate the 'gravitational' draw of God's will for community.

Accordingly, the popes persistently decry atheism as a variformed font of divine and human disunity.

The idea of community recurs in the popes' theological interpretation of the world. Again, on one level the discussions are dissimilar: the pre-Leonine period portrait of the world as a nourishing, yet dangerous, pasture; the Leonine period picture of a benign, cosmic hierarchy of being; and the post-Leonine period image of the cultural, physical, and historical context wherein God and humanity journey together. But despite these shifting viewpoints, the popes collectively construe the world as a medium of God's ubiquity. Whether a pasture, a cosmos, or an unmarked path, the world is in constant communion with God. From this characteristically Roman Catholic perspective, says Monika Hellwig, "there is no realm whatsoever outside the dominion of that God."[19] Thus, the popes continually criticize atheistic naturalism and dialectical materialism, worldviews which sever all links between God and the world.

Belief in God's concern for community profoundly influences papal interpretation of human faith, morality, and worship. Every pope considers human life deficient without religious faith. Yet the link between life and faith is interpreted differently. Pre-Leonine period letters focus on human will and the necessity to persevere in the flock's customary faith. Leonine period letters highlight human nature and reason, and its built-in correspondence with divine creation and grace. Post-Leonine period texts take interest in human experience, stressing the link between affectivity and conversion. Yet, for all the popes, religious faith—whether nourished by custom, cosmos, or affection—is mediated by community. Thus, the encyclicals continually decry rationalist attacks on the veracity or necessity of religious faith.

God's interest in community is also reflected in the existence of an objective morality. In pre-Leonine period letters, God's objective morality is found in the customary interpretations of the Ten Commandments, the laws of Christ, and the precepts of the Church. Leonine period encyclicals position these sources within the wider natural law moral theory. Post-Leonine period popes highlight the moral values reflected in these objective prescriptions and proscriptions. Whether a written decree, a natural law, or a moral value, the popes consider morality objective by virtue of its origin in God's will and mediation through the community. Consequently, the popes unceasingly criticize ethical subjectivism and relativism.

Worship is a third sign of God's stake in human community. In pre-Leonine period letters, religious fellowship subsists in the one (Roman Catholic) flock of Christ. Leonine period letters theoretically broaden this fellowship, using the image of the Mystical Body of Christ. Post-Leonine period texts suggest a more practically inclusive view of religious fellowship through constant reference to the pilgrim People of God. Yet through it all, the popes agree: worship is necessarily communal; its reduction to private experience and expression is an error.

Social Recommendations

These perspectives on God, the world, and humanity undergird a cluster of community-oriented social recommendations and judgments which persist throughout the encyclical literature. Some of the instructions on religious, political, family, economic, and cultural relations are initiated in pre-Leonine period letters; others are introduced in subsequent periods without overtly contradicting earlier teachings.

A constant encyclical concern regarding religious ideas and practices is ecclesial unity. For the popes, authentic 'ecclesial' communion requires 'ecclesiastical' unity. Though the popes of each period interpret the practical requirements of their office in distinct ways—from a relatively narrow construal in pre-Leonine period letters to an expansive interpretation in Leonine period texts—no pope fails to assert the juridic and pastoral primacy of the Petrine office and the lines of clerical authority which descend therefrom.

Operationally, all popes emphasize the general importance of missionary evangelization, religious education, and spiritual renewal. Specific methods prescribed for each activity, however, vary over the three encyclical periods. Theologians are reminded on a regular basis of their responsibility to ecclesiastical unity, while laity are encouraged to participate in social affairs as a necessary dimension of religious lives.

The popes also issue a number of persistent warnings concerning religious life. An ongoing problem is religious indifference, though the popes interpret the phenomenon in various ways. Theories of ecclesiological reorganization calling for dismantling the Church's hierarchical structure are continually reproved. Priests are warned against insubordination, as are theologians who limit the justification of religious truth to private experience and interpretation. Problems of insufficient religious vocations, withdrawal from clerical vows, and deficiencies in lay religious practice are also regularly cited.

In the area of political life, the popes uniformly identify God as the ultimate source of political authority, though citizens may designate holders of state power through democratic means. The purpose of the state is to serve the national and international common good. The popes gradually identify several tasks related to the common good: creation of just law, maintenance of criminal justice, oversight of public morality and spiritual well-being, coordination of social institutions, care of the poor and minority groups, monitoring of national population growth, support for education, protection of human rights, promotion of world peace and international social improvement, and encouragement of global structures of governance. Though encyclical teachings on Church-state relations vary, each pope recognizes the institutional distinction between Church and state, the rights of both bodies to exist and wield authority, and the necessity of Church involvement in political affairs affecting religion and morality.

According to the popes, human beings possess political obligations and prerogatives. Citizens should participate in government and obey the law. They may resist the dictates of political tyrants, though the popes differ on appropriate methods of resistance. Citizens must realize, however, that true political freedom is not simply the absence of tyranny, but the presence of moral rectitude. From the standpoint of a communitarian ethic, writes Unger, freedom is "the measure of an individual's capacity to achieve the good."[20] Similarly, the popes agree that human beings possess rights, but these are understood as grounded in God's will and linked to a moral requirement that their exercise not impair the common good. Mouffe captures this approach, in part, when he says "communitarians . . . affirm that one cannot define the right prior to the good for it is only through our participation in a community which defines the good that we can have a sense of the right and a conception of justice."[21] The growing list of incontrovertible rights in papal encyclicals includes: Roman Catholic worship, social freedom consonant with right reason, political participation, resistance to injustice, life and bodily integrity, marriage, parental control over adolescent education, vocational choice, individual ownership of property, goods necessary to human survival, work, just wage, safe working conditions, rest, occupations consistent with individual competence, strike, association, benefits and pensions, emigration, cultural and ethnic identity, language, respect, and state promotion and protection of human rights.

The popes continually criticize several political concepts and practices. The major encyclical adversary is the secular social contract theory. In the papal view, this theory bases political authority, law, freedom, and rights on human will expressed individually (despotism) or collectively (majoritarianism). Encyclical citations of state offenses against citizens increase with the popes' growing list of human rights. Oppressive practices include: restrictions on Roman Catholic worship, unjust imprisonment, torture, forced oaths and memberships in state-run organizations, denial of parental control over children, legalized euthanasia, abortion and sterilization, state-imposed contraception, suppression of worker associations, unjust expropriation of property, and racial or ethnic discrimination. The popes also decry excessive nationalism, weapons production, and interstate violence through either economic imperialism or outright war. Terrorism and civil violence motivated by the theory of class warfare are also reproved.

Encyclical teachings on family life persistently emphasize the centrality of a sacred and indissoluble marriage. Spousal relations are characterized by functional complementarity, with husbands given ultimate family authority consistent with justice. Beginning in Leonine period letters, the importance of affective relations between husband and wife is given increasing attention. Spouses are responsible for raising and educating their children. Such education should include both religious and beneficial secular knowledge. For their part, children must obey their parents and contribute to family maintenance.

The popes inaugurate encyclical discussion of spousal sexual relations during the Leonine period. These instructions include proscriptions of extramarital sex, abortion, sterilization, artificial birth control, and the acceptance of family planning through periodic continence. In the post-Leonine period, the notion of the unitive and procreative nature of conjugal relations is introduced. Throughout their letters, the popes believe the bedrock of society is a complementarily organized and sexually upright family.

The popes constantly reject the idea that marriage is simply a secular, or artificial, contract. This view promotes divorce and the demise of family life. Similarly destructive are economic conditions which force not only women, but also children, out of the home and into the workplace. Oppressive political regimes and warfare also threaten family life, as do sexual promiscuity, abortion, sterilization, and artificial birth control.

In the realm of economic life, the popes accept a market system morally and legally monitored to meet the needs of the common good. Although they approve individual ownership of productive and nonproductive property, no pope elevates this right to a moral absolute. Private possession is always conditioned by communal need, though estimating this need and determining when the communal right of use supersedes the personal right of possession varies in encyclical letters. Similarly, each pope insists that the rich have a material responsibility to the poor, but their interpretations of this responsibility differ.

Beginning in Leonine period letters, work is increasingly honored as a human activity fraught with profound psychological, familial, communal, and religious significance. In consequence, employers must respect employees by abandoning work structures and schedules harmful to religious and family life, overseeing occupational safety, providing just wages, permitting some degree of employee participation in decisions affecting the firm, and respecting worker associations. For their part, employees must honestly perform their work and avoid any direct physical harm to the employer's person or property. Employees also possess rights to organize, strike, rest, receive a family wage, work in safe conditions and in occupations respecting individual competence, and receive benefits and pensions.

On the macroeconomic level, capitalists, laborers, state, and Church have unique economic responsibilities. Capitalists must reinvest earnings into job-producing enterprises, make credit available to individuals and small firms, oversee corporate administration, and assist countries hosting their enterprises. Laborers should avoid economic theories and actions threatening permanent social damage. The state has an obligation in justice to guide and adjudicate employer-employee and capital-labor relations. This prerogative is simultaneously promoted and reined by the principle of subsidiarity. Cooperative management and worker associations beyond the local firm should be encouraged. Productive employment and equitable distribution must be enhanced with particular consideration for the needs of the poor. Inputs and outputs of the economy's industrial, service, and agricultural sectors require local and regional balance, with emphasis on the needs of farmers. Internationally, states should provide direct aid to underdeveloped nations and establish a world relief fund supplied by monies normally appropriated for armaments. Each nation's right to equal opportunity in international trade should be respected. For its part, the Church must maintain special care for the poor of every nation, encourage a global perspective on economic issues, and divest itself of riches in cases of emergency need.

The central economic problems cited in encyclical literature are greed and the postulation of amoral economic laws. These problems infect individuals and groups. Capitalist theory can augment individual greed by placing ultimate economic power and authority in private hands. This approach distorts the purpose of economic life, the status of individual property ownership, and the meaning of economic freedom. Capitalists are also prone to separate economics and morality by interpreting justice as the raw outcome of automatic free market operations. This ideology unduly minimizes the role of the state and completely severs wage and price levels from any consideration of human need. Socialism, on the other hand, can augment group greed by locating ultimate economic power and authority in the leaders of the state. This theory misinterprets both the role of the state and the communal right to use property. Marxist socialism separates economic life from morality by defining justice as the victory of the proletariat in a class war determined by the material dialectic of history. This ideology misinterprets both capital-labor relations and history.

Throughout their letters, the popes also identify a growing number of economic abuses committed by employers, employees, corporations, and states. Unjust employer practices include: poor working conditions, long hours, inadequate wages, immigrant exploitation, child labor, abuse of women, lack of illness and old age compensation, resistance to worker associations and worker participation in management, and neglect of the disabled. Employees are warned against subscribing to the Marxist theory of class warfare and engaging in union practices threatening permanent damage to the common good. Corporate injustices involve monopoly, undue influence over the state, avoidance of social responsibility through the legal mechanism of limited liability, and inappropriate behavior in underdeveloped countries. Problematic state practices include economic imperialism, actions against worker associations, disregard for unemployment, and support for increased arms production.

The popes believe cultural life should reflect God's objective morality. Informational and artistic media should communicate truth, impart an uplifting aesthetic message, and expose conditions of inhumanity requiring alleviation. Life-styles should reflect sexual modesty and moderation in both work and leisure. The best adolescent education combines beneficial secular knowledge and religious training, though the popes differ on how this should be structurally achieved. A morally prudent advance of science and technology is praiseworthy. Peace and cooperation between different social groups is critical. In particular, minority racial and ethnic groups should receive equal treatment. As a social group, the handicapped should receive special care. Rights of women must be respected consistent with the stability of the family.

The persistent encyclical complaint concerning cultural life is secularization—understood as the elimination of religiously inspired moral considerations from social communication, life-style, education, science, and group relations. Licentious communications are decried throughout the papal texts, as is the theory that art need respect no standard. Sexual promiscuity, consumerism, and violence are routinely condemned, along with irreligious education of children. Scientific and technological developments threatening the environment and world peace are also reproved. Concerning group relations, the problems of racism, generational conflict, and physical abuse of women in home and workplace are cited.

Self and Society

Internal to all the popes' social recommendations and judgments is a communitarian understanding of the self and society. Whether rooted in territorial custom, cosmological nature, or affective sentiment, the self is invariably "defined by the totality of its relations with other beings and, particularly, with other selves."[22] Hence, the encyclicals constantly protest liberalism's Enlightenment-inspired notion of the self as a "radically unencumbered," "autonomous chooser of ends."[23]

In the papal view, mutuality is a characteristic of embedded selves. This quality, in turn, defines society. Whether construed territorially, cosmologically, or affectively, the notion of society as 'koinonia'—or, community of mutuality—"responds to the deepest aspirations of God's human creatures."[24] Concomitantly, all realms of human interaction—religious, political, family, economic, cultural—must reflect a 'coordinate' interest in mutual aid. Thus, the popes perennially decry the classical liberal model where society is understood as an artificial contract between autonomous individuals "undertaken for self-interested rather than fraternal reasons."[25] Similarly, they condemn the notion that the realms of human interraction in society can be morally segregated. The "principle of continuity" wherein all dimensions of life are seen as interdependent is a fundamental assumption of papal thought throughout.

The social teaching of the papal encyclicals is not an "uncritical eclecticism or an opportunistic syncretism of unrelated parts."[26] Nor is it a teaching tightly unified by natural law moral theory or the concept of human dignity. Rather, encyclical social teaching coheres around a theologically inspired communitarian ethic which has, since the eighteenth century, yielded an enduring cluster of shared, double-pulsed insights on human relations in society. Thus, prescinding from a judgment on the ultimate adequacy of papal thought to the problems of modern society, the social teaching of papal encyclicals possesses an internal rationale and credibility. It represents a 'tradition,' not simply of texts, but argument.

But, as Sander Griffioen notes, "a single worldview may be the basis for a variety of theories."[27] Such has been the case with the papal encyclicals. Each encyclical period displays a particular slant on communitarian social ethics. Like artists, popes make unique "moves, gambits, stratagems, or procedures" reflecting their particular historical circumstances and theological perspectives.[28] In some cases, this has resulted in contradictory teaching. But frank recognition of this fact should not detract from the substantial—and coherent—contribution encyclical literature has made to the enterprise of Christian social ethics in the modern world.

NOTES

1.   Barry Gross, *Discrimination in Reverse: Is Turnabout Fair Play?* (New York: New York University Press, 1978), p. 26.

2.   Dorr, *Option for the Poor*, p. 8.

3.   Charles' study includes the following encyclicals: Benedict XIV's *Vix pervenit*; Leo XIII's *Libertas* and *Rerum novarum*; Pius XI's *Rappresentanti in terra*, *Casti connubii*, *Quadragesimo anno*, *Mit brennender Sorge*, and *Divini Redemptoris*; John XXIII's *Mater et Magistra* and *Pacem in terris*; Paul VI's *Populorum progressio* and *Humanae vitae*; and John Paul II's *Redemptor hominis* and *Laborem exercens*.

4.   On eternal law, see Charles, *Social Teaching of Vatican II*, p. 9. On the true and unchanging quality of the eternal law, see ibid., p. 12. On the natural law, see p. 86. On human judgment, see p. 363. On Church interpretation, see p. 10.

5.   On marriage, see ibid., 115. On the fundamental orientation of marriage, see p. 117. On the wife's rsponsibility, see p. 118. "Patriarchy," says Charles, ". . . has continued to be and is the ideal of marriage held forth by the Church." Ibid., p. 166. On artificial contraception, see p. 141.

6.   On representative government, see ibid., p. 379. On separation of powers, see pp. 243-44. According to Charles, Catholic social teaching contends that "the Church is not to be identified with any particular party or political system, but transcends them all." Ibid., p. 373. On violence, see p. 373. On freedom, see pp. 12-13. On world order, see p. 260.

7.   On the market system, see ibid., p. 296. On private property, see p. 377. On egalitarianism, see p. 318. On subsidiarity, see p. 372.

8.   On salvation outside the Church, see ibid., p. 153. On seeking the truth, see p. 12.

9.   Ibid., p. 148. Charles accepts a "concept of development of doctrine which indeed does involve 'change' but not 'contradiction' in the teaching of the Church." Borrowing the approach utilized by John Courtney Murray, Charles explains contradiction in encyclical teaching as difference in historical circumstance, not disagreement in principle. See pp. 234-43.

10.   Hollenbach, *Claims in Conflict*, p. 42.

11.   On Leo XIII, see ibid., p. 43; Pius XI, p. 50; Pius XII, p. 56; John XXIII, p. 63; Paul VI, p. 77-84.

12. On reason, see ibid., p. 90; on culture, p. 109. On human dignity as the fundamental norm, see p. 130.

13. Ibid., p. 68. On Leo XIII, see p. 47; Pius XI, p. 56; John XXIII, p. 66. John XXIII's *Pacem in terris* represents a "systematic recapitulation of the rights claims made in the tradition since Leo XIII." Ibid., p. 67.

14. Ibid., p. 68.

15. Ibid., p. 83.

16. In her study of encyclical teaching on human rights, Elsbernd similarly criticizes Hollenbach for overstating the link between human rights and human dignity in papal thought before Pius XII. Analyzing Hollenbach's interpretation of passages from Leo XIII and Pius XI, Elsbernd concludes he has "decontextualized" these statements to suggest a greater degree of papal attachment to the contemporary notion of human dignity than actually existed." "Statement on Rights," p. 568, n. 1.

17. Deny Turner, *Marxism and Christianity* (Totowa, N.J.: Barnes & Noble, 1983), p. 15.

18. This phrase comes from David Tracy's discussion of the two conceptual languages in theological discourse: analogic and dialectic. According to Tracy, the purpose of analogical language is to develop, from the "prime analogue," an order of "similarities-in-difference" among the various items (God, world, self, others) "constituting the whole of reality." David Tracy, *The Analogical Imagination: Christian Theology and the Culture of Pluralism* (New York: Crossroad, 1981), p. 408. Contrariwise, dialectical language stresses God's inscrutable, "unsettling" revelation. Ibid., p. 415. Given these alternatives, papal encyclicals predominantly employ analogical language. This study suggests that the letters (when read as a whole) do not ultimately succumb to the potential weakness of the analogical method—what Tracy calls the "false harmony, the brittle sterility, the cheap grace of an all-too canny univocity." Ibid., p. 421. However, some commentaries unfortunately present the papal letters in such a light.

19. Monika Hellwig, *Understanding Catholicism* (New York: Paulist Press, 1981), p. 185.

20. Unger, *Knowledge and Politics*, p. 278.

21. Mouffe, "American Liberalism," p. 199. Curran is incorrect when he claims that "Catholic social teaching only recently has developed the important concept of human rights." Charles E. Curran, "The Common Good and Official Catholic Social Teaching," in *The Common Good and U.S. Capitalism*, ed. Oliver F. Wllliams and John W. Houck (Lanham, Md.: University Press of America, 1987), p. 123. The concept is long-standing in papal letters, but understood in a manner unlike the secular liberal view.

22. Unger, *Knowledge and Politics*, p. 216.

23. Buchanan, "Assessing the Communitarian Critique," p. 866.

24. John Mahoney, *The Making of Moral Theology: A Study of the Roman Catholic Tradition* (Oxford: Clarendon Press, 1987), p. 345.

25. Plant, "Community," p. 105.

26. Remark of Alfred Diamant, quoted in Coleman, "Church Social Teaching." p. 177.

27. Sander Griffioen, "The Worldview Approach to Social Theory: Hazards and Benefits," in *Stained Glass: Worldviews and Social Science*, ed. Paul A. Marshall, Sander Griffioen, Richard Mouw (Lanham, Md.: University Press of America, 1989), p. 107.

28. Karl Aschenbrenner, *The Concept of Coherence in Art* (Dordrecht: D. Reidel Publishing, 1985), p. 5.

29. John P. Boyle, "The 'Ordinary Magisterium': Towards a History of the Concept (2)," *Heythrop Journal* 21 (January 1980): 28.

CONCLUSION

This book presents the social teaching of the papal encyclicals and addresses the question of their coherence. In pursuing these objectives, several new ideas are introduced with implications for future encyclical commentary.

Three novel claims are suggested for interpreting encyclical social teaching. First, it is suggested that correct interpretation of the conventionally designated 'social' encyclicals requires reading these texts in conjunction with a given pope's total encyclical corpus. This method (1) provides collaborative data for understanding a single text's specific words or phrases, (2) discloses the broader theological framework within which each encyclical stands, and (3) relates individual letters to the pope's overall pontifical program. While it is commonplace to insist that individual encyclicals be interpreted in their historical context, it has not been previously suggested that each letter be read within the context of a pope's entire encyclical collection.

The call for inclusive reading generates a second recommendation. When read in their entirety, papal letters show serious interest in social relations involving not only economic affairs, but also political, religious, family, and cultural life. As a result, interpretation of encyclical social teaching should include these additional areas. Occasional commentators have made this observation since Vatican II, but none had heretofore analyzed and incorporated these areas of encyclical social thought.[1]

Opening the investigation of encyclical social thought to a wider range of texts and topics invites new analysis of the pre-Leonine period encyclicals. Because conventional wisdom has long located the beginning of papal social thought in Leo XIII's *Rerum novarum*, no comprehensive treatment of pre-Leonine period teachings exists. This study provides the first investigation of these papal texts and asserts that dismissing pre-Leonine period letters distorts the understanding of encyclical teaching as a whole.

These new methodological claims generate novel ideas regarding the content and coherence of encyclical social teaching. First, this study claims that papal encyclicals persistently critique a series of general notions regarding God, the world, and humanity, and a set of specific ideas concerning religious, political, family, economic, and cultural life inaugurated during the Enlightenment. While some commentators recognize the critical dimension of encyclical teaching, most dismiss it as historical artifact. This book argues that the popes' critical judgments of several Enlightenment premises are a constitutive aspect of encyclical social teaching.

This study also claims that a comprehensive investigation of encyclical thought exposes several contradictory teachings. Though commentators have long recognized textual inconsistencies, many smooth them over by identifying troublesome papal statements as 'historical' and not substantive. The present study holds that substantive contradictions occur in encyclical social thought.

Third, it is argued that the sources utilized in encyclicals and the methods employed in arriving at social teachings are eclectic. No single source or method molds encyclical thought as a whole. Thus, conventional association of Thomistic Neoscholastic theology and natural law moral theory with the whole of encyclical social teaching is inaccurate.

Despite their contradictions and eclecticism, the papal letters share several common recommendations concerning general concepts of God, the world, and humanity, and specific issues affecting religious, political, family, economic, and cultural life. These communitarian recommendations, combined with the popes' persistent negative judgments, constitute the coherence of encyclical social teaching.

The interpretation of encyclical social teaching offered here has two suggestive implications for the general field of Christian social ethics. By identifying one persistent function of encyclical teaching as social critique, a new dialogue is opened between papal thought and both European political theology and Third World liberation theology.[2] Second, by loosening the hold of Thomistic Neoscholastic theology and natural law moral theory on encyclical interpretation, similar dialogue may be possible between papal thought and Protestant social ethics in North America and Europe.[3]

The research presented in this study also suggests new links between encyclical social teaching and contemporary discussions in secular political philosophy. Several of the new communitarian analyses and critiques of Western liberalism possess an uncanny relationship with encyclical teachings.[4]

These implications, prompted by the interpretation of encyclical content and coherence offered here, suggest that papal social teaching deserves a fresh appraisal. The texts provide a multitude of fascinating insights for professionals and nonprofessionals interested in public affairs and social ethics. At the same time, the encyclicals are a major installment in the ongoing Christian effort to satisfy Jesus' prayer to the Father "that they be one, even as we are one."

NOTES

1.   Calls for a broader understanding of encyclical social teaching have recently been made by Jean-Yves Calvez and Paul Surlis. Jean-Yves Calvez, "Economic Policy Issues," p. 15 and Paul Surlis, "The Relation between Social Justice and Inculturation in the Papal Magisterium," *Irish Theological Quarterly* 52 (1986): 253. A preconciliar effort at presenting a broad-gauged social ethic based, in part, on papal letters is Eberhard Welty, *Handbook of Christian Social Ethics*. A postconciliar effort is Charles' *Social Teaching of Vatican II*.

2.   From the standpoint of European political theology, both Johannes B. Metz and Edward Schillebeeckx want the Church to adopt a "theology of social criticism," without observing that several elements of this theology are already present in encyclical teaching. See Johannes B. Metz, "The Church's Social Function in the Light of a 'Political' Theology" and Edward Schillebeeckx, "The Magisterium and the World of Politics," in Johannes B. Metz, ed., *Foundational Theology: Faith and the World of Politics, Concilium*, vol. 36, trans. Theodore L. Weston (Edinburgh: T. & T. Clark, 1968). See also Karl Rahner, "Theological Reflections on the Problem of Secularization," in *Theological Investigations*, trans. David Bourke (New York: Herder and Herder, 1973), 10:330. The presentation of encyclical social teaching on political, family, economic, and cultural life offered in this study is fully compatible with the "open system" interpretation of papal thought which Clodovis Boff believes is in "no contradiction" with liberation theology. See Clodovis Boff, "The Social Teaching of the Church and the Theology of Liberation: Opposing Social Practices?," in Jacques Pohier and Deitmar Mieth, eds., *Christian Ethics: Uniformity, Universality, Pluralism, Concilium*, vol. 150 (Edinburgh: T. & T. Clark, 1981). See also Enrique Dussel, *Ethics and Community*, trans. Robert R. Barr (Maryknoll, N.Y.: Orbis Books, 1988), pp. 205-18.

3.   Despite his own dislike of encyclical teaching, many claims advanced by Stanley Hauerwas are compatible with papal thought as interpreted in the present study. See Stanley Hauerwas, *A Community of Character: Toward a Constructive Christian Social Ethic* (Notre Dame, Ind.: University of Notre Dame Press, 1981). Suggestive links also exist between encyclical social teaching and the Protestant evangelical social ethic presented in Norman Geisler, *Options in Contemporary Christian Ethics* (Grand Rapids, Mich.: Baker Book House, 1981), and M. Douglas Meeks, *God the Economist: The Doctrine of God and Political Economy* (Minneapolis: Fortress Press, 1989). This is also the case with the European Protestant ethicist Jan Milič Lochman. See Lochman, "Ideology or Theology of Human Rights?" in Müller and Greinacher, *Church and the Rights of Man*.

4.   See Benjamin R. Barber, *Strong Democracy: Participatory Politics for a New Age* (Berkeley: University of California Press, 1984); Andrew Levine, *Liberal Democracy: A Critique of Its Theory* (New York: New York University Press, 1981); Alasdair MacIntyre, *After Virtue: A Study in Moral Theory* (Notre Dame, Ind.: University of Notre Dame Press, 1981); Carole Pateman, *The Problem of Political Obligation: A Critical Analysis of Liberal Theory* (Berkeley: University of California Press, 1985); Michael Sandel, *Liberalism and the Limits of Justice* (Cambridge: Cambridge University Press, 1982); William Sullivan, *Reconstructing Public Philosophy* (Berkeley: University of California Press, 1982); Charles Taylor, *Hegel and Modern Society* (New York: Cambridge University Press, 1979); Roberto Mangabeira Unger, *Knowledge and Politics* (New York: The Free Press, 1975); and Michael Walzer, *Spheres of Justice: A Defense of Pluralism and Equality* (New York: Basic Books, 1983).

BIBLIOGRAPHY

Books

Abbott, Walter, M., ed. *The Documents of Vatican II.* New York: Guild Press, 1966.

Adriányi, Gabriel. "The Church in Northern, Eastern, and Southern Europe." In *The Church in the Modern Age,* edited by Gabriel Adriányi et al., translated by Anselm Biggs. 505-31. New York: Crossroad, 1981.

Adriányi, Gabriel, et al., eds. *The Church in the Modern Age.* Translated by Anselm Biggs. New York: Crossroad, 1981.

Alexander, Edgar. "Church and Society in Germany." In *Church and Society: Catholic Social and Political Thought and Movements 1789-1950,* edited by Joseph N. Moody. 325-583. New York: Arts, Inc., 1953.

Aschenbrenner, Karl. *The Concept of Coherence in Art.* Dordrecht: D. Reidel Publishing, 1985.

Aubert, Roger. "Concern for Pastoral Improvements: Seminaries, Catechetical Instruction, Catholic Action." In *The Church in the Industrial Age,* edited by Roger Aubert et al., translated by Peter Becker. 413-19. New York: Crossroad, 1981.

_____. "Old and New in Pastoral Care and Moral Theology." In *The Church in the Age of Liberalism,* edited by Roger Aubert et al., translated by Peter Becker. 14-31. New York: Crossroad, 1981.

_____. "The Modernist Crisis." In *The Church in the Industrial Age,* edited by Roger Aubert et al., translated by Margit Resch. 420-80. New York: Crossroad, 1981.

_____. "The Other European Churches." In *The Church between Revolution and Restoration,* edited by Roger Aubert et al., translated by Peter Becker. 142-62. New York: Crossroad, 1981.

Aubert, Roger, et al., eds. *The Church between Revolution and Restoration.* Translated by Peter Becker. New York: Crossroad, 1981.

_____, et al., eds. *The Church in the Age of Liberalism.* Translated by Peter Becker. New York: Crossroad, 1981.

_____, et al., eds. *The Church in the Industrial Age.* Translated by Margit Resch. New York: Crossroad, 1983.

Barber, Benjamin R. *Strong Democracy: Participatory Politics for a New Age.* Berkeley: University of California Press, 1984.

Barry, James D., ed. *The Catholic University and the Urban Poor: The 1987 Loyola Symposium on Values and Ethics*. Chicago: Loyola University Press, 1988.

Bartell, Ernest. "Private Goods, Public Goods and the Common Good: Another Look at Economics and Ethics in Catholic Social Teaching." In *The Common Good and U. S. Capitalism*, edited by Oliver F. Williams and John W. Houck. 179-211. Lanham, Md.: University Press of America, 1987.

Baum, Gregory. *The Priority of Labor: A Commentary on 'Laborem Exercens,' Encyclical Letter of Pope John Paul II*. New York: Paulist Press, 1982.

Baumgartner, Jakob. "The Expansion of Catholic Missions from the Time of Leo XIII until World War II." In *The Church in the Industrial Age*, edited by Roger Aubert et al., translated by Margit Resch. 527-75. New York: Crossroad, 1981.

Bentham, Jeremy. "An Introduction to the Principles of Morals and Legislation." Excerpts in *British Moralists: 1650-1800*, edited by D. D. Raphael. 2 vols. 2:313-46. Oxford: Oxford University Press, 1969.

Berger, Peter L. "Empirical Testing." In *Aspiring to Freedom: Commentaries on John Paul II's Encyclical 'The Social Concerns of the Church'*, edited by Kenneth A. Myers. 110-18. Grand Rapids, Mich.: William B. Eerdmans Pub., 1988.

Bianchi, Renzo. *Liberalism and Its Critics, with Special Attention to the Economic Doctrine of the Roman Catholic Church*. Northfield, Minn.: Carleton College Economics Club [1958].

Bigongiari, Dino, ed. *The Political Ideas of St. Thomas Aquinas: Representative Selections*. New York: Hafner Press, 1953.

Boff, Clodovis. "The Social Teaching of the Church and the Theology of Liberation: Opposing Social Practices?" In *Christian Ethics: Uniformity, Universality, Pluralism*, edited by Jacques Pohier and Deitmar Mieth. *Concilium*, 150. 17-22. Edinburgh: T. & T. Clark, 1981.

Bowe, Gabriel. *The Origin of Political Authority: An Essay in Catholic Political Philosophy*. Dublin: Clonmore & Reynolds, 1955.

Burke, Redmond A. *What Is the Index?* Milwaukee: Bruce, 1952.

Burghardt, Walter J. "Critical Reflections." In *Religious Freedom: 1965 and 1975, A Symposium on a Historic Document*, edited by Walter J. Burghardt. 69-72. New York: Paulist Press, 1977.

_____, ed. *Religious Freedom: 1965 and 1975, A Symposium on a Historic Document*. New York: Paulist Press, 1977.

Calvez, Jean-Yves. "Economic Policy Issues in Roman Catholic Social Teaching: An International Perspective." In *The Catholic Challenge to the American Economy: Reflections on the U. S. Bishops Pastoral Letter on Catholic Social Teaching and the U. S. Economy*, edited by Thomas M. Gannon. 15-26. New York: Macmillan, 1987.

Calvez, Jean-Yves and Jacques Perrin. *The Church and Social Justice: The Social Teaching of the Popes from Leo XIII to Pius XII (1878-1958).* Translated by J. R. Kirwin. Chicago: Henry Regnery Co., 1961.

Camp, Richard. *The Papal Ideology of Social Reform: A Study in Historical Development 1878-1967.* Leiden: E. J. Brill, 1969.

Carlen, Claudia, ed. *The Papal Encyclicals.* 5 vols. [Wilmington, N.C.]: McGrath Publishing Co. 1981.

Carrier, Hervé. "Understanding Culture: The Ultimate Challenge of the World-Church?" In *The Church and Culture since Vatican II: The Experience of North and Latin America*, edited by Joseph Gremillion. 13-30. Notre Dame, Ind.: University of Notre Dame Press, 1985.

Catechism of the Council of Trent. Translated by J. Donovan. Dublin: James Duffy, 1906.

Catholic Social Guild. *The Social Thought of John XXIII.* Hinckley, England: Samuel Walker, 1964.

Cathrein, Victor. *Socialism: Its Theoretical Basis and Practical Application.* Translation of 8th German ed. by Victor F. Gettelmann. New York: Benziger Bros., 1904.

Chadwick, Owen. *The Popes and the European Revolution.* Oxford: Clarendon Press, 1981.

_____. *The Secularization of the European Mind in the Nineteenth Century.* Cambridge: Cambridge University Press, 1975.

Charles, Roger, with Drostan Maclaren. *The Social Teaching of Vatican II: Its Origin and Development.* San Francisco: Ignatius Press, 1982.

Chenu, Marie-Dominique. *La 'doctrine sociale' de l'église comme idéologie.* Paris: Les éditions du Cerf, 1979.

_____. "Les signes des temps: réflexion théologique." In *L'église dans le monde de ce temps: constitution pastorale 'Gaudium et Spes'*, edited by Y. M.-J. Congar and M. Peuchmaurd. Tome 2. 205-25. Paris: Les editions du Cerf, 1967.

_____. "The Church's 'Social Doctrine.' " In *Christian Ethics and Economics: The North-South Conflict*, edited by Dietmar Mieth and Jacques Pohier. *Concilium*, 140. 71-75. Edinburgh: T. & T. Clark, 1980.

_____. *The Scope of the Summa*, edited and translated by Robert Edward Brennan. Washington, D.C.: Thomist Press, 1958.

Cipolla, Carlo M. *Before the Industrial Revolution: European Society and Economy, 1000-1700.* 2d ed. New York: W. W. Norton & Co., 1980.

Clark, Mary T., ed. *An Aquinas Reader.* Garden City, N.Y.: Image Books, 1972.

Coleman, John. "Development of Church Social Teaching." In *Readings in Moral Theology No. 5: Official Catholic Social Teaching*, edited by Charles E. Curran and Richard A. McCormick. 167-87. New York: Paulist Press, 1986.

Congar, Y. M.-J., and M. Peuchmaurd, eds. *L'église dans le monde de ce temps*. 3 vols. Paris: Les éditions du Cerf, 1967.

Connery, John. *Abortion: The Development of the Roman Catholic Perspective*. [Chicago]: Loyola University Press, 1977.

Cooper, Helen. *Pastoral: Mediaeval to Renaissance*. Totowa, N.J.: D. S. Brewer, Rowman, and Littlefield, 1977.

Copleston, Frederick. *A History of Philosophy*, vol. 2, *Mediaeval Philosophy, Part 2: Albert the Great to Duns Scotus*. Garden City, N.Y.: Image Books, 1962.

Cornforth, Maurice. *Materialism and the Dialectical Method*. New York: International Publishers, 1971.

Cragg, Gerald R. *The Church and the Age of Reason: 1648-1789*. Harmondsworth, England: Penguin Books, 1970.

Cremona, Paul. *The Concept of Peace in Pope John XXIII*. Malta: Dominican Publication, 1988.

Curran, Charles. "The Changing Anthropological Bases of Catholic Social Ethics." In *Readings in Moral Theology No. 5: Official Catholic Social Teaching*, edited by Charles E. Curran and Richard A. McCormick. 188-218. New York: Paulist Press, 1986.

_____. "The Common Good and Official Catholic Social Teaching." In *The Common Good and U. S. Capitalism*, edited by Oliver F. Williams and John W. Houck. 111-29. Lanham, Md.: University Press of America, 1987.

Curran, Charles E., and Richard A. McCormick, eds. *Readings in Moral Theology No. 5: Official Catholic Social Teaching*. New York: Paulist Press, 1986.

Daniel-Rops, H. *A Fight for God: 1870-1939*. Translated by John Warrington. London: J. M. Dent & Sons, 1965.

_____. *The Church in the Age of Revolution: 1789-1870*. Translated by John Warrington. New York: E. P. Dutton, 1965.

_____. *The Church in the Eighteenth Century*. Translated by John Warrington. New York: E. P. Dutton, 1964.

Davis, Henry. *Moral and Pastoral Theology*. Heythrop Series 2, 4th ed., rev. and enl., 4 vols. London: Sheed and Ward, 1945.

Diamant, Alfred. *Austrian Catholics and the First Republic: Democracy, Capitalism, and the Social Order, 1918-1934*. Princeton, N.J.: Princeton University Press, 1960.

Dorr, Donal. *Option for the Poor: A Hundred Years of Vatican Social*

Teaching. Maryknoll, N.Y.: Orbis Books, 1983.

Dougherty, Kenneth. *Cosmology: An Introduction to the Thomistic Philosophy of Nature*. Peekskill, N.Y.: Graymoor Press, 1952.

Dunn, Dennis J. *Détente and Papal-Communist Relations, 1962-1978*. Westview Replica Editions. Boulder, Colo.: Westview Press, 1979.

Dupanloup, Félix. *La convention du 15. septembre et l'encyclique du 8. décembre*. Paris: Charles Douniol, 1865.

Dussel, Enrique. *Ethics and Community*. Translated by Robert R. Barr. Maryknoll, N.Y.: Orbis Books, 1988.

Eagleson, John, and Philip Scharper, eds. *Puebla and Beyond: Documentation and Commentary*. Translated by John Drury. Maryknoll, N.Y.: Orbis Books, 1979.

Ederer, Rupert J., ed. *The Social Teachings of Wilhelm Emmanuel von Ketteler*. Washington, D.C.: University Press of America, 1981.

d'Entrèves, Alexander Passerin. *The Medieval Contribution to Political Thought: Thomas Aquinas, Marsilius of Padua, Richard Hooker*. New York: Humanities Press, 1959.

Ettin, Andrew. *Literature and the Pastoral*. New Haven: Yale University Press, 1984.

Fanfani, Amintore. *Le origini dello spirito capitalistico in Italia*. Milan: Società editríce 'Vita e Pensiero,' 1933.

Fisher, Eugene J., and Daniel F. Polish, eds. *Formation of Social Policy in the Catholic and Jewish Traditions*. Notre Dame, Ind.: University of Notre Dame Press, 1980.

Fremantle, Anne, ed. *The Papal Encyclicals in Their Historical Context*. Introduction by Gustave Weigel. New York: The New American Library, Mentor Books, 1956.

Fromm, Erich. *Marx's Concept of Man*. Milestones of Thought Series. New York: Frederick Ungar Publishing Co., 1961.

Gannon, Thomas A., ed. *The Catholic Challenge to the American Economy: Reflections on the U. S. Bishops Pastoral Letter on Catholic Social Teaching and the U. S. Economy*. New York: Macmillan, 1987.

Gardiner, Harold C. *Catholic Viewpoint on Censorship*. Rev. ed. Garden City, N.Y.: Image Books, 1961.

Gaskin, J.C.A. *The Quest for Eternity: An Outline of the Philosophy of Religion*. New York: Penguin Books, 1984.

Geisler, Norman. *Options in Contemporary Christian Ethics*. Grand Rapids, Mich.: Baker House Book, 1981.

Golding, John. "Whistler." In *'Atlantic' Brief Lives: A Biographical Companion to the Arts*, edited by Louis Kronenberger and Emily Morison Beck. 866-68. Boston: Little, Brown and Co., Atlantic Monthly Press Books, 1965.

Granfield, Patrick. "The Rise and Fall of 'Societas Perfecta.' " In *May Church Ministers Be Politicians?*, edited by Peter Huizing and Knut Walf. *Concilium*, 157. 3-8. Edinburgh: T. & T. Clark, 1982.

_____. *The Limits of the Papacy: Authority and Autonomy in the Church*. New York: Crossroad, 1987.

Greeley, Andrew. *No Bigger than Necessary: An Alternative to Socialism, Capitalism, and Anarchism*. New York: Meridian, 1977.

Gremillion, Joseph, ed. *The Church and Culture since Vatican II: The Experience of North and Latin America*. Notre Dame, Ind.: University of Notre Dame Press, 1985.

_____. *The Gospel of Peace and Justice: Catholic Social Teaching since Pope John*. Maryknoll, N.Y.: Orbis Books, 1976.

Griffioen, Sander. "The Worldview Approach to Social Theory: Hazards and Benefits." In *Stained Glass: Worldviews and Social Science*, edited by Paul A. Marshall, Sander Griffioen, and Richard Mouw. 81-118. Lanham, Md.: University Press of America, 1989.

Groethuysen, Bernard. *The Bourgeois: Catholicism and Capitalism in Eighteenth Century France*. Translated by Mary Ilford, introduced by Benjamin Nelson. New York: Holt, Rinehart and Winston, 1969.

Gross, Barry R. *Discrimination in Reverse: Is Turnabout Fair Play?* New York: New York University Press, 1978.

Gudorf, Christine E. *Catholic Social Teaching on Liberation Themes*. Washington, D.C.: University Press of America, 1981.

Hales, E. E. Y. *Pio Nono: A Study in European Politics and Religion in the Nineteenth Century*. New York: P. J. Kenedy & Sons, 1954.

_____. *Revolution and the Papacy 1769-1846*. London: Eyre & Spottiswoode, 1960.

Hansen, Eric O. *The Catholic Church in World Politics*. Princeton, N.J.: Princeton University Press, 1987.

Hauerwas, Stanley. "Work as Co-Creation: A Critique of a Remarkably Bad Idea." In *Co-Creation and Capitalism: John Paul II's 'Laborem Exercens'*, edited by John W. Houck and Oliver F. Williams. 42-58. Washington, D.C.: University Press of America, 1983.

_____. *A Community of Character: Toward a Constructive Christian Social Ethic*. Notre Dame, Ind.: University of Notre Dame Press, 1981.

Haughey, John C., ed. *The Faith That Does Justice: Examining the Christian Sources for Social Change*. New York: Paulist Press, 1977.

Haynes, Renée. *Philosopher King: The Humanist Pope Benedict XIV*. London: Weidenfeld & Nicolson, 1970.

Hehir, Bryan. "Religion and International Human Rights: A Catholic Perspective." In *Formation of Social Policy in the Catholic and Jewish*

Traditions, edited by Eugene J. Fisher and Daniel F. Polish. 109-22. Notre Dame, Ind.: University of Notre Dame Press, 1980.

Heilbroner, Robert L. *The Making of Economic Society.* 3d ed. Englewood Cliffs, N.J.: Prentice-Hall, 1970.

Hellwig, Monika. *Understanding Catholicism.* New York: Paulist Press, 1981.

Heyer, Friedrich. *The Catholic Church from 1648 to 1870.* Translated by D.W.D. Shaw. London: Adam & Charles Black, 1969.

Hilgers, Joseph. *Der Index der verbotenen Bücher.* Freiburg im Breisgau: Herdersche Verlagshandlung, 1904.

Hobbes, Thomas. *Leviathan.* Edited and introduced by C. B. MacPherson. Harmondsworth, England: Penguin Books, 1968.

Hollenbach, David. *Claims in Conflict: Retrieving and Renewing the Catholic Human Rights Tradition.* New York: Paulist Press, 1979.

————. "Global Human Rights: An Interpretation of the Contemporary Catholic Understanding." In *Readings in Moral Theology No. 5: Official Catholic Social Teaching,* edited by Charles E. Curran and Richard A. McCormick. 366-83. New York: Paulist Press, 1986.

Hollenbach, David. "Modern Catholic Teachings Concerning Justice." In *The Faith That Does Justice: Examining the Christian Sources for Social Change,* edited by John C. Haughey. 207-31. New York: Paulist Press, 1977.

Holman, C. Hugh. *A Handbook to Literature.* 3d ed. Indianapolis: Bobbs-Merrill Co., Odyssey Press, 1972.

Holmes, J. Derek. *The Papacy in the Modern World.* New York: Crossroad, 1981.

Houck, John W., and Oliver F. Williams, eds. *Co-Creation and Capitalism: John Paul II's 'Laborem Exercens'.* Washington, D.C.: University Press of America, 1983.

Hughes, Emmet John. *The Church and the Liberal Society.* Notre Dame, Ind.: University of Notre Dame Press, 1961.

Huizing, Peter, and Knut Walf, eds. *May Church Ministers Be Politicians? Concilium,* 157. Edinburgh: T. & T. Clark, 1982.

Iserloh, Erwin. "History of the Ecumenical Movement." In *The Church in the Modern Age,* edited by Gabriel Adriányi et al., translated by Anselm Biggs. 458-73. New York: Crossroad, 1981.

Janson, H. W., with Dora Jane Janson. *History of Art: A Survey of the Major Visual Arts from the Dawn of History to the Present Day.* 2d ed. Englewood Cliffs, N.J.: Prentice-Hall, 1977.

Jarlot, Georges. *Doctrine pontificale et histoire: L'enseignement social de Léon XIII, Pie X et Benoît XV vu dans ambiance historique: 1878-1922.* Rome: Presses de l' Université Grégorienne, 1964.

Jedin, Hubert. "The Second Vatican Council." In *The Church in The Modern Age*, edited by Gabriel Adriányi et al., translated by Anselm Biggs. 96-151. New York: Crossroad, 1981.

Jossua, Jean-Pierre, and Claude Geffré. *Indifference to Religion. Concilium*, 165. Edinburgh: T. & T. Clark, 1983.

Kamenka, Eugene, ed. *Community as a Social Ideal*. New York: St. Martin's Press, 1982.

Kirwin, J[erome] R. "Christianising the New Society: A New Translation of 'Mater et Magistra.'" In *The Social Thought of John XXIII*, Catholic Social Guild. 1-96. Hinckley, England: Samuel Walker, 1964.

Köhler, Oscar. "Catholic Self-Awareness in the British Empire." In *The Church in the Industrial Age*, edited by Roger Aubert et al., translated by Margit Resch. 135-50. New York: Crossroad, 1981.

_____. "The Condemnation of 'Americanism.'" In *The Church in the Industrial Age*, edited by Roger Aubert et al., translated by Margit Resch. 331-34. New York: Crossroad, 1981.

_____. "The Development of Catholicism in Modern Society." In *The Church in the Industrial Age*, edited by Roger Aubert et al., translated by Margit Resch. 190-219. New York: Crossroad, 1981.

Kronenberger, Louis, and Emily Morison Beck, eds. *'Atlantic' Brief Lives: A Biographical Companion to the Arts*. Boston: Little, Brown and Co., Atlantic Monthly Press Books, 1965.

Lamennais, F. *Paroles d'un croyant*. Paris: Ancienne maison Michel Lévy Frères, 1877.

La Mettrie, Julien Offray de. *Man a Machine*. Notes and translation by Gertrude Bussey. LaSalle, Ill.: Open Court, 1912.

Langan, John. "Human Rights in Roman Catholicism." In *Readings in Moral Theology No. 5: Official Catholic Social Teaching*, edited by Charles E. Curran and Richard A. McCormick. 110-29. New York: Paulist Press, 1986.

Lee, Andrea, and Amata Miller. "Feminist Themes and 'Laborem Exercens.'" In *Readings in Moral Theology No. 5: Official Catholic Social Teaching*, edited by Charles E. Curran and Richard A. McCormick. 411-41. New York: Paulist Press, 1986.

Levine, Andrew. *Liberal Democracy: A Critique of Its Theory*. New York: New York University Press, 1981.

Lochman, Jan Milič. "Ideology or Theology of Human Rights?" In *The Church and the Rights of Man*, edited by Alois Müller and Norbert Greinacher. *Concilium*, 124. 11-19. Edinburgh: T. & T. Clark, 1979.

Locke, John. *An Essay Concerning Human Understanding*. 2 vols. Edited by Alexander Campbell Fraser. New York: Dover Publishing, 1959.

Lukàcs, József. "The Problem of Poverty and the Poor in Catholic
Social Teaching: A Marxist Perspective." In *Readings in Moral
Theology No. 5: Official Catholic Social Teaching*, edited by Charles E.
Curran and Richard A. McCormick. 301-12. New York: Paulist
Press, 1986.

McCool, Gerald. *Catholic Theology in the Nineteenth Century: The Quest
for a Unitary Method*. New York: Seabury Press, Crossroad Books,
1977.

McCormick, Richard A. *Notes on Moral Theology, 1981 through 1984*.
Lanham, Md.: University Press of America, 1984.

Machlis, Joseph. *The Enjoyment of Music: An Introduction to Perceptive
Listening*. 3d ed. New York: W. W. Norton Co., 1970.

MacIntyre, Alasdair. *After Virtue: A Study of Moral Theory*. Notre Dame,
Ind.: University of Notre Dame Press, 1981.

Mackin, Theodore. *What Is Marriage?: Marriage in the Catholic Church*.
New York: Paulist Press, 1982.

McManners, John. *Church and State in France, 1870-1914*. New York:
Harper & Row, Harper Torchbooks, 1973.

Macquarrie, John. *Existentialism*. Theological Resources. Philadelphia:
Westminster Press, 1972.

Mahoney, John. *The Making of Moral Theology: A Study of the Roman
Catholic Tradition*. Oxford: Clarendon Press, 1987.

Mandel, Ernest. *An Introduction to Marxist Economic Theory*. New York:
Pathfinder Press, 1970.

Marinelli, Peter. *Pastoral*. London: Methuen, 1971.

Marshall, Paul A., Sander Griffioen, and Richard Mouw, eds. *Stained
Glass: Worldviews and Social Science*. Lanham, Md.: University Press
of America, 1989.

Marx, Karl. *Capital: A Critic of Political Economy*. Edited by Frederick
Engels, translated by Samuel Moore and Edward Aveling. 3 vols.
New York: International Publishers, 1967. Vol. 1.

Meeks, M. Douglas. *God the Economist: The Doctrine of God and Political
Economy*. Minneapolis: Fortress Press, 1989.

Metz, Johannes B. "The Church's Social Function in the Light of a
'Political Theology.'" In *Foundational Theology: Faith and the World of
Politics*, edited by Johannes B. Metz. Concilium, 36. 2-18. New York:
Paulist Press, 1968.

_____, ed. *Foundational Theology: Faith and the World of Politics*.
Concilium, 36. New York: Paulist Press, 1968.

Mezzardi, Luigi. "Catholicism in Italy." In *The Church in the Modern
Age*, edited by Gabriel Adriányi et al., translated by Anselm Biggs.
569-83. New York: Crossroad, 1981.

Mieth, Dietmar, and Jacques Pohier, eds. *Christian Ethics and Economics: The North-South Conflict. Concilium*, 140. Edinburgh: T. & T. Clark, 1980.

Moody, Joseph, N. "The Church and the New Forces in Western Europe and Italy." In *Church and Society: Catholic Social and Political Thought and Movements 1789-1950*, edited by Joseph N. Moody. 21-92. New York: Arts, Inc., 1953.

_____, ed. *Church and Society: Catholic Social and Political Thought and Movements 1789-1950*. New York: Arts, Inc., 1953.

Moody, Joseph N., and Justus George Lawler, eds. *The Challenge of 'Mater et Magistra'*. New York: Herder and Herder, 1963.

Mosse, George L. "Nationalism, Fascism, and the Radical Right." In *Community as a Social Ideal*, edited by Eugene Kamenka. 27-42. New York: St. Martin's Press, 1982.

Mueller, Franz H. "The Church and the Social Question." In *The Challenge of 'Mater et Magistra'*, edited by Joseph N. Moody and Justus George Lawler. 13-154. New York: Herder and Herder, 1963.

Müller, Alois, and Norbert Greinacher, eds. *The Church and the Rights of Man. Concilium*, 124. Edinburgh: T. & T. Clark, 1979.

Müller, Wolfgang, et al. *The Church in the Age of Absolutism and Enlightenment*. Translated by Gunther J. Holst. New York: Crossroad, 1981.

Murphy, Charles. "Action for Justice as Constitutive of the Preaching of the Gospel: What Did the 1971 Synod Mean?" In *Readings in Moral Theology No. 5: Official Catholic Social Teaching*, edited by Charles E. Curran and Richard A. McCormick. 150-66. New York: Paulist Press, 1986.

Murstein, Bernard. *Love, Sex, and Marriage through the Ages*. New York: Springer Publishing, 1974.

Myers, Kenneth A., ed. *Aspiring to Freedom: Commentaries on John Paul II's Encyclical 'The Social Concerns of the Church'*. Grand Rapids, Mich.: William B. Eerdmans Pub., 1988.

National Literary Commission. *Study Guide to the 'Index Librorum Prohibitorum' and the Censorship Regulations*. Detroit: Marygrove College, n.d.

Nau, Paul. *Une source doctrinale: les encycliques*. Paris: Les éditions du Cèdre, 1952.

Nell-Breuning, Oswald von. *Reorganization of Social Economy: The Social Encyclical Developed and Explained*. Translated by Bernard W. Dempsey. New York: Bruce, 1936-37.

_____. "The Drafting of 'Quadragesimo Anno.'" In *Readings in Moral Theology No. 5: Official Catholic Social Teaching*, edited by

Charles E. Curran and Richard A. McCormick. 60- 68. New York: Paulist Press, 1986.

Neuner, J., and J. Dupuis. *The Christian Faith in the Doctrinal Documents of the Catholic Church*, rev. ed. New York: Alba House, 1982.

Noonan, John T., Jr. "An Almost Absolute in History." In *The Morality of Abortion: Legal and Historical Perspectives*. Edited by John T. Noonan. Cambridge, Mass.: Harvard University Press, 1970.

_____. *Contraception: A History of Its Treatment by the Catholic Theologians and Canonists*, enl. ed. Cambridge, Mass: Harvard University Press, 1986.

_____. *The Scholastic Analysis of Usury*. Cambridge, Mass.: Harvard University Press, 1957.

_____, ed. *The Morality of Abortion: Legal and Historical Perspectives*. Cambridge, Mass.: Harvard University Press, 1970.

Novak, Michael. "Creation Theology." In *Co-Creation and Capitalism: John Paul II's 'Laborem Exercens'*, edited by John W. Houck and Oliver F. Williams. 17-41. Lanham, Md.: University Press of America, 1983.

_____. "The Development of Nations." In *Aspiring to Freedom: Commentaries on John Paul II's Encyclical 'The Social Concerns of the Church'*, edited by Kenneth A. Myers. 67-109. Grand Rapids, Mich.: William B. Eerdmans Publishing, 1988.

_____. *The Spirit of Democratic Capitalism*. New York: Simon & Schuster, 1982.

O'Brien, David J., and Thomas A. Shannon. *Renewing the Earth: Catholic Documents on Peace, Justice and Liberation*. Garden City: N.Y.: Image Books, 1977.

O'Connor, Daniel A. *Catholic Social Doctrine*. Westminster, Md.: Newman Press, 1956.

O'Dwyer, Margaret M. *The Papacy in the Age of Napoleon and the Restoration: Pius VII, 1800-1823*. Lanham, Md.: University Press of America, 1985.

Overberg, Kenneth R. *An Inconsistent Ethic? Teachings of the American Catholic Bishops*. Lanham, Md.: University Press of America, 1980.

Padover, Saul K., ed. and trans. *On Religion: Karl Marx*. The Karl Marx Library, vol. 5. New York: McGraw-Hill Book Co., 1974.

Pastor, Ludwig Freiherr von. *The History of the Popes*. Translated by E. F. Peeler. 39 vols. St. Louis: Herder, 1956. Vol. 36.

Pateman, Carole. *The Problem of Political Obligation: A Critical Analysis of Liberal Theory*. Berkeley: University of California Press, 1985.

Pavan, Pietro. "Ecumenism and Vatican II's 'Declaration on Religious Freedom.'" In *Religious Freedom: 1965 and 1975, A Symposium on a*

Historic Document, edited by Walter J. Burghardt. 7-38. New York: Paulist Press, 1977.

Pegis, Anton, ed. *Introduction to Saint Thomas Aquinas.* New York: Modern Library, 1948.

Perroux, François. " 'Populorum progressio': l'encyclique de la résurrection." In *L'église dans le monde de ce temps,* edited by Y. M.-J. Congar and M. Peuchmaurd. 3 vols. 1:201-12. Paris: Les éditions du Cerf, 1967.

Pfürtner, Stephen H. P. "Human Rights in Christian Ethics." In *The Church and the Rights of Man,* edited by Alois Müller and Norbert Greinacher. *Concilium,* 124. 57-66. Edinburgh: T. & T. Clark, 1979.

Poggioli, Renato. *The Oaten Flute: Essay on Pastoral Poetry and the Pastoral Ideal.* Cambridge, Mass.: Harvard University Press, 1975.

Pohier, Jacques, and Dietmar Mieth, eds. *Christian Ethics: Uniformity, Universality, Pluralism. Concilium,* 150. Edinburgh: T. & T. Clark, 1981.

Poplin, Dennis E. *Communities: A Survey of Theories and Methods of Research.* 2d ed. New York: Macmillan Pub. Co., 1979.

Postgate, Raymond, ed. *Revolution from 1789 to 1906.* Gloucester, Mass.: Peter Smith, 1969.

Prümmer, Dominic M. *Handbook of Moral Theology.* New York: P. J. Kenedy and Sons, 1957.

Rabb, Theodore K., and Robert I. Rotberg, eds. *The Family in History.* New York: Harper & Row, Harper Torchbooks, 1971.

Rahner, Karl. *Theological Investigations.* Translated by David Bourke. 20 vols. New York: Herder and Herder, 1973. Vol. 10.

_____. "Theological Reflections on the Problem of Secularization." In Karl Rahner, *Theological Investigations.* Translated by David Bourke. 20 vols. 10:318-48. New York: Herder and Herder, 1973.

Randall, John Herman, Jr. *The Making of the Modern Mind: A Survey of the Intellectual Background of the Present Age.* 50th Anniversary ed. Foreword by Jacques Barzun. New York: Columbia University Press, 1976.

Ranney, Austin. *The Governing of Men.* 3d ed. New York: Holt, Rinehart and Winston, 1971.

Raphael, D. D., ed. *British Moralists.* 2 vols. Oxford: Oxford University Press, 1969.

Redpath, Peter A. *A Simplified Introduction to the Wisdom of St. Thomas.* Lanham, Md.: University Press of America, 1980.

Refoulé, François. "Efforts Made on Behalf of Human Rights by the Supreme Authority of the Church." In *The Church and the Rights of Man,* edited by Alois Müller and Norbert Greinacher. *Concilium,* 124. 77-85. Edinburgh: T. & T. Clark, 1979.

Repgen, Konrad. "Foreign Policy of the Popes in the Epoch of the World Wars." In *The Church in the Modern Age*, edited by Gabriel Adriányi et al., translated by Anselm Biggs. 35-96. New York: Crossroads, 1981.

Rhodes, Anthony. *The Power of Rome in the Twentieth Century: The Vatican in the Age of Liberal Democracies, 1870-1922*. London: Sidgwick & Jackson, 1983.

_____. *The Vatican in the Age of Dictators: 1922-1945*. New York: Holt, Rinehart and Winston, 1973.

Ritter, Harry. *Dictionary of Concepts in History*. Reference Sources for the Social Sciences and the Humanities, no. 3. New York: Greenwood Press, 1986.

Rommen, Heinrich A. *The State in Catholic Thought: A Treatise in Political Philosophy*. St. Louis: B. Herder Book Co., 1945.

Rouse, Ruth, and Stephen Charles Neill, eds. *A History of the Ecumenical Movement: 1517-1948*. 2d ed. Philadelphia: Westminster Press, 1967.

Rousseau, Jean-Jacques. *The Social Contract*. Translated and introduced by M. Cranston. Harmondsworth, England: Penguin Books, 1968.

Sandel, Michael. *Liberalism and the Limits of Justice*. Cambridge: Cambridge University Press, 1982.

Schacht, Richard. *Classical Modern Philosophy: Descartes to Kant*. London: Routledge and Kegan Paul, 1984.

Schapiro, Salwyn. *Condorcet and the Rise of Liberalism*. New York: Octagon Books, 1963.

Schillebeeckx, Edward. "The Magisterium and the World of Politics." In *Foundational Theology: Faith and the World of Politics*, edited by Johannes B. Metz. *Concilium*, 36. 19-39. New York: Paulist Press, 1968.

Schmitter, Philippe C. "Still the Century of Corporatism?" In *Trends toward Corporatist Intermediation*, edited by Philippe C. Schmitter and Gerhard Lehmbruch. Contemporary Political Sociology, vol. 1. 7-52. London: Sage Publications, 1979.

Schmolke, Michael. "Information and the Mass Media." In *The Church in the Modern Age*, edited by Gabriel Adriányi et al., translated by Anselm Biggs. 410-36. New York: Crossroad, 1981.

Schoof, Mark. *A Survey of Catholic Theology: 1800-1970*. Translated by N. D. Smith and introduced by E. Schillebeeckx. Paramus, N.J.: Paulist Newman Press, 1970.

Schuck, Michael J. "The Bishops' Letter, Loyola University, and the Urban Poor." In *The Catholic University and the Urban Poor: The 1987 Loyola Symposium on Values and Ethics*. 59-68. Chicago: Loyola University Press, 1988.

Seven Great Encyclicals. Introduced by William J. Gibbons. New York: Paulist Press, 1963.

Shorter, Edward. "Illegitimacy, Sexual Revolution, and Social Change in Modern Europe." In *The Family in History*, edited by Theodore K. Rabb and Robert I. Rotberg. 48-84. New York: Harper & Row, Harper Torchbooks, 1971.

Sleumer, Albert. *Index Romanus*. Osnabruck, Germany: Jul. Jonscher, 1951.

Smith, Adam. *The Wealth of Nations: Books I-III*. Introduced by Andrew Skinner. Harmondsworth, England: Penguin Books, Pelican Classics, 1974.

Soderini Eduardo. *Leo XIII, Italy and France*. Translated by Barbara Barclay Carter. London: Burns Oates and Washbourne, 1935.

Solomon, Robert C. *Introducing Philosophy: Problems and Perspectives*. 2d ed. New York: Harcourt Brace Jovanovich, 1981.

Sommet, Jacques. "Religious Indifference Today: A Draft Diagnosis." In *Indifference to Religion*, edited by Jean-Pierre Jossua and Claude Geffré. *Concilium*, 165. 3-10. Edinburgh: T. & T. Clark, 1983.

Stalin, Joseph. *Dialectical and Historical Materialism*. New York: International Publishers, 1940.

Stasiewski, Bernhard. "Catholicism in the Slavic World until 1914." In *The Church in the Industrial Age*, edited by Roger Aubert et al., translated by Margit Resch. 166-98. New York: Crossroad, 1981.

————. "State and Church in Poland-Lithuania to the End of the Republic of the Aristocracy." In *The Church in the Age of Absolutism and Enlightenment*, edited by Wolfgang Muller et al., translated by Gunther J. Holst. 489-91. New York: Crossroad, 1981.

Sullivan, William. *Reconstructing Public Philosophy*. Berkeley: University of California Press, 1982.

Tanquerey, A. *Manual of Dogmatic Theology*. 2 vols. Translated by John J. Byrnes. New York: Desclee Co., 1959.

Tawney, R. H. *Religion and the Rise of Capitalism: A Historical Study*. New York: New American Library, 1954.

Taylor, Charles. *Hegel and Modern Society*. New York: Cambridge University Press, 1979.

Thomas Aquinas. *Summa Contra Gentiles, Book One: God*. Translated and introduced by Anton C. Pegis. Notre Dame, Ind.: University of Notre Dame Press, 1975.

————. *Summa Contra Gentiles, Book Three: Providence, Part I*. Translated and introduced by Vernon J. Bourke. Notre Dame, Ind.: University of Notre Dame Press, 1975.

————. *Summa Contra Gentiles, Book Three: Providence, Part II*.

Translated and introduced by Vernon J. Bourke. Notre Dame, Ind.: University of Notre Dame, 1975.

_____. *Summa Contra Gentiles, Book Four: Salvation.* Translated and introduced by Charles J. O'Neil. Notre Dame, Ind.: University of Notre Dame Press, 1975.

Tomkins, Oliver Stratford. "The Roman Catholic Church and the Ecumenical Movement: 1910-1948." In *A History of the Ecumenical Movement: 1517-1948,* edited by Ruth Rouse and Stephen Charles Neill. 2d ed. 677-93. Philadelphia: Westminster Press, 1967.

Tracy, David. *The Analogical Imagination: Christian Theology and the Culture of Pluralism.* New York: Crossroad, 1981.

Tracy, David. *Blessed Rage for Order: The New Pluralism in Theology.* New York: Seabury Press, 1975.

Trippen, Norbert. "Developments in the Clergy since 1914." In *The Church in the Modern Age,* edited by Gabriel Adriányi et al., translated by Anselm Biggs. 336-52. New York: Crossroad, 1981.

Tuck, Richard. *Natural Rights Theories: Their Origin and Development.* Cambridge: Cambridge University Press, 1979.

Turner, Deny. *Marxism and Christianity.* Totowa, N.J.: Barnes and Noble, 1983.

22nd Congress of the C.P.S.U. *Programme of the Communist Party of the Soviet Union.* Moscow: Foreign Languages Publishing House, 1961.

Unger, Roberto Mangabeira. *Knowledge and Politics.* New York: The Free Press, 1975.

Vaquero, Quintín Aldea. "Spain." In *The Church in the Modern Age,* edited by Gabriel Adriányi et al., translated by Anselm Biggs. 600-11. New York: Crossroad, 1981.

Wackenheim, Charles. "The Theological Meaning of the Rights of Man." In *The Church and the Rights of Man,* edited by Alois Müller and Norbert Greinacher. *Concilium,* 124. 49-56. Edinburgh: T. & T. Clark, 1979.

Wallace, Lillian P. *Leo XIII and the Rise of Socialism.* [Durham, N.C.]: Duke University Press, 1966.

Wallace, William. *The Elements of Philosophy: A Compendium for Philosophers and Theologians.* New York: Alba House, 1977.

Walzer, Michael. *Spheres of Justice: A Defense of Pluralism and Equality.* New York: Basic Books, 1983.

Watzlawik, Joseph. *Leo XIII and the New Scholasticism.* Cebu City, Philippines: University of San Carlos, 1966.

Weber, Wilhelm. "Society and State as a Problem for the Church." In *The Church in the Modern Age,* edited by Gabriel Adriányi et al., translated by Anselm Biggs. 229-59. New York: Crossroads, 1981.

Weigel, George. "The Democracy Connection." In *Aspiring to Freedom: Commentaries on John Paul II's Encyclical 'The Social Concerns of the Church'*, edited by Kenneth A. Myers. 119-33. Grand Rapids, Mich.: William B. Eerdmans Pub., 1988.

Welty, Eberhard. *A Handbook of Christian Social Ethics*. 2 vols. New York: Herder and Herder, 1963.

Weulersse, Georges, ed. *Le mouvement physiocratique en France (de 1756 à 1770)*. 2 vols. Paris: Félix Alcan, 1910; reprint ed., Paris: Editions Mouton, 1968.

Williams, George Huntston. *The Mind of John Paul II: Origins of His Thought and Action*. New York: Seabury Press, 1981.

Williams, Oliver F., and John W. Houck. *The Common Good and U.S. Capitalism*. Lanham, Md.: University Press of America, 1987.

Yoder, John Howard. *When War Is Unjust: Being Honest in Just-War Thinking*. Introduction by Charles P. Lutz. Minneapolis, Minn.: Augsburg Publishing House, 1984.

Journal Articles

Anderson, Ken, Paul Piccone, Fred Siegel, and Michael Taves. "Round-table on Communitarianism." *Telos* 76 (Summer 1988): 2-32.

André-Vincent, Ph. J. "A propos de l'enseignement pontifical et des droits de l'homme." *La pensée catholique* 185 (March-April 1980): 91-93.

Arnal, Oscar L. "Why the French Christian Democrats Were Condemned." *Church History* 49 (June 1980): 188-201.

Baldwin, John. "The Medieval Theory of Just Price: Romanists, Canonists, and Theologians in the 12th and 13th Centuries." *Transactions of the American Philosophical Society* 49 (1959).

Baum, Gregory. "Class Struggle and the Magisterium: A New Note." *Theological Studies* 45 (December 1984): 690-701.

Boyle, John P. "The 'Ordinary Magisterium': Towards a History of the Concept (2)." *Heythrop Journal* 21 (January 1980): 14-29.

Briefs, Goetz. "Catholic Social Doctrine, 'Laissez-Faire' Liberalism, and Social Market Economy." *Review of Social Economy* 41 (December 1983): 246-58.

Buchanan, Allen E. "Assessing the Communitarian Critique of Liberalism." *Ethics* 99 (July 1989): 852-82.

Christiansen, Drew. "On Relative Equality: Catholic Egalitarianism after Vatican II." *Theological Studies* 45 (December 1984): 651-75.

Clark, David B. "The Concept of Community: A Re-examination." *The Sociological Review* 21 (August 1973): 397-416.

Congregation for Catholic Education. "Guidelines for the Study and Teaching of the Church's Social Doctrine in the Formation of Priests." *Origins* 19 (August 1989): 169-92.

Congregation for the Doctrine of the Faith. "Instruction on Christian Freedom and Liberation." *Origins* 15 (April 1986): 713-28.

Dorr, Donal. "John XXIII and Option for the Poor." *Irish Theological Quarterly* 47 (1980): 247-71.

_____. "The New Social Encyclical." *Furrow* (November 1981): 700-12.

Griffin, Leslie. "The Integration of Spiritual and Temporal: Contemporary Roman Catholic Church-State Theory." *Theological Studies* 48 (March 1987): 225-57.

Grima, George. "Method in the Social Teaching of the Church." *Melita Theologica* 33 (1982): 11-33.

Habiger, Matthew. "Is the Magisterium a Reliable Moral Guide? The Case of Usury." *Social Justice Review* 80 (May-June 1989): 73-79.

Harrison, Brian W. "Vatican II and Religious Liberty: Contradiction or Continuity?" *Social Justice Review* 80 (July-August 1989): 104-12.

Hehir, Bryan. "Church and State: Basic Concepts for an Analysis." *Origins* 8 (30 November 1978): 377-81.

Hehir, Bryan. "The Church and the Population Year: Notes on a Strategy." *Theological Studies* 35 (March 1974): 72-81.

Hellman, John. "French Left-Catholics and Communism in the Nineteen-Thirties." *Church History* 45 (December 1976): 507-23.

Hennesey, Joseph. "Leo XIII's Thomistic Revival: A Political and Philosophical Event." *The Journal of Religion* 58, supplement (1978): S185-97.

Higgins, George G. "Issues of Justice and Peace." *Chicago Studies* 20 (Summer 1981): 191-206.

Jacob, Margaret C. "Newtonianism and the Origins of the Enlightenment: A Reassessment." *Eighteenth Century Studies* 11 (Fall 1975): 1-25.

Johnson, Humphrey J. T. "The Roman Index of Prohibited Books." *Downside Review* 73 (April 1955): 160-73.

Kirwin, Jerome R. "'Mater et Magistra.'" *The Wiseman Review* 489 (1961): 123-32.

Knapp, Thomas. "The Red and the Black: Catholic Socialists in the Weimer Republic." *Catholic Historical Review* 61 (July 1975): 386-408.

Komonchak, Joseph A. "The Enlightenment and the Construction of Roman Catholicism." *Catholic Commission on Intellectual and Cultural Affairs* (1985): 31-59.

Luža, Radomir. "Nazi Control of the Austrian Catholic Church, 1939-1941." *The Catholic Historical Review* 63 (October 1977): 537-72.

Mackin, Theodore. "Conjugal Love and the Magisterium." *The Jurist* 36 (1976): 263-301.

Maza, Sarah C. "An Anatomy of Paternalism: Masters and Servants in Eighteenth Century French Households." *Eighteenth Century Life* 7 (October 1981): 1-24.

McCool, Gerald. "Twentieth Century Scholasticism." *The Journal of Religion* 58 supplement (1978): S198-S221.

McKee, A. F. "The Market Principle and Roman Catholic Thought." *Kyklos* 17 (1964): 65-80.

Miles, Margaret. "Pilgrimage as Metaphor in a Nuclear Age." *Theology Today* 45 (July 1988): 166-79.

Mouffe, Chantel. "American Liberalism and Its Critics: Rawls, Taylor, Sandel and Walzer." *Praxis International* 8 (July 1988): 193-206.

Murray, John Courtney. "Leo XIII on Church and State: The General Structure of the Controversy." *Theological Studies* 14 (March 1953): 1-30.

_____. "Leo XIII: Separation of Church and State." *Theological Studies* 14 (June 1953): 145-214.

_____. "Leo XIII: Two Concepts of Government." *Theological Studies* 14 (December 1953): 551-67.

_____. "Leo XIII: Two Concepts of Government II, Government and the Order of Culture." *Theological Studies* 15 (March 1954): 1-33.

_____. "The Church and Totalitarian Democracy." *Theological Studies* 13 (December 1952): 525-63.

O'Riordan, Sean. "The Teaching of the Papal Encyclicals as a Source and Norm of Moral Theology." *Studia Moralia* 14 (1976): 135-57.

Paulus, Normand J. "Uses and Misuses of the Term 'Social Justice' in the Roman Catholic Tradition." *The Journal of Religious Ethics* 15 (Fall 1987): 261-82.

Pettovich, Piero. "'Pacem in Terris' and Human Rights." *World Justice* 4 (June 1964): 452-67.

Plant, Raymond. "Community: Concept, Conception, and Ideology." *Politics & Society* 8 (1978): 79-107.

Refoulé, François. "L'église et les libertés de Léon XIII à Jean XXIII." *Le supplément* 125 (May 1978): 243-59.

Rhodes, Anthony. "The Pope of the First World War: Benedict XV (1914-1922)." *The Month* 250 (June 1989): 248-52.

Riga, Peter. "'Pacem in Terris': An Analysis." *World Justice* 6 (September 1964): 20-49.

Schmitter, Philippe C. "Corporatism is Dead! Long Live Corporatism!" *Government & Opposition* 24 (Winter 1989): 54-73.

Selznick, Philip. "The Idea of a Communitarian Morality." *California*

Law Review 75 (1987): 445-63.

Stange, Douglas. "Popes, Peace and People: Marxist Comment on Three Encyclicals." *Una Sancta* 25 (1968): 64-70.

Storck, Thomas. "The Problem of Religious Liberty." *Faith and Reason* 15 (Spring 1989): 59-67.

Surlis, Paul. "The Relation between Social Justice and Inculturation in the Papal Magisterium." *Irish Theological Quarterly* 52 (1986): 245-67.

Vallin, Pierre. " 'Laborem Exercens.' " *Etudes* (November 1981): 546-50.

Volf, Miroslav. "On Human Work: An Evaluation of the Key Ideas of the Encyclical 'Laborem Exercens.'" *Scottish Journal of Theology* 37 (1984): 65-79.

Willebrands, Johannes. "Vatican II's Ecclesiology of Communion." *Origins* 17 (28 May 1987): 27-33.

Encyclopedia Articles

Encyclopaedia Britannica, 1968 ed. s.v. "Duel," by Charles-Louis de Beaumont.

_____. s.v. "Eugenics," by Frederick Osborn.

_____. s.v. "Freemasonry," by Ray Baker Harris.

Encyclopaedia Judaica, 1971 ed. s.v. "Church, Catholic," by Egal Feldman.

_____. s.v. "Pius X," by Willehad Paul Eckert.

Encyclopaedia of Religion and Ethics, 1961 ed. s.v. "Naturalism," by W. D. Niven.

New Catholic Encyclopedia, [n.d.] s.v. "Catholic Action," by D. J. Geany.

_____. s.v. "Education, I: Modern European Education," by J. J. O'Brien.

_____. s.v. "Freemasonry," by W. J. Whalen.

_____. s.v. "Modernism," by J. J. Heaney.

_____. s.v. "Social Thought, Catholic," by T. J. Harte.

_____. s.v. "Social Thought, Papal: 1. History," by T. J. Harte.

_____. s.v. "Social Thought, Papal: 2. Basic Concepts," by P. Pavan.

_____. Supplement 1967-1974. s.v. "Missionary Adaptation," by J. Boberg.

Unpublished Materials

Elsbernd, Mary. "Papal Statements on Rights: A Historical Contextual Study of Encyclical Teaching from Pius VI-Pius XI (1791-1939)." Ph.D. dissertation, Catholic University of Louvain (Belgium), 1985.

Griffin, Leslie C. "The Integration of Spiritual and Temporal: Roman Catholic Church-State Theory from Leo XIII to John Paul II." Ph.D. dissertation, Yale University, 1984.

Handwerker, Valentine, N. "'Take of Your Substance, and not Just of Your Abundance': The Modern Catholic Social Tradition on the Distribution of Surplus Wealth." Ph.D. dissertation, Lateran University (Rome), 1981.

Habiger, Matthew H. "Papal Teaching on Private Property: 1891-1981." Ph.D. dissertation, The Catholic University of America, 1986.

Munier, Joseph David. "Some American Approximations to Pius XI's 'Industries and Professions.'" Ph.D. dissertation, The Catholic University of America, 1943.

INDEX

Unger, Roberto, 155, 183
unions, 123
United Nations Organization, 143
United States, 99n, 108n
unitive meaning, 121-22, 145
unity: communitarian social ethic, 182;
    ecclesial unity, 21; Leonine period, 48
Universal Declaration of Human Rights, 144
universal purpose of goods, 147
urbanization, 124
use, right of use, 81, 110n
usury, 7
utilitarianism, 15, 58, 62
utopianism, 9

Vatican Council I, 143
Vatican Council II, 138, 140, 143, 160n,
    161n, 163n, 178
Vehementer nos, 61, 75
verism, 65, 101n
Vermeersch, Arthur, 113n
Vigilanti cura, 53, 87
violence, 51, 83: communitarian social
    ethic, 184; Leonine period, 95n, 101n;
    natural law theory, 175; post-Leonine
    period, 120, 123, 143; violent citizen
    resistance, 177
virtue in moral life, 58
Vix dum a Nobis, 26-27
Vix pervenit, 7
vocational groups, 112n-13n, 169n
vocations (religious vocations), 48
Volf, Miroslav, 168n
volonté générale, 38n
Voltaire (F. M. Arouet), 12
"voluntary association of citizens," 61

wages, 64, 83, 148, 166n
Wallace, Lillian, 10
warfare, 51, 54, 120, 142
"we-feeling," 155
wealth and poverty, 8-9, 29, 30, 64, 82-84,
    120, 124, 142, 147, 177, 184-85
Weber, Wilhelm, 141
Weigel, George, 164n
Western civilization, 91, 115n, 153, 176,
    177
wheel image, 179
Whistler, James, 102n
will: communitarian social ethic, 181;
    Leonine period, 68; post-Leonine
    publication, 130
Willebrands, Johannes, 163n
Williams, George Huntston, 162n, 165n
women, 170n: Leonine period, 51, 54, 80,
    90, 114n; post-Leonine period, 152. *See
    also* husband and wife; men and
    women.
work, 84, 147, 168n
workers' rights, 148
working conditions, 166n
working women, 152
world government, 142
World War I, 46
World War II, 47
world: Leonine period, 56-57; post-Leonine
    period, 127, 135, 161n
worship: communitarian social ethic, 181-
    82; post-Leonine period, 118

Zigliara, Tommaso Maria, 78
Zionism, 114n
Zola, Emile, 101n